Playing Under the Piano

Playing Under the Piano

From Downton to Darkest Peru

Hugh Bonneville

Other Press
New York

First published in Great Britain in 2022 by Little, Brown

Production editor: Yvonne E. Cárdenas
This book was typeset in Jenson by M Rules

1 3 5 7 9 10 8 6 4 2

Printed in the United States of America on acid-free paper. For information write to Other Press LLC, 267 Fifth Avenue, 6th Floor, New York, NY 10016.
Or visit our Web site: www.otherpress.com

Library of Congress Cataloging-in-Publication Data
Names: Bonneville, Hugh, author.
Title: Playing under the piano : from Downton to darkest Peru / Hugh Bonneville.
Description: New York : Other Press, [2022] | "First published in Great Britain in 2022 by Little, Brown."
Identifiers: LCCN 2022030571 (print) | LCCN 2022030572 (ebook) |
ISBN 9781635423426 (hardcover) | ISBN 9781635423433 (ebook)
Subjects: LCSH: Bonneville, Hugh. | Actors—Great Britain—Biography.
Classification: LCC PN2598.B6625 A3 2022 (print) | LCC PN2598.B6625 (ebook) |
DDC 792.02/8092 [B]—dc23/eng/20220815
LC record available at https://lccn.loc.gov/2022030571
LC ebook record available at https://lccn.loc.gov/2022030572

For Lulu & Felix

Contents

Part Three: Roll Sound

Introduction

They're Going in a Different Direction

"Not really my cup of tea," said my agent.

"Well, Donna, I think it's going to be a global phenomenon," I said.

It was 2009, and the script under discussion was *Downton Abbey*. I didn't in fact predict the show's worldwide success but we're only a few lines in here and I want you to think I'm smart.

Nine years and fifty-two episodes later we were about to do the readthrough for the first *Downton Abbey* film. A memo came through from the publicity team saying that Focus Features, the financiers of the movie, had come up with a shiny idea with which to tease our audience. As we assembled on a sound stage at Twickenham Studios, a film crew would capture us clasping each other as we reunited after three years apart. Moments of coffee drinking and satsuma peeling would be caught on camera for posterity as the returning heroes prepared for another foray into the world of the British aristocracy between the wars; the show that its creators had first pitched as "Merchant Ivory meets *The West Wing*." Then, during the readthrough itself, a supercool 360°

camera would record the experience in a digitally shimmering way and there would be a photographer snapping it for all eternity.

A knot tightened in my stomach.

Readthroughs in any genre of entertainment are awkward at the best of times. For the writer(s) it's like giving birth on the centre spot of a football pitch in front of a capacity crowd. For everyone else it's first day at Big School. Because of the number of personnel involved, it usually takes place in an anonymous hall, deconsecrated church or, if at a British film studio, in an airless condemned sound stage with what looks worryingly like asbestos billowing out of the chicken-wire walls.

On a table in one corner next to the scalding/freezing urn is a tower of Styrofoam cups, tea bags, coffee (granulated if it's theatre, cafetière if it's TV, barista – chain or possibly in-house – if it's a movie), a smattering of fruit and biscuits and a stack of croissants that no one dares touch because you're on a diet, obviously; now that you've got a job you're no longer prone to stuffing your face with the unfairness of it all.

If you're lucky you'll know a couple of people from other jobs and if so you cling to each other like shipwreck survivors, reliving the horrors of Harrogate '88, or *Peak Practice* '09. Some real car crashes of productions, some invented but worth amplifying anyway in these nerve-shredding circumstances.

Over there is a producer, in a daze because he or she never thought they'd actually get to this point without either having a nervous breakdown or being fired by the money people. Nearby is the director, either quivering because they've finally agreed that the schedule is unshootable, or worryingly relaxed (beta blockers) for the same reason – knowing they too may be relieved of their duties before long, or may just walk.

If you're a guest artist on a series then, however welcoming the principals might be, you are by definition An Outsider. As everyone else mingles and brays and says See You in a Bit, like they're at a glittering cocktail party that's never going to end, you hang around the edges of the room gradually deconstructing your Styrofoam cup until it resembles a piece of failed origami with a brown drip. Alternatively, you sit in your allocated spot at the trestle table which has a place card on it with your real name misspelled and beneath it in brackets your character – "AN OUTSIDER (ep. 2)." You want the floor to open up and put you out of your misery, preferably plunging the cliquey overpaid stars to their deaths as well, along with their hilarious in-joke wrap-gift mugs from last season with the special herbal drink in it that some runner had to get them from the production office because that's what they're meant to do and Christ how they hate it but as Dad said, everyone has to start somewhere, Tiger.

I guess whoever had the task of telling Maggie Smith about the bright shiny marketing idea of filming up our nostrils throughout this emotionally complex rendezvous had been met with a brief and final "Oh I don't think so," because there were, thank God, no 360° cameras in evidence as we assembled for the day. The reunion.

Our hugs and smiles went unrecorded. It was three years since we'd last been together in the same room but I can tell you that the bond of those six seasons working with largely the same group of people was tangible. In a good way.

As we started to read I looked round the huge square of tables, catching Lesley's eye, now Brendan's – Mrs. Patmore, Mr. Bates. A shared smile and a shake of the head, almost of disbelief. Who would have thought it? And then Liz Trubridge, one of our executive producers, the one closest to the cast and its welfare from day one, who had been going to leave after the second season to pursue other projects but had said to me one day, "I can't leave. This show's in my blood now."

I suppose that's how we all felt as the series continued to roll out around the world.

*

We were standing in a garden in Dorset watching a camera track being laid for the next shot when Julian Fellowes first told me about *Downton Abbey*. He was directing me in a film called *From Time to Time*. Maggie Smith is brilliant in it. Well, what else would you expect? Seemingly half the future cast of *Downton Abbey* were in it too.

"You writing anything else at the moment?" I asked.

Julian's statuesque wife Emma was nearby, chaperoning her elderly mother who was sitting in a chair next to the sound recordist, a rug over her knees. "Now Mummy, when that man over there with the walkie-talkie says 'Action' you *zzzzp*," said Emma firmly, zipping her mouth with one hand and adjusting Mummy's blanket with the other.

"Well, yes," Julian answered me, "a number of things on the go, as a matter of fact."

In a blazer and tie, he was without doubt the most smartly dressed director I had ever worked with.

"There's a four-parter about the *Titanic*. I've got two book adaptations in the works. Oh, and one idea that's set in a country house before the Great War. *Gosford Park* territory but earlier." He paused before adding, "You probably think you're too young to play a dad."

"I am a dad."

"Of three girls, marriageable age."

"Hmm."

"Well. Once it's ready, let's see."

Ten months later I read the first episode. I couldn't put it down. The way the characters, as yet uncast, popped off the page was rare. I could see them in my mind's eye and I could hear them, too. All too often you can blank out the name of a character in a script and not be able to tell who is speaking. The setting was grand yet homely, the pacing snappy, like that of a soap opera (it was no surprise to learn that Julian was a fan of *Coronation Street*), the characters intriguing, endearing and convincing. And as I turned the final page, I wanted to know What Happens Next.

At the time, period dramas were out of fashion with British broadcasters and none of the US channels were interested either; only PBS Masterpiece put its hand up. Nevertheless, Carnival, the production company commissioned to make the show for ITV in the UK, wanted a three-year option on its cast. "But as we all know," said Gareth Neame, the executive producer and managing director of Carnival, "it probably won't run beyond the first seven episodes."

"Well, Donna, I quite like it," is what I actually said to my agent.

She shrugged. "OK. It's up to you."

Some people change their agents like they change their underwear. I've worn mine for more than thirty years. In fact, I've been with my UK agency longer than my agent has. Donna started as an office junior at Marina Martin Management; after ten years, she and a colleague, Cally Gordon, then my agent, bought out Marina and changed the name to Gordon and French Ltd. Then Cally hung up her headset, leaving Donna holding the baby. Or at least holding the actors, some of whom need treating like babies because sometimes we behave like babies. I don't, obviously, but you know what I mean. You've heard the stories. As a breed we're notoriously thin-skinned, prone to door-slamming and lying on dressing room floors flailing feet and fists until one of them connects with something hard, which justifies upping the screeching by a couple of decibels.

That's the public perception of the indulged actor, who can't handle criticism or rejection and has to be protected from painful truths at all costs. A good supply of euphemisms is probably the most valuable tool in the agent's toolbox, if he or she is to have a chance of getting through a Bad News phone call with a client without it descending into a silent sulk or a tearful tirade, or sometimes both in the space of half a minute. I'm made of sterner stuff. I can't bear being let down gently by means of a euphemism.

"Hugh, it's me," says Agent Donna. "I'm afraid they're going in a different direction."

"If by that you mean I haven't got the job," I say, "then just say so. Please don't treat me like an imbecile."

"OK. You didn't get the job."

"Fine. Thank you. I didn't want it anyway. We move on."

As an actor you are the chairman, chief financial officer, production manager, marketing director and product all in one. At least that's the way I see it. Being rejected is nine-tenths of the job. One in ten times you get the part.

American agents are often more straightforward and to the point. There's certainly no gushing down the phone about how exciting it is to have got as far as an audition. In my experience, it's usually a dispassionate email from an assistant.

> In anticipation of your conversation with Jeremy Barber about RADIATOR MOON, please find attached the script. This is a Bottleneck/Turnip Production directed by Ming Vase, produced by Curly Wurly, for Ginger Snap Productions. Please consider the role of JESSICA. Also attached to star are Sprouting Broccoli (AMY), Crème Caramel (COUNT SERGE), Pina Colada (MIKEY) and Pickled Onion (DAPHNE).

I'm always interested by the "Also attached to star" bit – which is sometimes "Interest has been expressed by," or perhaps "Offers are out to" – because they rarely reflect reality. By the time the film eventually comes to be made (if indeed it does get made) most of the cast originally mentioned have either jumped ship, or died.

The one time I had to eat my words was when a note came

through about playing the role of Donald Jeffries in a film called *The Monuments Men*. Aside from George Clooney, who as co-writer, director and co-producer was fairly likely to turn up, "Also attached to star" were Bill Murray, Bob Balaban, Jean Dujardin, Cate Blanchett, Gary Oldman and John Goodman. For once they did show up. All, that is, except Gary Oldman. He had presumably "expressed interest" initially but at some point had become less interested or in some other way uncoupled from the project but the assistant forgot to take him off the "Also attached to star" paragraph. So when the script and covering note reached my inbox it didn't take much to deduce the clerical error. Still, it was flattering to think that if you can't get Gary Oldman you might eventually end up with me.

Most actors are wise enough to know that you're often second, third or even eightieth choice for the role, however much the producer, director, casting director and agent try to convince you otherwise, gushing waves of superlatives in your direction about how thank *God* you agreed to accept the role because you are the only person in the universe who could *possibly* play the part.

What's hard to take is when you know you're perfect casting but no one else does. I was so convinced that I was right for the lead in David Nicholls' TV mini-series *I Saw You* that I was prepared to cancel the holiday I was taking soon after the audition because I knew I'd be required in London for the recall. I was about to break the news to my wife about having to sacrifice our romantic jaunt on the altar of my career when Donna rang to tell me I wouldn't be needed for a second audition and so we could go on our mini-break after all.

"Well, that's great! That's fantastic!" I was grinning from ear to ear.

"Is it?" Donna said doubtfully.

"I mean, that doesn't happen very often, does it – no need to bring him back in, he's our man. Wonderful!"

"I don't think you understand. They don't want you."

Time stopped. The world went silent. Somewhere in a park a mile away a crow flapped its wings. Tumbleweed.

"I beg your pardon?" I husked, my voice now a winded whisper.

"You haven't got the part."

The air chilled, the tumbleweed began to dance, precursor to some terrible change in the weather. A plume on the horizon.

The bluntness of those words was so painful, her directness so utterly, appallingly insensitive, that really I should have fired her on the spot. And lo, the plume funnelled, grew taller and taller, spiralling upwards as it approached, gathering speed, until the tornado roared into the foreground and down the telephone line.

"How could you? How COULD you? I cannot believe you just called me up and ruined my day, my week, my whole fucking year actually, by being so callous. Christ, don't you ever THINK before you speak? Do you have any IDEA what it's like going into auditions, baring your very soul to these people, putting your life on the line, time and time again, and then – *bang* – 'You haven't got the part.' Just like that. Jesus! And anyway, he's wrong. He is so fucking wrong. That is MY PART, it has MY NAME ON IT."

"No it doesn't, Hugh."

"Oh doesn't it, Donna Marie French? Well, I'm going to write to David fucking Nicholls and tell him he's wrong."

"Don't."

"Don't," said my wife Lulu as she stepped out of the shower in the crummy hotel we were now in for our mini-break.

Three days later I was still fuming. I'd cleared the rickety little table of the kettle with the implausibly short lead, the sachets of tea, instant coffee and UHT milk pouches in order to create a desk from which I could launch a nuclear strike via the medium of words. I wrote a brilliant, pithy defence of my position – that I was the only person on the planet who could do justice to the lead role in this brilliant piece. You, David Nicholls, may have given birth to the character and the script, you may have crystal-clear ideas about how the role should be played, you may indeed be the executive producer on the show and involved in the casting, but you really don't know what you're talking about and your project will be a catastrophe if I don't play the part. I jabbed the last full stop and tore the page from its binder – I thought using the reverse of the final page of the actual script was a *brilliant* touch – folded it and put it in the envelope I'd brought from home for the purpose.

"You're not *actually* going to send that, are you?" sighed Lulu, searching for a plug socket for the hairdryer without which she never travelled. "At least sleep on it."

"I'll be right back," I said as I licked the stamp and flung open the hotel room door for a full-flounce exit. Or I would have done if it hadn't been one of those self-closing doors that has a ridiculous pressure hinge on it, so you can't slam, fling, or do anything remotely dramatic with it for punctuation.

I woke next morning and lay in a sweat wishing I hadn't found that post box in Malmesbury, Wiltshire, quite so easily the night before.

The letter didn't make the blindest bit of difference, of course, and Paul Rhys was excellent in the part. I met David Nicholls again eighteen years later. We were both on a jury for something or other. He said hello as he reached across the table for a ginger biscuit.

Sometimes you read of actors going into the audition room and smashing up the furniture and impressing the director so comprehensively with their I Don't Give a Shitness that they instantly get the part. Other times the police turn up. Tricky to know how to pitch it. Or there are times when your agent believes in you in a way that you yourself don't. Because you're now in your fifties and have concluded that no one's going to let you try anything different any more.

"I've got this script, Hugh. Nina Gold's casting. We love Nina."

"Donna, you love Nina. You go skiing with Nina. I don't ski."

"There's a part in it which Nina doesn't think is right for you but I know, I absolutely *know*, you can play it."

"She's Nina Gold. She skis. She's bound to be right."

"Hugh, I've represented you for thirty years. This part is you."

"Describe it."

"He's a bitter misanthrope who drinks too much, wafts his own farts round the office, looks a mess and nobody likes him."

"Hugh?"

"Hugh, are you still there?"

"Yes, I'm still here, Donna."

"The thing is, the girls have been looking through your clips and they can't find anything suitable to put together as a mini-showreel. And Nina assumes you won't go in and read."

The weird thing about being in a few telly shows and films that do well is that it is immediately assumed you are (a) constantly in work and (b) too grand to meet directors and casting directors to discuss a project let alone read for a role. Mind you, I've heard of actors in the USA being paid a fee just to read a script in their own bathtub.

"If the script's good, of course I'll go in and read."

"Phew," said Donna. "I'll ping it over."

You can usually tell within the first five pages whether or not a project has potential. I'm a stickler for spelling and punctuation. If they're sloppy then I wonder if the writer doesn't care, or if the producer/director doesn't care, or if they do care whether they're too scared of the writer to correct him or her. Whatever the reason, it distracts me. Like covering letters that often accompany a script, which on the one hand tell me I'm their fantasy casting for the role and wouldn't they be so lucky if I so much as deigned to read the first page, while on the other hand addressing me as Dear Huw or Mr. Bonvile or Hew Bournville. Yes, I get the gist, but I can tell immediately you don't actually give a monkey's whether I'm involved in your project or not, you've just been told to write a covering letter to make me feel special. "Dear Huge" is the most common, by the way, but that's just autocorrect being hilarious. I think.

This particular script is great. And it is indeed a terrific role, which anyone who knows me would agree shares much of my emotional DNA. The challenge is how to convince "them."

The meeting will be with Nina Gold and the creator of the show. The reading will be taped and forwarded to myriad faceless executives and deskbound decision-makers. But I'll really need to be in character, Donna says. "Make them forget about *Downton* and *Paddington* and *W1A* and just be the filthy heap of shit I know and love."

As the day of the audition approaches, I put personal hygiene on hold and hide my razor. I choose my wardrobe carefully. A grey (not white) T-shirt, on to which I carefully flick some tea around the neck. I find a collarless grandpa shirt that's seen better days and rip a hole in its forearm. I drip a tell-tale splish of oil on the groin of some pale trousers and rummage in a cupboard for my manky old trainers.

So far so good. Nina Gold's office is brilliantly convenient if you live in her part of North London, which I don't. I live in West Sussex and rarely go up to town, so when I do I always try and condense appointments as much as possible. On the day in question, I have a meeting with a TV drama commissioner first thing, a voice over, then the dentist, the Nina Gold audition at 2 p.m., followed by a podcast interview. My dentist would be fairly relaxed about how I look – it's my gummy version of the Forth Bridge he's interested in – and I could do a voice over and a podcast in bra and knickers and no one would bat an eyelid, but I do need to look presentable for the breakfast meeting. After all, I'm pitching a show to a broadcaster and don't want him to spend the meeting wondering where on earth it all went wrong for me and if this really is what I look like off camera, kudos to the wardrobe and make-up departments of the British film and television industry.

I opt for a suit for the morning, a quick change into my rundown civvies at lunchtime and off to Nina's torture chamber.

Looking suitably suited and stubbled, I select a couple of supermarket bags (Tesco, not Waitrose), ram the script and Outfit B into them and set off. The breakfast pitch meeting goes fine, as does the voice over. Things start to go wrong at the dentist.

"Ooh. That looks interesting. Does it hurt if I—"

"YEG! Cucksake! Yeg, it dug!"

I emerge nearly an hour later with a sore mouth, carrying my two Tesco bags. I'm now running forty-five minutes late, just time to change and head north-west for two o'clock. I'm near the Marylebone Road and have already planned my next stop: the Gentlemen's toilets opposite Baker Street tube station. I'm not overfamiliar with the facilities in question but am confident I'll be able to pop into one of the cubicles for a Superman-style change. I last visited these particular loos in my twenties. The sort of place that boasted ceramic tiles and a forelock-tugging assistant on whose dish you'd pop 5p in gratitude for keeping the place spick and span. It probably never looked like that but in my imagination all public loos in days gone by were civilised establishments; you might even run into Sir John.

By September 2019 things have changed substantially, I can tell you. I skip jauntily down the steps in my suit, expecting to find the place empty, or at most occupied by a good-natured assistant with a mop.

Not a bit of it.

Three men standing at urinals, their heads slowly craning round to take in the newcomer. Another man, humourless and starey, in a smelly anorak, waiting to take his place in one of the eight cubicles, only two of which are occupied. I've never felt more uncomfortable. Worst of all, these are not the cubicles of my recollection, protected by reassuring floor-to-ceiling solid oak doors, with chunky brass latches and locks. No, the modesty protectors of this facility are the toilet architecture equivalent of the thong, revealing way too much above and below and not hiding that much in the middle.

I bravely push against the saloon door of the cubicle furthest away from Mr. Starey. Oh my God, it's like Armageddon in there. I retreat and try the next one. Marginally better. I enter. The floor is damp and has gritty footprints of previous visitors, who've shuffled their dance across the tiles. The hook on the low-level door is broken. I put my bags down gingerly but where am I going to hang my things as I manoeuvre out of my suit and into Outfit B without dropping anything? Oh terrific: now Mr. Starey has gone into Armageddon next door. Why in God's name would anyone willingly enter that hell hole?

Oh.

Oh, I see.

Life is coming at me in a rush. There's no way I can get changed in here. What little dignity I have left is not worth shedding in front of Mr. Starey, who is now standing in the dystopian wasteland of the adjoining cubicle, eyes apparently fixed on the downpipe of the cistern, but ready to swivel his glassy gaze on to anything fleshy that might come into his peripheral vision.

I'm up the stairs and on to the pavement in a flash, my Tesco bags moist at the base. Christ, it's 1:17 p.m. Think. Think, man, think!

Marks & Spencer, Edgware Road. They're civilised. Their loos are bound to be nice and way less predatory. Having lived in this neck of the woods in my teens I have The Knowledge and am as nifty as a taxi driver. I sprint off along Marylebone Road, past the Old Marylebone Town Hall, slant left down Old Marylebone Road, right on to Chapel Street. And there she is up ahead, M&S, a shining beacon of welcome and reliability and hopefully a better class of cottaging. My aunt always referred to Peter Jones in Sloane Square as the Mothership. That my mum thought of M&S as Home says a lot about different branches of the family. I am nearly Home. And I can buy some socks if I have time, like a proper customer. But I haven't *got* time and, alarmingly, there's a notice on the door stating "Marks & Spencer, Edgware Road, is closed for refurbishment. We apologise for the inconvenience."

It's 1:24 and I'm in a grey suit with visibly wet patches under the arms. And then a solution doesn't so much occur to me as appear like a mirage. The soundtrack switches to *Lawrence of Arabia* as the dark dot looms larger and larger, taking shape in this desert of inconveniences. It may not be Omar Sharif on a camel but it is the Hilton London Metropole, shimmering in the heat haze of diesel exhausts this September lunchtime on the Edgware Road. And suddenly I am O'Toole on camel-back, hurtling towards Aqaba, as I dart through the traffic, my supermarket bags flailing, making for the front door of the hotel.

Once inside, the music scratches to *Mission Impossible* as I move calmly and swiftly across the lobby, nodding hello to the concierge, dividing my ocular capabilities by scoping for security cameras with one eye while with the other scanning the horizon for the lavatories. Time check: 1:29.

I round the corner of the lobby, nearing the banqueting suites. Wisely, I don't break into a run because I'm now being picked up by a second bank of cameras. A gender neutral sign indicates that the bogs are in range.

But it's not my day. The music stops abruptly. Outside the toilets is one of those yellow hazard caution cones indicating that operatives are on manoeuvres. On cue, a woman appears from within holding a bucket, gesturing that I'd better come back later. Using the universal language of grunting, I apologise and enter anyway, the man in the grey suit leaving her marooned in the corridor.

In seconds I'm down to my pants in a cubicle the size of a phone box but at least I'm on my own and, even better, I have a disgruntled hotel employee standing guard outside. I whip off my tie and, using my shirt as a towel, pat down the wetter patches of my body as best I can. Next, it's on with the T-shirt, ripped overshirt and soiled trousers. Stylish brogues are swapped for old flappy trainers, smart watch for some weird bracelet I found from another life. I squish my suit into the Tesco bags, topping things off with a strategically placed half-drunk bottle of whisky. At the basin, I sluice my hair with water and assess myself in the mirror. I look like I've just died.

I exit the toilets and smile at the woman with the bucket,

who does a fantastic double-take – what happened to the man in the suit?

I have twenty minutes to get to Nina Gold's lair in fucking Greenland or wherever. More running and sweat and screw the bus, get an Uber. Painful minutes watching the little car wander round and round my screen.

Eventually I am deposited outside Nina's fortress and I go in. Nina looks at me with suppressed curiosity. The show's creator is equally puzzled but too polite to comment.

"Apologies about the ripped shirt," I say. "You should see the bush!"

If I don't stink, I am definitely sweating. And as I put my Tesco bags down with a satisfying clink, I fart. I suspect more through nerves than being in character.

"Let's crack on, shall we?"

I read pretty well, I think. Nina and the writer/producer give me some notes. I read again, differently but still in the manner of a man who's had a hideous ninety minutes getting here.

Two days later Donna calls to tell me that they're going in a different direction.

"Who different direction?"

"Well, they'd offered it to someone a while ago but he'd hummed and hawed and they thought he was no longer interested, which is why they started looking again. I mean Nina really was ... really was surprised and, don't get me wrong, *interested* by your, by your—"

"Who different direction?"

"Gary Oldman."

Actors are characterised as self-indulgent, greedy, lazy and feckless.

Q: How do you wipe out fifty actors in one go?
A: Lob a chicken leg on to the M25.

Q: Why don't actors look out of the window in the mornings?
A: Because otherwise they'd have nothing to do in the afternoons.

Keen to find out how much dogs resemble their owners, researchers conducted an experiment. They took three dogs, one belonging to an architect, one to a scientist and one to an actor, and put them in a room with three piles of bones. The results were revealing. The architect's dog swiftly organised its pile of bones into a perfect pyramid, the scientist's dog shuffled the bones around to form a double helix, while the actor's dog ate all the bones, shagged the other two dogs and asked for the afternoon off.

I am one of the luckiest actors I know. I have managed to keep working since 1986 in theatre, radio, television and film but beyond turning up on time and not punching the director if you can possibly help it, I have no great tips of the trade to impart. This isn't a manual or a map, it's a series of snapshots I've taken along the way.

PART ONE

Beginners Please

1

Hurry Up and Wait

Dad was sleeping when I arrived at 7:45 a.m. A February morning in 2018. I was taking over from the carer who had an urgent appointment. I was free that day anyway, in a holding pattern, waiting to hear if a film about Roald Dahl was going to happen, or not happen. It had been in development for two years and after several false starts was nearly ready to go into pre-production.

Nearly.

As is so often true of independent films, delicately put together by a coalition of the willing rather than one studio with a cheque book, we'd hurried to the start line and were now waiting for one last piece of the jigsaw – financing dependent on confirmation of my co-star – to slot into place. Then we could mix metaphors and start taxiing along the runway.

So I had time spare to spend with Dad. And time was precious. He was in the early stages of dementia. While I waited for him to wake up I sat on the sofa by the baby grand piano in the living room of his flat, the downstairs of a converted Edwardian house. I picked up a family album from the coffee table and began to leaf through it . . .

*

My darling mum had passed away three Christmases previously, my brother ten months ago. Then my dad's twin brother died. My father had suffered a great deal of loss lately, but strangely, because of the softening of his brain and the inevitable loosening of his attachment to the world, he had not seemed particularly emotional about any of these events. Then again, I never saw Dad cry. That's not to say he was a hard or heartless man. On the contrary, you could not meet a more twinkly-eyed, good-natured soul; when introduced to ladies of any age he'd usually kiss their hand, theatrically. But he was never one to express deeper feelings. As I've tried to fathom him more in recent years I think I've put this sense of emotional distance down to his own father before him. He greatly admired his father, a surveyor, who suffered from shell shock in the First World War. It was one of the five or so stories my dad still had access to and repeated on a regular basis, weekly if not daily.

"My father was blown up on the first day of the Somme, y'know. Thrown right up in the air. Have I not told you this story?"

"Well, ye—"

"And when he landed he said he felt like he was a blob of jelly on a slab of ice. He never rode a bike or drove a car after that." Nor did he ever talk about the war, apparently. After his experience in the fields of France he became a man of few words and even fewer gestures.

My father rarely gave me a hug on impulse when I was a kid – a kiss at bedtime, sure, if I was still awake when he got home from work at the hospital. I don't think his parents hugged him or his twin brother much, although they loved them both. Once I had got over the awkwardness of being a teenager, when any familial expression of emotion was quite frankly hideous, I consciously started to hug Dad hello and goodbye. It's not that he recoiled in embarrassment when I kissed him on the cheek or put my arm round his shoulder but I think he found it unusual, just not part of his make-up.

My grandfather, John Pritchard Williams – same name as my dad – died before I was born. Grandma Dorothy was a Methodist, serious but sweet in her own way; bird-like and quietly spoken. Dad said the only time he saw her drink alcohol was the night they went to see Donald Wolfit in *King Lear*. She was so traumatised by his performance that in the interval she ordered a port and lemon.

Saturday afternoons in East Sheen in south-west London, where we lived when I was a kid, saw me being deposited round the corner at Grandma's. A trip to the toy shop, Fred Cross, on the corner of Thornton and the Upper Richmond roads was the bribe. Grandma lived in the ground-floor flat of a two-storey conversion in Palewell Park. My Cassie lived upstairs. For years I assumed a Cassie was some sort of relative that everyone had, like an aunt twice removed or something. But in fact she wasn't a blood relative at all and had evidently married into the family in a manner that was never fully explained to me. Only recently did I discover that she had in fact been nanny to my father and his brother and when their grandmother died, Cassie married their grandfather. Perhaps some of the family didn't approve.

By the time I came along, Cassie had a fantastic beard. Both she and Grandma smelt of Old. Although Cassie had better biscuits and her bright kitchen upstairs looked out over the rooftops of Sheen, I felt duty bound to have tea with Grandma in her altogether more gloomy flat below. She would put the television on just as the afternoon's sports were coming to an end. Time for *Final Score*. The living room was sepulchral, with dark Edwardian furniture and heavy curtains. Add to that the incantation of football results emanating from the telly and the whole thing was like being in a brown tomb listening to Gregorian chant without the laughs.

"West Bromwich Albion [slight upward inflection] two ... Manchester City [depressing downward tone] one."

Even today hearing the football results being read out causes a feeling of dread to wash over me. But it wasn't just the dirge of the scores being intoned like an executioner's death scroll, it was also because, back then, it meant it was nearly *that* time. Time to hide behind the sofa. Time for *Doctor Who*.

I can still feel the rough bobbled texture of the fabric on my upper lip as my hands gripped the top edge of Grandma's dark green settee, my nose just resting on the rim, between the antimacassars. The room fills with the creepy, haunting electronic slithers of the theme tune, my eyes are glued to the weird pulsating diamond shape emanating from the screen of the television as Patrick Troughton's face warps into view.

Most of my father's family on his mother's side lived within a few streets of each other in East Sheen. Uncle Ron had been gassed in the First World War and was forever being doused in cow's cream – great big thick dollops of it – to soothe his skin; it came in a pot, prescribed. And he ate industrial quantities of ice cream. The house in which he lived with Auntie Ethel was preternaturally dark. She had OCD. The curtains were always closed, the furniture was heavy and depressing – what you could see of it anyway. Most of it was covered in dust sheets. Reluctantly, Auntie Ethel would reveal the dining table for meals and polish it while eating.

During the war years much of my father's extended family lived in the same house, Greenfields, in East Sheen. After lunch on Sundays Grandpa Bates, the patriarch – he had founded Luxfer, a pavement glass company, had a driver and smoked a cigar – used to stroll across the lawn to the old coach house and cottage at the bottom of the garden where the chauffeur lived. But it wasn't the chauffeur he was visiting for a post-prandial moment, it was Miss Slatter, his former secretary, who he had installed in the same property. Maybe the chauffeur was asked to vacate for the afternoon. Maybe she dressed up as the chauffeur. Maybe she had a stick-on moustache and a cap? History doesn't relate.

*

Dad's bedroom door opened and out he came, dressed neatly in pale cavalry twill trousers and brown suede brogues, a checked shirt and burgundy lambswool V-neck sweater. Something of a uniform. A country gentle man. Seeing me in the living room, leafing through the album, he spread his arms wide in a showman's expression of delight. "My dear old chap! I didn't know you were coming!" – even though we had gone over his diary many times just yesterday.

"How are you, Dad?"

"All the better for seeing you."

It was a familiar rhythm of speech. Sometimes the same question elicited the response "God has been merciful to me, a sinner." It was usually one of the two.

"Coffee? Tea? Glass of something stronger?"

"It's eight a.m., Dad. Let me get you some breakfast."

In the grey haze of dementia, time of day has no real meaning. In recent months Dad had taken to getting fully dressed at three in the morning and shaking his carer awake because he had an urgent engagement. One night there were half a dozen people waiting in the car, apparently. Another time he was going to be late for the Queen. Good to know his subconscious was mixing in the right circles.

After the Leys School and Emmanuel College, Cambridge, Dad went to St. Mary's, Paddington, to train as a doctor. It was the era evoked in the film *Doctor in the House* and its sequels, a world in which carefree medical students tried to avoid the professional wrath of big, blustery surgeons like James Robertson Justice and the wards were run by matrons of the firm but fair variety. The early years of the NHS, a time when there were fewer middle managers, when medical students worked hard and played hard and, as Dad never tired of telling me, "we didn't spend all our time filling in forms."

Clearly thinking themselves rakish and debonair, my father

and his two best friends called themselves The Three Musketeers. There was one particularly pretty trainee nurse they'd spotted in the canteen, so they drew straws for who was going to ask her to the annual dance. You can probably guess the rest.

The album on my lap was open at an informal photograph of Dad and Mum, newly engaged. A handsome couple, he in a suit and tie, she beautiful in a floral dress, dark brown wavy hair, swept back.

"Tell me, old fellow, who is that? Priddy gal!"

I told him Mum's name but it didn't mean anything to him now.

John Pritchard (JP) Williams married Patricia Adele Freeman in March 1952 and they lived happily together for sixty-four years, bringing up three children: Nigel, Clare and me. There were two years between Nigel and Clare and I was youngest by six years; an afterthought perhaps but hopefully not a mistake.

After St. Mary's, Dad went on to become a surgeon, and, from what I gather from the medics I occasionally meet whom he trained, a good and kind one. He was a urologist – "I'm just a plumber, really. Waterworks and all that." However much he downplayed his occupation the fact is he improved and often saved lives. He made a difference to the world around him and he did it with modesty and a lightness of touch.

My mother, the pretty nurse the musketeers had spied in the canteen, was born in Alexandria in 1929, to Richard Freeman, an RAF doctor from Howth, Dublin, one of eleven children, and his wife Muriel White, who was from a family of bulb growers in Spalding, Lincolnshire. If you're not in the know, family nicknames can be embarrassing. There was no problem using the name Granny for Muriel (to distinguish her from Grandma Dorothy) but I could never really understand why classmates at my primary school sniggered and held their noses when I said, "My PooPoo's coming this weekend."

PooPoo – my mother's father – made me laugh. The sort of laughter that pushed me to a pitch of tearful hysterics where I'd plead, "Stop it! Please stop it, it hurts!" There would be a truce and a moment of respite, until he pulled some other silly face or made some other farty noise and I'd be off again, fast on the way to bursting something. I don't remember much else about him – he died before I turned five – other than the bath times whenever he came to stay. As Mum and I went through the general washing procedure, this spooky shape would appear against the mottled glass of the bathroom door and his fingers would drum on the pane, transporting me to so many squirming giggles that the water would slosh and sloosh and overflow.

Granny smoked Benson & Hedges, drank gin and tonic and had a telephone on the table by her armchair so she could call the bookies. She loved watching horse racing on the television, which as her years advanced and her hearing retreated was turned up louder and louder. After PooPoo died, whenever I went to stay with her in her bungalow in Pinchbeck, Lincolnshire, there was no escaping the climaxes of Peter O'Sullevan's commentary on the 4:05 at Doncaster. Granny's was the first colour TV I had ever seen. It was miraculous and vibrant, mainly because she usually mistook the colour knob for the brightness knob and so the hues on the jockeys' silks throbbed like an acid trip.

"What's that noise, old fellow?" asked Dad, as the beep of my mobile phone broke the reverie. I put down the photo album and looked at the text. It was John Hay, the producer/director of the Roald Dahl film, *To Olivia,* telling me our leading lady had become unattached. Not as in deranged, she had got a better offer than our small-budget project.

So, it was back to the drawing board. Just another iteration of the industry catchphrase Hurry Up and Wait.

2

Playing Under the Piano

Fledglings was a nursery school in a house in East Sheen. I know the building at least is still there because I drove past it not long ago and a single image popped into my mind: me under the upright piano near the bay window, wearing a green painting smock, looking like Christopher Robin in a drawing by Shepard.

Was I hiding under the piano? Or was I just playing?

I couldn't remember at first, and then, as I passed through the gates into Richmond Park, it came back to me. The teacher had asked me to do something in front of the class. I think it might even have been a bit of the Nativity play. Except – no – there's a stream of sunshine lancing down through the window and piercing my hiding place like a spotlight. And the sunlight is flickering, so there must be leaves of some sort. So, it's not Christmas. No, not leaves, it's blossom. There's pink blossom on the tree and sunshine and a blue sky beyond. And I am terrified of having to do something in front of the dozen or so other boys and girls. Are they wearing poncey green smocks too? I can't see now, not from this distance. Am I the only one looking this ridiculous, aged three or four? Maybe the terror that's gripping me there beneath the piano has more to do with looking like a green meringue than performing. And that's the tension, I suspect, that I have sensed within me ever since. The instinct to keep it in the shadows, this acting lark, just playing under the piano for fear of looking a fool, yoked to the thrill of stepping into the spotlight in character, as someone "other" (and certainly more interesting) than me, and, by doing so, sharing stories with others.

I was about six when we moved to Kidbrooke Grove, Blackheath. The house seemed huge to me. Solid red-brick entrance pillars marked the In and Out of the semi-circular gravel drive. It was quite imposing, with three stone steps up to the front door, a big bay window to the left of it – a playroom with piano – and my dad's study window to the right.

It was built at the beginning of the last century, with a large rear garden divided by a pergola that ran the whole way across its width. In summer, which of course in my memory was most of the time, the pergola was shrouded with yellow laburnum and twice a year the rear façade of the house was a sea of purple as the wisteria, the bane and beauty of my father's gardening pleasure, wafted its intoxicating scent to my various camps and hiding places. One of these was a tree house in the copper beech that stood sturdy and ancient. A rope ladder from Raggity Ann's toy shop in Blackheath Village provided access to this turret of adventure and a swing hanging from one of its muscular grey branches was the source of bruises and scrapes from aggressive pirates and repelled Roundheads.

Whenever Billy Smart's Circus pitched camp on the Heath, the circus kids used to come to our school for the duration of their stay, on one occasion on an actual elephant, which was totally thrilling. Had the Health & Safety Executive existed at the time it would have had a coronary. All Saints School was tucked in a vale on the Heath itself. The circus kids were earthy and different but I felt sorry for whichever of them had to sit next to my friend Phoebe who seemed to pee non-stop, bless her. You only had to say "Good morning, Phoebe" or something equally upsetting and there it was, lemoning its way down her leg. She played 1st Shepherd to my 3rd Shepherd in the Nativity play, so at least I didn't have to stand directly next to her. As well as my first acting role I was also given the stage management duty of Manger Wrangler, a dual skillset that I like to think has served me in good stead over the years.

Poor Phoebe. Mind you, my own bladder function wasn't exactly robust.

One winter, snowballing on the Heath, dressed in the sixties equivalent of a giant furry onesie, I felt the call. On the treeless Heath everyone can hear you scream and there's absolutely nowhere to hide, or, for that matter, take a leak. So, looking like something out of Scott's Antarctic expedition, I started waddling home as fast as I could.

Crunch, crunch through the snow – which way's quickest? Along the road past the houses, or take the alleyway footpath down the side of Morden College?

Decision, decision.

Crossing the road now, icy, nearly slipped, decision, decision.

Stick to the road and the pavement. Waddle, waddle.

You so want to pee, but don't worry, you're going to make it.

The turning into our street now coming into view.

Fast waddle, faster waddle, bladder burning. You're going to make it.

"By the way," your tour-guiding brain intervenes unhelpfully, "just up that road on the left lives someone called Wedgwood Benn. His family have something to do with politics. And in that house there lives a famous conductor called Downes – his children are Caractacus and Boudicca, Crack and Boo for short," which always makes my mum raise her eyebrows and shake her head.

"And look, there's Adrian Thingy's house, and here's the corner coming up."

Oh how fantastic, it's going to be absolutely fine. Right turn approaching, then a hundred-yard dash along the slushy pavement and I'll be home.

The turning's nearly upon me now, the pollarded tree on the corner looking stubbled and bald. I don't even know what pollarding means but Dad used the word the other day so I've been telling friends about the pollarded trees in our road as a matter of importance, showing off my new word. "There are a lot of them about you know and—"

Uh-oh.

Too late. There's a sudden, unexpected warmth inside my furry jumpsuit. And it's wet.

As the camera cranes up I see a six-year-old boy leaning against the pollarded chestnut tree at the corner of Kidbrooke Grove, panting, beginning to cry, a dark stain spreading across his khaki snowsuit.

Oh, the humiliation.

It was at that same spot, a few years later, that I told my sister about the boy up the road who made me rub myself up against him. He was several years older than me. We shared the school run and so I would often go to his house for tea on afternoons when Mum was at work. While his mother prepared sandwiches, we'd go up to his room to play. Except my idea of play and his were evidently quite different. He had recently been to see *Diamonds Are Forever* at the Odeon in Lewisham and wanted to act out a scene in which James Bond apparently rubbed up against someone. He instructed me to lie on the bed and let him demonstrate quite how amazing the scene in the film was. Intrigued, and a devoted fan of 007, I did as I was told. He then frotted away against me like a dog against a leg. But I wasn't the corner of a table, nor insensible. Even at the time I thought it was fairly peculiar behaviour for a secret agent but anyway it made me rampantly curious for about a year and a half and I went round James Bonding with anyone who was vaguely interested.

3

Emperor Salazar

The time spent between getting back from school and doing my homework was a patchwork of rubbish attempts at making Airfix models, and yelling *"Achtung!"* as Guy Bonser, Mark Spurgeon and Adrian Thingy from round the corner besieged or escaped from the fortresses we had constructed in the occupied territory of various back gardens along our road. But more sharply in focus than any of these images is me, cross-legged on the carpet in front of the telly. Prep school shorts, a downy moustache of orange squash, a Garibaldi biscuit if I was lucky. And there, glowing from the box in front of me, three gods of the small screen, whose every word was gospel.

You see, I was one of the anointed who between 1967 and 1972 bore witness to the tripartite divinity of John Noakes, Peter Purves and Valerie Singleton. Verily they said unto me *sticky back plastic* and *send your milk bottle tops to* and *Down, Shep!*

This was the world according to *Blue Peter* and it was the religion of my childhood certainties. Of course, there was an alternative doctrine, but *Magpie* was on something called ITV which, if not the work of Satan, was certainly to be considered with suspicion because it was New and had Adverts.

A lot of my time was spent on my own. I didn't have imaginary friends but I certainly developed a vivid imagination. At this stage in my young life I wanted to kill my sister. Really seriously murder her. I was about seven. At breakfast I had done something innocuous like kick her under the table. Just for something to do, really. Looking for a reaction. I was an irritating younger brother, it was in the job description. She'd kicked me back, so I had probably shrieked or cried and in any event complained loudly to Mum, who was in the kitchen, half visible through the hatch in the small dining room.

"Clare!" snapped Mum. "You are thirteen, for heaven's sake."

"Ow!" I shrieked again, even though nothing so much as a fly had touched me. But Mum wasn't to know.

"Oh stop it, both of you!"

Suddenly, Clare was out of her chair and round my side of the table to "get me." She pulled my ears and dashed on past, making for the twelve-paned door in the corner of the dining room that gave on to the garden. Furious, I squealed like a stuck pig and, abandoning my toast, leaped up.

Cut to: me chasing my sister round the perimeter of the back garden. She was laughing. I was chubby and slow. I sweated after her, my blood boiling as she glanced over her shoulder at me, skipping easily ahead. After two laps, she darted off the lawn, through the back door and into the house, swiftly pulling the door shut, at the same time turning the key in the lock. As she dangled the key smugly, she did the most irritating thing any sibling can do when in a momentary position of power: she stuck her tongue out at me.

A red mist descended and the world went into slow motion.

A sledgehammer was leaning against the wall next to the back door, minding its own business. Cutting short its coffee break, I reached for its handle. It was incredibly heavy. With superhuman strength I managed to pick it up and with one wobbly slo-mo roar launched it towards Clare's scrunched-up face and pointy tongue. To reach its target the sledgehammer obviously had to pass through the multiple glass panes of the door, which it did with impressive ease, thanks to various laws of physics relating to force, momentum and angry little boys. The glass from a dozen panes shattered into a thousand shards as the door splintered.

Cut to: Dad chasing me round the back garden. While I panted my way religiously around the perimeter my dad simply cut the corner and headed me off, tackling me to the ground in about six seconds. I pleaded for mercy, blamed my sister, society, the dog – bad call, since we didn't have one at the time – but to no avail. Dad spanked me with a slipper, or it might have been a hairbrush. The only time he did so.

On the upside, the back door subsequently let in a lot more light, now containing as it did a single sheet of glass instead of those annoying little panes. So much easier for Mum to clean. Frankly, I had done everyone a favour. I dug a shallow grave behind the garage for Clare and plotted ways to put her in it, but as the months went by my animosity waned and I decided to bury the hatchet rather than my sister.

The upstairs landing of the house had two exits either side of the staircase, left and right. As far as I was concerned it was a proscenium arch theatre in London, SE3. Perfect for the great performances I was destined to give to my bored family and hired locals. Or for my more avant-garde creations there was the playroom downstairs, a room that back in the day must have been the formal dining room but to me was a gigantic blank canvas. Here I could put on big-budget productions that required things like actual sets (cardboard box), rather than the simple request of "now shut your eyes" between scenes while I effected a quick change from Granny's fox fur stole to an Arabian headdress. Now I was the Emperor Salazar or, with Grandpa's waistcoat added, a Sultan of Some Description.

The dressing-up box in the walk-in airing cupboard was a

haven for me. This was where I spent an inordinate amount of time inventing characters. Inside Dad's National Service Royal Navy trunk were endless cast-offs, ripe for new stories. Guy Bonser and Mark Spurgeon and Adrian Thingy from round the corner were far more interested in football and shooting things (Guy once took out my ankle from thirty yards with my brother's air rifle as I hid behind the wheelbarrow). But all the commando stuff in our garden, or in the allotments at the top of the road, was really a ploy. I was reeling them in. While by day I feigned interest in Leeds United and declared Peter Bonetti the best goalkeeper in the world until Guy pointed out he played for Chelsea, by night I crafted theatre tickets and drew up playbills. Ultimately my humouring of their preferred interests had the desired effect: one by one, my neighbourhood friends succumbed, allowing me to dive into the dressing-up box and drape them in some musty old clothes, so that they could play a supporting role in one of my Plays on the Landing, starring ME.

In my bed in the small room that in olden days would have been a dressing room, I would lie awake and listen to sounds from downstairs, a long, long way away.

There'd be the ring-ring of the telephone. Mum answering, "Ayt fiyve ayt, three double ayoh wun, haylayo?" – putting on her telephone voice, which sounded like the Queen on Christmas Day. I used to wonder if the Queen put on a special voice for her Broadcast to the Commonwealth and the rest of the year she sounded like a Welsh miner. Not that I'd heard many Welsh miners speak, to be honest, but it did seem such an extraordinarily fabricated sound.

The creaking of the ancient water pipes.

A wisteria branch scraping against the paint-cracked and possibly-rotten-but-we-won't-talk-about-it window frame.

A scratching from deep behind a skirting board somewhere.

And then the sound of a car pulling into the gravel drive.

My pulse quickens. It's Dad. It's Daddy!

The heavy front door opening and closing, the steady, confident tread of his leather shoes as he crosses the hall to the kitchen. The kiss on the cheek, the murmur of catching-up chat, and then, my pulse still quicker now, his footsteps on the wide wooden stairs that creak on the fourth step, two extra paces at the turn, then up the final flight on to the landing. The soft pad of footsteps on carpet, the standard lamp rattling a little as he passes it, closer and closer to my room. But then – oh no! – a diversion: he veers off into his and Mum's bedroom, next door to mine. I hear his jacket come off and get re-bodied round a chair in a swift single movement, coins out of his pocket on to a tray on his dressing table. Then the sound of him blowing his nose into his hanky, as loud as a foghorn and familiar and ordinary to me. And then he comes into my room with a cheerily whispered, "Hello, old chap. Are you awake?"

As if I wouldn't be.

He kneels down at the side of my bed, his head level with mine, and ruffles my hair with his left hand and nuzzles my cheek with a brief kiss. The scratch of his bristle and the smell of the hospital, clinical and clean. Maybe he asks about my day, maybe I'm meant to ask him about his, but frankly I'm not interested. I'm about eight and all I want is to keep him close and to hear The Story. This is what I have been waiting for.

He begins.

"Once upon a time, a long, long time ago, when Richmond Park was all forest, in a clearing in the wood lived a Mummy and a Daddy and their three children: Niggle the Giggle, Clare-a Bear-a Butterskin and Hugh de Boo de Boo. And in the trees nearby lived a squirrel. But this was no ordinary squirrel because instead of storing his nuts in his cheeks this squirrel kept them in his ears, so that when he shook his head, they rattled. Rattle-rattle-rattle. The other thing that made this squirrel particularly special was that he had one red eye and one green eye . . ."

Only in later years did I realise that he always began The Story the same way each night in order to give his tired brain time to shake off the tensions of the day. The blips and bleeps of the machines in the operating theatre, the worried patients on the ward, the diagnoses and the decisions. This autopilot opening was a way of pushing the real world to one side while he gathered his thoughts, giving him time to come up with whatever adventure Hugh de Boo de Boo and the wise and wonderful squirrel might go on next. I look back now with nothing but admiration for my dad, finding these moments of calm for his youngest son.

Dad was so tall, to me, back then. Dark hair, balding, strong nose. Distinguished. Like a Roman statue but not pompous or condescending. He was intelligent, talented at the piano; he played squash and loved sailing, was funny without being a comedian, flirty without being a lech. Modest. Patient. And he loved my mum. And she loved him. Their contentment was sometimes boring to be around and is boring to write about, so I won't stay here long. I could try and make it more interesting and say I had to duck flying furniture but I never did. The most turbulent it got, in fact, was on a trip to visit cousins in Norfolk. Just the three of us in the car, Mum with the map on her lap. We approached a T-junction.

"Eyand it's right heeyah, darling."

For some reason she put on her Queen-at-Christmas voice when map reading. I think it made her feel more in control of something she might not fully understand, like the telephone.

"No, I think it's a left," said Dad, flicking the indicator accordingly.

"Darling, it's right."

"No, I'm quite sure it's left."

"John!"

She never called him John. It was always Darling or, in polite company, JP. As in, "JP, where are the tonics? Sorry, Fabia, I tell him where they're meant to go but he never puts them in the right place. Honestly!"

"Men, eh, Pat?"

"Oh dear me, Fabia, I know. I know!"

You heard exchanges like that all over our part of the London suburbs. Anyway, it was JP, never John. So, calling him by his proper Christian name could mean only one thing. I felt a surge of panic. I lurched forward between the seats as, through mounting sobs, I pleaded with them at the top of my voice.

"Please, Mummy! Please, Daddy! Please don't get divorced!"

4

Don Ferolo

I looked up to my brother Nigel, literally. I wanted him to show me the way. He did, to an extent, but with the eight-year age gap I was never going to be his closest buddy. He taught me Funny, though. Through his LP collection he introduced me to Flanders & Swann, Tony Hancock, *Round the Horne* and the Goons. He had collected scripts, biographies of the writers and performers as well as recordings of Tom Lehrer, Lenny Bruce, Peter Sellers, Joyce Grenfell, Spike Milligan and Kenneth Williams. He would point out to me their vocal idiosyncrasies, what made them stand out from the crowd. He also talked ad infinitum about *Beyond the Fringe*, educating me that satire was the way forward and battering it into my head that performers were nothing without the writers. I was beginning to know what he meant, as my own writing – superlative as it was – did not appear to be going down as well as, say, Alan Ayckbourn's, who had written a play for children called *Ernie's Incredible Illucinations*.

We put it on at my prep school as part of an evening of Informal Drama. Ernie is the lead and I played him. There is a moment at the end when, in reference to the "illucinations" he has experienced, Ernie says to the audience, "I hope you don't get 'em!" It was the first time I had ever looked out at an audience in character. Up until then any glances out front during plays had been furtive, checking whether or not Mum was laughing at the bit we all found funny. But for that moment, with all eyes on Ernie and my eyes sweeping across all of them, the pleasure I took in seeing *their* pleasure, the delight in us all being connected in this entertainment, was an incredibly potent feeling.

My brother had latched on to *Monty Python* straight away and introduced it to my father. Having heard them laughing their heads off one evening I tiptoed downstairs in my dressing gown to see what was going on. They were on the sofa transfixed by the surreality of the show. Because it was smart as well as daft, from then on I was sometimes allowed to stay up and watch it, as a treat. However, it was on way past my bedtime, sometimes as late as eleven o'clock. So, any outstanding chores (thank you letters, have you cleaned your shoes?) had to have been completed if I was even to have a chance, and only then on occasion, and only during the holidays. Its late-night scheduling led to one significant life lesson.

Dad and I were going to the Boat Show at Earls Court. I liked collecting brochures from exhibitors' stands and poring over them in bed where I would fantasise about life at sea in impossibly big sailing yachts. We never went to the speedboat stands, nor took our shoes off to board one of the gin palaces; anything that wasn't powered principally by sail was, in Dad's book, The Enemy.

"We're leaving at eight o'clock tomorrow morning, old chap. So tonight it's straight to bed after your bath."

"But *Monty Python*'s on tonight."

Dad looked at Mum, who put up her hands as a sign that whatever negotiation was to follow had nothing to do with her. But as far as Dad was concerned there was no negotiation. I could either stay up late to watch *Monty Python* and not go to the Boat

Show because I would be over-tired, or go to bed on time and join him for the Earls Court adventure. The choice was simple and it was mine. I obviously opted to stay up and watch *Monty Python*, because I knew that with my boundless charm and long eyelashes, come the morning I would be able to tag along with Dad no problem.

That night I laughed at the Gumbys and the lumberjacks and the grown men dressed as gossipy housewives whose sons were clever little boys who worked in the Ministry. Next morning, I yawned awake, dressed quickly and hurried downstairs, slightly behind schedule.

Dad had left without me.

I suppose I always associated my brother with acting because it was on stage that I saw him most prominently, at least once he was away at boarding school. It was the same with my sister. Clare, six years older than me, boarded at Westonbirt School in Gloucestershire for sixth form. I would be dragged along for visits at weekends: a desultory walk in the nearby arboretum (oooh look, another tree) or for the end-of-year festivities, which did at least feature cake. However, I really sat up and paid attention when I saw her on stage in a production of Sheridan's *The Critic*. It was in a grim school Nissen hut that was trying its best to be a theatre. She played Don Ferolo Whiskerandos and was brilliantly funny. My sister? Funny? The one whose grave I had dug only a year or so before, who sang on the loo and was altogether older and therefore annoying, funny? Proper side-splittingly funny. This stage lark changed people, clearly. I held both my brother's and sister's talent in high esteem. However, to them I was probably little more than an irritant, a buzzing fly wanting to get in on their act. In fact, I know I was.

There was the Sunday afternoon when they were going with their friends to see the latest Bond film at Studio 6 & 7 in Lewisham. A bus trip from the top of our road, upstairs seats hopefully – always more exciting – across the Heath and down the hill to the faraway land of Lewisham. A real proper outing with the big boys and girls. Popcorn, the works. I hadn't yet told anyone the good news that I was going with them, least of all my brother and sister, but it was going to be a great afternoon, I knew it. After lunch they went to fetch their coats. I followed.

"What are you doing?" asked my brother.

"I'm coming with you," I said, standing on the little bench to get my own coat from the hook.

"Mum?" said my sister, a pleading tone in her voice.

"Sorry but it's a double A," said my brother quickly, heading to the front door.

"Yes, sorry," added Clare, whipping the belt round her coat. "You have to be fourteen."

My Sunday afternoon turned into a crashing bore of leafing through old copies of *Look and Learn* as I reluctantly accepted the fact that it would be a while before I was allowed to watch Roger Moore running across a load of crocodiles' noses.

A few days later Mum was driving me to Ladywell Baths for a chlorine overdose followed by an evening of stinging eyes, otherwise known as a swimming lesson. We turned off Lewisham Hill and on to the High Street. As we passed the cinema I looked across at the marquee hoarding, with its signage for *Live and Let Die*. Just beneath it and to the right was a smaller sign indicating its certification: "A." This meant a child could attend, unless his name was Hugh and his big brother and sister didn't want him spoiling their Sunday afternoon fun.

When I was growing up my parents only knew one person in show business, an actor called Michael Bates. He had found national fame in television series like *Last of the Summer Wine* and *It Ain't Half Hot Mum*, in which he was all tanned up with a cod-Indian accent as the punkah-wallah Rangi Ram. The mind boggles now but this was then. He was an acclaimed stage actor too, having salvaged the role of Inspector Truscott in Joe Orton's *Loot*, after its inauspicious start in the hands of Kenneth Williams.

In the spring of 1971 Michael appeared at our local theatre in the first production of *Forget Me Not Lane*, by Peter Nichols, directed by Michael Blakemore. It later transferred to the Apollo Theatre but during the try-out in Greenwich, rather than commute each night across South London to his home near Richmond, Michael stayed with us in Blackheath.

He was a bit older than my father, with a high forehead, close-cropped greying hair and a tight military moustache, like a stiff brush, which made him look eerily like Field Marshal Montgomery, whom he once played. I only really saw him at breakfast and at first I didn't know who he was or why he was in our house. The main thing was he let me get on with my cornflakes without doing annoying grown-up things like asking me about school, so I thought he was OK. As far as I was concerned he was just Our Lodger . . . until one day.

I had been in the dressing-up box in the airing cupboard since supper, losing myself in Dad's cropped dress jacket that he must have worn for mess dinners in Singapore. It was white and (on him) short and would (on him) have looked smart and chic. On me it looked baggy and messy. So I decided I was a fine dining waiter called Enrico who was never going to make it in the hospitality business, not with sleeves so long they kept dragging in the soup.

Dad poked his head round the door and asked if I'd like to go with him to pick Michael up after the evening performance. The most exciting thing about this opportunity was that it meant staying up way past my normal bedtime.

We parked near the theatre and went into the foyer. After a word with one of the ushers, Dad beckoned me to follow him up the stairs. As the usher opened the heavy door at the top of the raked auditorium, Dad shushed a finger to his lips.

I stepped into the darkness.

There in the distance, brightly lit on stage, was Our Lodger Michael and some other people, performing to an audience of three hundred plus, completely captivated by the show. You could hear a pin drop. As the lights dimmed the silence was broken first by one pair of hands clapping, then a dozen, then hundreds – thunderous applause. All because of what Our Lodger had been doing.

The next morning at breakfast I sat staring at Michael as he tapped the shell of his boiled egg. He had transformed from being Bloke at Brekky to The Giant with Extraordinary Power. This titan, now dipping his toasted soldiers into the yolk and chatting to Mum, was, quite simply, a breed apart. I wanted to know the secret of whence this power came, oh Giant. He had a unique talent, which I was hungry to understand and acquire: the ability to inhabit a role and weave magic in the dark in front of hundreds of people, holding them enchanted, entranced and entertained. He was no longer Our Lodger, he was Our Actor.

Bernard Miles became another hero, because he frightened the life out of me when I saw him play Long John Silver in *Treasure Island* at The Mermaid, the theatre near Blackfriars that he himself had opened in 1959. Apparently Spike Milligan was in the show too, but he didn't make a lasting impression on the eleven-year-old me, transfixed as I was by the glinting avarice of the pirate leader. I knew I was in a theatre watching something entirely artificial but nevertheless I was swept away by the power of make-believe.

Mum and Dad enjoyed the theatre in the same way they enjoyed galleries, the opera and concerts. They were cultured but not obsessed about being up on the latest exhibition or show. It was just part of their diet, like Dad playing squash, or Mum and her flower arranging. In the same way, they introduced us kids to the arts as part of the curriculum of our everyday life. I couldn't stand most of it, to be honest. Being dragged round museums bored me to tears. So did stopping off at National Trust houses en route to visiting a relative. Grinling Gibbons and his bloody carvings – yes, OK, Mum, I'm sure they're genius but can we please just get to the gift shop, I need toffee and a keyring. But thanks to repeated family visits and any number of school trips, I learned a basic amount about the cultural fabric around me. Opera just wasn't my thing, classical concerts didn't hit the spot either, nor did art galleries particularly, not then. But theatre really landed. My parents regularly took me to Greenwich Theatre to see shows like *The Firebird*. I sat in the front row and felt the swish of air from its feathers as this magical creature leaped around the stage in a flurry of oranges and reds and blacks. Peter Brook's famous production of *A Midsummer Night's Dream* at the Aldwych was my first Shakespeare play and featured a huge red feather that descended from the top of this magic toybox, for that's what theatre seemed to me to be (it also accurately described this particular set). But plays were balanced with shows like *Behind the Fridge*, Peter Cook and Dudley Moore's spin-off from *Beyond the Fringe*.

Everyone considers their childhood normal until they get away from it and see it in perspective. For me, it wasn't until years later, once I joined the National Youth Theatre in my mid-teens and began to get to know kids my age from completely different upbringings and parts of the country, that I started to realise that not everyone had the same background hum of medium-level culture in their lives as I had experienced. I may not have been born with a silver spoon in my mouth but I realised I had a nice set of crockery compared to so many others.

A few years ago I got together with Paul Roseby, the artistic director of the National Youth Theatre, to discuss how I could help broaden the accessibility of the company that had been so important to me in my teens. There were two things I was adamant about: neither where someone lived nor their financial circumstances should be a barrier to being able to audition. As I myself had experienced time and again, it's getting to the door of the interview that is the hardest part. Once you're in the room, then your talent can reveal itself. So, we established the Audition Access Fund. It enabled NYT audition teams to travel to more distant corners of the British Isles than they had ever done before and those auditions, where applicable, were free. In year two I was thrilled to read the stats: some 26 per cent of the NYT's overall intake had gained entry via the Fund.

It was during a visit to a school in Kent to promote the Fund that something really hit home about successive governments' approach to the way young people are educated, in the broadest sense. The school was an academy, a bright, newly built campus, with the capacity for some two thousand students. I was with Joe Duggan from the NYT and we were there to meet students who were working on scenes from *Romeo and Juliet*. The English teacher met us at reception and led us through the impressive interior – high open atrium, lots of natural light – and up the stairs to the rehearsal space. As we walked along a broad balcony – a lot of thought had gone into the design of the building – she explained that while there was no official drama at the school there was plenty of enthusiasm. She opened the door to what I was expecting to be a studio of some sort. In fact it was the small school library. My heart sank and an emotion like anger began to bubble inside me. The six students were in the process of pushing the bookshelves to one side in order to create a modest rehearsal space.

The teacher clocked the look on my face and shrugged a smile. "We have to make the most of what we can get."

I asked her what other arts were on offer for the pupils.

"Oh, we have a great art department," she said.

"And music?" I asked.

"There isn't any."

There was no choir, band, orchestra, no musical instruments, nor the chance to learn one. This modern chrome cathedral of education had been built in the last year or two, so the only excuse for not incorporating in the design even a small designated studio space for drama, dance or music must have been a policy decision to exclude such experiences from the school. I later looked up the school's prospectus.

> As well as the core subjects of English, maths and science, students have the chance to find their interests and talents across many other disciplines including history, geography, technology, art, textiles, food technology, computer science, PSHE, Spanish, religious studies and PE.

Sure enough, no mention of drama or dance, no mention of music. Perhaps things have changed in the few years since my visit. I hope so. Because without an introduction to the performing arts at school level, quite apart from the intellectual and emotional nourishment they can provide a human being, how on earth is the next generation of those who drive the multi-billion-pound entertainment and creative industries to be discovered, or even to take part?

5

Davy Crockett

My first attempt at playing a romantic lead was a prime example of how not to improvise your way out of a situation.

Chetnole in Dorset is a quiet village, at least it was in the early 1970s, with a pub, a shop opposite the church, and a baker, all within a long throw of the tufty cricket pitch. A mixture of traditional stone farm buildings, more modern council houses, a couple of imposing Lord of the Manor type mansions and, at the end of the lane past the former village school, a disused smithy with its two-bedroomed cottage, Moonfleet. There was a well in the back garden and a cluster of pylon-tall pines in the adjacent paddock, in which crows nested, their sinister caws forming as much a part of the soundscape as the distant tractor and the church bell on a Sunday. This was my family's weekend and holiday destination for several years during my childhood, where some experiences glow warm through rose-tinted, scratched spectacles while others make me shudder at the gaucheness of the young boy I can see from this distance of fifty years.

There he is in gumboots, aged nine or so, alone but content, idling through the field behind the house, prodding the crust of a cow pat with a stick and watching the flies swarm and disperse, or sitting in the hollow of a tree with an air rifle in his lap, waiting for the poor old myxy rabbits to emerge for a twilight forage. Two fields over, the single-track railway line, connecting Yeovil and Weymouth. In the distance, the Halt, a request stop, a raised prefab concrete platform and never more than a handful of passengers flagging down the train.

Hattie Hanley lived in a cottage at the far end of the village past the rectory. She was without doubt the most beautiful girl who had ever lived, ever ever ever. Unfortunately, I was nine and she was nearly twice my age, so my crush was not only unrequited, it went completely unnoticed. But her younger sister, Susan, was a tomboy, my age, who liked climbing trees and going down to the river with me, where we'd build "beavers' dams" and lie on the bank and listen to the water rush over the barriers of sticks we'd created and watch the sky up there through the trees and listen to the cows mooing on their way to or from milking. By now, being familiar with re-runs of a few black and white US TV shows like *The Virginian*, *Casey Jones* and *Davy Crockett*, I reckoned I knew a thing or two about the outdoor life and tried to interest her in an al fresco production I had in mind, featuring me as a King of the Wild Frontier, wearing a hat crafted from the fur of the imaginary beavers who built our dams. She could play a squaw of some sort, or maybe even the beaver, I hadn't worked it out yet. But riverside theatre wasn't really her thing. Once, she lifted up her vest to complain about her tits not "doing anything" yet. I didn't know what to say really because her sister Hattie's did loads, but I didn't want to sound mean, so I offered her some of Mrs. Fudge's fudge that I'd bought from Fudge's shop that morning.

Between our cottage and the top of the lane was a run of semi-detached houses in one of which lived the Tanner family. Old Man Tanner was probably called that because he really was very old. I only saw him once, in a black suit for some reason, which makes me think it might have been in his coffin, which they'd somehow squeezed into the front room. The house was a two up, two down. They must have had a Tardis in there because seemingly dozens of kids thumped up and down those stairs, all of them answering to the name of Tanner and all of them presumably sleeping somewhere. With any number of children and the bustle, it's no wonder Ma Tanner looked so knackered. She had an army to feed. Her usual pose was by the bubbling saucepan, greying straw-like hair, gin-rimmed eyes and a fag permanently in the corner of her mouth, the ash always on the brink of falling into the . . . oh, there it goes. Seasoning.

I'd pitch up at the kitchen door on a Sunday before lunch to say hello, keen for company, to listen to the cacophony and inhale whatever was boiling over. There she'd be, stirring at the stove, yelling for one of two hundred Tanners to get the frog out of the water tank, or put them pheasants in the lean-to or there'd be a slipper on someone's backside. I can't picture any of her children's faces now but I can see hers: tired and worn but with a gummy smile that made me know that the little posh boy from up London was welcome. She'd wink and give me a sip of cooking sherry and then I'd head back home.

Next door to the Tanner tribe lived another family, the daughter of which, Jane, was the second most beautiful girl who had ever lived, ever ever ever, and the good news was she was only a couple of years older than me. I might still have been a snowball in hell but dammit I had a better chance with Jane than ever I had with Hattie Hanley. Jane had dark curly hair and freckles.

As my heart began to melt for Jane I'd come and hang around the Tanners' back doorstep more frequently than just on Sundays and so the offers of sherry increased. While chatting to Mrs. T I'd make a point of standing just outside the open back door, hoping that Goddess Jane might appear out of her own back door, which was directly adjacent, so I could nonchalantly toast her with my schooner and begin casual conversation. Sometimes I got lucky. The neighbouring back door would open and Jane would appear. However, nine times out of ten she was late for an assignation with twelve-year-old Sean, or thirteen-year-old Kevin, or any other human being who wasn't me. After a few crushingly awkward hellos, usually addressed to her departing ankles, I knew I had to change tack and up the stakes. I was doing it all wrong. I should do as they do on the telly. I'd seen the adverts when sneaking a peek at the commercial channel.

Opposite the church on the corner next to the pub was the village shop. My mum had an account there and so my occasional errands didn't usually involve cash, unless I was buying sweets with my own pocket money. One afternoon, unable to take Jane's fleeting, disinterested "hiyas" any longer, I marched into the store, the delicate little bell tinkling in counterpoint to my ferocious determination. Mrs. Barnes the shopkeeper barely looked up from her magazine as I placed a few groceries on the counter. She started to tot them up on the mechanical till.

"And a box of Milk Tray, please," I said in a surprisingly strong voice.

"We haven't got any I'm afraid," said Mrs. Barnes.

My world and my confidence collapsed.

"Oh. Oh, I see. Well . . . well, have you got anything else?"

She pointed to the bars of Fruit & Nut on the shelf behind me.

"Oh. No. No, that won't do. It's for a present, you see. A gift . . ."

Mrs. Barnes looked at me. I looked at Mrs. Barnes. Then, after a stupidly long pause, I added . . .

"For my mum."

A sniff of disbelief whistled up Mrs. Barnes's nose. She distrusted the smell. Then, like a poker player calling another's bluff, her eyes never leaving mine, she reached below the counter and brought out the largest box of chocolates known to man. It was enormous. Nothing else in the very ordinary shop would lead you to think that Mrs. Barnes would have such a gigantic luxury lurking out of sight, unless she'd been planning for years to embarrass a nine-year-old into admitting he was lying and that finally her moment had come.

"Black Magic. Perfect. Thank you," I said, my throat now dry.

"You paying cash for that, then?" she asked, her smile curling with a hint of cruelty.

"No, no, on account with everything else, please."

"You're buying a present for your mum and you're charging it to her account, is you?"

She sounded like a sardonic police officer pulling out their little notebook and licking the end of their pencil.

"Er, yes please, Mrs. Barnes, thank you." I'd never consciously done blasé before but I was certainly trying it now.

I exited the shop and ran across the village with a carrier bag of unnecessary groceries and a vast pizza box of chocolates. Panting, I arrived at Jane's back door and knocked.

It was opened not by sultry, freckly Jane but by her wild-haired uncle Frank, the one-armed woodsman. Frank, who invariably dressed in old trousers with braces and an oil-stained naval shirt, lived with Jane's family and was a complete enigma to me. Not in the sense that he spoke in riddles or had hidden depths, more in the sense that it was a total mystery to me how Frank, a man with one arm, had found gainful employment as a woodsman. Any job involving the wielding of an axe demands a certain level of hand-to-eye co-ordination and in the woodsman's job description surely two of the former would be the *sine qua non* of being contracted. Right now the absent arm, or rather the smooth leather stump that dropped from Frank's left shoulder where his arm should be, was just above my head.

"Awlright, Yugh?" coughed Frank in his Dorset drawl, as with one hand he opened a tin of tobacco and, with extraordinary dexterity, extracted a cigarette paper and somehow wedged it against his stump. I was mesmerised. His fingers fluttered and danced as he sprinkled the tobacco, rolled the paper, licked the gummed strip, put the lid back on the tin and replaced it in his pocket.

I followed this impressive ballet with my eyes and, as he took an old brass lighter from his pocket and lit the cigarette, I pointed to where the scene of the hypnotic dance had taken place and muttered in awe and wonder, "How did you do that?"

Frank peered at me through an eye-stinging first plume of smoke as he inhaled. "Slipped when I was splittin' logs in the rain."

I looked at him, nonplussed.

"Slipped," he repeated, "an' chopped it off with an axe, din I, see?"

I still find it hard to put in order the emotions and words that ricocheted through me as the misunderstanding sank in. Embarrassment; shame that he should think I would ask such an insensitive question; revulsion as I saw the axe flash-frame into his arm above the elbow (but how so high up? How could he actually chop it off so high up?); plus the unspoken jumbled sentence in my defence, explaining that no no, Frank, I was simply asking how you rolled your fag so amazingly with one hand.

I said nothing. I just stood there gawping as he smoked, the polished brown stump catching the glow of the setting sun.

I handed him the enormous box of chocolates.

"Ta."

I think he heard me say "for Jane" as the door shut. I hoped he had.

That night, Mum came in and sat on the end of my bed.

"Mrs. Barnes rang. She said you bought a box of chocolates this afternoon."

"Did she? Did I?"

"A very big box. As a present for me. And she wanted to make sure I'd received it because it was rather expensive. Five pounds. Five pounds!"

Blimey, I thought, that's a bloody fortune.

"So where are the chocolates?" she continued.

"They were . . . they were for Frank," I said, with as much piety and charity in my voice as possible.

Mum didn't believe a word of it.

The following day, as I was heading along the lane to meet flat-chested Susan at Beaver's Dam, I looked across to Jane's house. She was sitting at the table at the downstairs window, picking out a chocolate from a box the size of a Monopoly board and popping it sensually into the waiting mouth of thirteen-year-old Kevin.

And for the next four months my pocket money was reduced by 50 per cent.

6

Lean and Hungry

At prep school in Dulwich I dived into the Play Reading Club and got a couple of decent parts on stage, despite the man in charge of drama, who looked like Dirk Bogarde in *Death in Venice*, with a black moustache and a cigarette held pertly between his fingers, rarely giving me a break. So, when I arrived at Big School, Sherborne, I had one goal in mind: get a girlfriend by acting in a play. However, being at an all-boys boarding school, the former proved tricky, and for the same reason my first role, with my unbroken thirteen-year-old voice, was to play a girl, Agave in *The Bacchae*. The bloke playing blind Tiresias was very good and projected quite a lot of phlegm across the stage in the angry bits. I got to carry his severed head at one point – a triumph of the art department, although in the haste of its creation, strips of the *Sunday Times* still showed through the outer mould. The review in the school magazine described me as only becoming "self-conscious" in the final scene. Mum had to explain to me what "self-conscious" actually meant.

"Aware of who you really are, darling. It's a sort of compliment really."

Only after a further year's development and my grasp of the

English language having improved somewhat did I realise that it was in fact my first bad review.

Sherborne is a beautiful town, dominated by an abbey which dates back to the eighth century. Buildings of honeyed limestone which change colour with the sun's journey. All very romantic, except when you were up with the lark doing Long Slopes, a daft punishment that involved running a circuit of the town and adjacent Dorset countryside before plunging into a cold bath, hurriedly dressing in your Sunday suit, out of it, cold bath, games kit, out of it, cold bath, into the suit again, all against a stopwatch and reporting at each stage to a bored house prefect, before the rest of the boarding house had woken up. The general tone among the boys was benign cynicism; sports were approved of, the arts so-so, working hard was treated with suspicion while being secretly admired. For some, being put in a school play was the equivalent of detention. Not so for me.

Heading back to the boarding house between lessons one day, I found myself walking alongside one of my house tutors, Charles Mitchell-Innes. He asked me what I'd been up to. I told him I'd just auditioned for *Julius Caesar*.

"Oh very good. Very good. Which part are you hoping for?"

"Cassius, sir," I said, confidently.

He hesitated in his stride, trying to hide his surprise at my certainty. It should be pointed out that I've always been, shall we say, big-boned. At my prep school I had to go to a special outfitter's in Herne Hill to get "sturdy fit" shorts. Some smart alec nicknamed me Batman, not due to my prowess as a caped crusader but because calling me B(elly)-A(rse)-T(it)-man made people laugh. Here at Sherborne, with my voice now fluctuating between treble and alto during any given sentence, I was still something of a chubster.

"Cassius?" Mr. Mitchell-Innes repeated, biting his cheek. "You mean the one with the 'lean and hungry look'?"

"Yes, sir. Cassius, absolutely, sir."

I was in complete denial that I was physically wrong for the part, and being a junior oik with a voice that hadn't properly broken made it even less likely that I was going to be cast in the role.

On the day the director was to put the cast list up I loitered round the noticeboard in the windy cloisters with the same excitement most other boys hung around the sports noticeboards to see if they'd made the team.

Messala was the part I'd been assigned. Not exactly memorable but at least he spoke. For some reason I learned Cassius's big speeches anyway and years later even trotted them out at drama school auditions. I can still blurt out "For once, upon a raw and gusty day . . ." from some strange recess of my brain where it has been stored, unused and unemployable, for decades.

Things improved once I started doing plays with one or other of the local girls' schools. Being in plays gave me a far better chance of meeting girls than playing second row in the 3rd XV rugby, which was the pinnacle of my sporting achievement.

Under Milk Wood was a co-production with Sherborne Girls School, with actual girls in it, which was a major plus. I loved the play with its swirling spirit of memory, melancholy, heartache, comedy and vivid characters. The sheer brilliant Welshness of it. The cast were good fun and I fell a bit in love with Gossamer Beynon and Lily Smalls. There was one moment on the second night that I look back on as a self-taught lesson in stagecraft. I can't even remember which of the several roles I was playing when it happened. I was evidently so in character that night – that elusive state of being "in the moment" – that when the girl playing my unrequited love passed by me on stage, hips swaying seductively, my left hand spontaneously shot out to touch her and in the same instant my right hand grabbed my left hand and pulled it back to my side, so that decorum prevailed. It wasn't rehearsed, I don't know where it came from, but it worked and was funny and true to the character's state of mind, and the audience laughed. Thrilled to bits with my bit of stage business, the next night I went for the same gesture at the same moment, expecting the same reaction. But I got nothing. Zilch. Spontaneity is one thing, planned spontaneity is another. Going for the laugh kills the laugh. Every actor knows when they've done it and instantly regrets it because it can take weeks or months in a run to regain it. Audiences smell fake a mile off.

There was a hall area in my boarding house that was the hub of house activity, known as the Open Space. It had a cold stone floor and strip lights on the low ceiling. It's where boys criss-crossed from the changing rooms to the stairs up to the dormitories, from the freezing outside loos to the boot room, or to the battered front door to the outside world. Along one side of it was an angled reading board where improving newspapers were placed. Not the *Sun* with its bare-breasted women on Page Three, of course, which was all we hormonally overloaded boys were interested in.

Opposite the newspaper boards was a row of prefects' studies, including that of the Head of House, which had the added privilege of a gas fire. And it was on the table outside this study that Mr. Rouse the housemaster would plonk the mail each morning and to which, on clumping downstairs from the dormitory, tucking in the dark blue shirt and pulling on the blue wool sweater of the school uniform, I would gravitate before heading for breakfast. Mum and Dad wrote at least once a week and there would be the odd postcard from my brother and sister. In turn, I dutifully wrote home on a Sunday about how stupid biology was and how Botty Blackburn had let off a firework under my chair and burned a hole in my trousers but Slug Rouse had told me there were more serious things in the world to worry about. And it was from this table, one late spring day in 1980, aged sixteen, that I picked up the letter.

I can put a pin in that image and mark it as a turning point in my life.

The envelope was typed, and it had a London postmark. I had been waiting weeks for it to arrive. "We'll let you know," the man had said. The sounds around me distorted – hard shoes with steel Blakey's heel plates to prevent wear, clacking over the stone floor on the way to breakfast, towel flicks and yelps from the changing rooms – as the thump of my heart took over the soundtrack. The contents of this letter meant everything to me and carry even more significance now that I look back at it from a distance of more than four decades. I sometimes wonder if I would be in the same place in life today were I to go back and open the tri-folded concertina of A4 paper once again and read something different. What if this time, beneath the orange logo on the headed notepaper, what if this time I read the words "Unfortunately, your application to join the National Youth Theatre has been unsuccessful?"

7

Finding the Tribe

When I joined the National Youth Theatre in 1980 the company was based entirely in London and was really only active over the summer months. Introductory courses were held over three weeks at Haverstock School in North London and members who had progressed through those went on to audition for the productions that were put on for the public each year. One afternoon each summer Michael Croft, the artistic director, would call the entire company together for a pep talk – all of us in our later teens – warning those unfamiliar with London about the perils of the bright lights, his five minutes on the birds and the bees being an annual highlight.

Michael was an ebullient figure who had founded the Youth Theatre in the late fifties, growing out of his teaching work at Alleyn's School in South London. By the mid-1960s the National Youth Theatre of Great Britain, as it had become, was the pre-eminent youth arts organisation in the country. Michael was in his late fifties when I joined. He had a chunky build and hair that resembled a greying crinkle-cut chip. He wore an unfortunate line in shirts that either caused or exacerbated a tendency to sweat, so a handkerchief was always on standby to dab bubbled beads from his brow. His voice was Mancunian by way of Shropshire and everyone in the company tried out their impersonation, bouncing along sentences, stressing unlikely syllables, one hand gesturing to his audience, the other scratching chest hairs, sometimes visible through a damply transparent shirt above the upturned horseshoe of his vest line.

"Now . . . I also need to *men*tion, *to* the unaware, the *poss*ibility of an activity known as *sex*."

In my first summer Bill Buffery, himself an NYT alumnus, led a company of ten newbies like me in a studio-scale production of Thomas Middleton's *A Chaste Maid in Cheapside*. Working on a play with kids from different parts of the country was a revelation. The bank clerk's daughter from Belfast, the miner's son from Newcastle, Fiona from Dumfries who had never been south of Carlisle – and yes, I had to look up Dumfries on the map. We were all chucked in together on a voyage of discovery, united in our interest in making a play come to life. I had found my tribe. Bill was great on text and, hallelujah, stood the play on its feet early on, knowing that sitting reading a play in a classroom setting, as if it is literature first and foremost, dulls its resonance and the author's intentions – such a change from some of my experiences reading plays aloud at school. He drummed into us the basic disciplines of professional theatre too, like turning up on time or risk losing if not your role then at least your prospects of a future with the company. Richard Dillane was a fit teenager but he got even fitter because Bill's company rule was one press-up for every minute you were late for rehearsals. Bill's whole approach was to treat us like grown-ups. We needed to raise our game and take the project and the material seriously. We weren't going to perform the play to the public, just to an audience of fellow NYT members, but that was pressure enough. Costumes were cobbled together by the resourceful designer and from early on the fight director was brought in to choreograph the sword fight between Rick and me. We practised with our foils every spare moment, every lunch break, and by the time the day came for our two-performance run, a Saturday, we were polished and proficient.

We had gathered as a company in the performance space and were just warming up when the stage manager appeared. He was ashen-faced.

"What's up?" asked Bill.

"I'm afraid it's the foils. You'd better come and see."

Rick and I looked at each other, then followed Bill and the stage manager out of the room and down the stairs. The building we had been rehearsing in was managed by a janitor whose lair was in the basement amid the clunking pipes of the boiler, which is where we now found ourselves. There was a table, an unwashed mug and a tall metal changing locker. To one side was a cage, bolted to the wall and padlocked. In it were housed the janitor's most nickable possessions: a step ladder, mops, buckets, dustpans and brushes . . . and two fencing foils. All safely under lock and key until Monday.

"He doesn't work weekends and I forgot to ask if I could borrow the key," said the stage manager sheepishly.

"What the hell are we supposed to do now?" I exclaimed. "We go up in forty minutes!"

I can't remember whose idea it was but when it came to the point in the show when Sir Walter drew his sword on Touchwood Junior, we simply did the fight using invisible foils. It worked, because every cut and thrust and parry we had rehearsed were as real to Rick and me as if we actually had flashes of steel in our hands. So the audience bought it too.

I spent the next few summers doing plays with the NYT. Plays with big, bustling casts: Ben Jonson's *Bartholomew Fair*; Peter Shaffer's *Royal Hunt of the Sun*; *For Those in Peril*, a play about the Invergordon mutiny (eighty boys on a ship, not a single girl, poor optics); and probably the best production of *Twelfth Night* I have ever experienced. I played Orsino but that's by the by. The design was a Christmas magic box of delights and Matthew Francis' direction was subtle, heartfelt, and drew the best Malvolio I've ever seen out of Matthew Townshend. I have absolutely no idea if Matthew went on to become an actor or a hairdresser but that's somehow the point of the NYT. What we teenagers learned at the NYT – discipline, communication, trying and failing in rehearsals through teamwork and trust, commitment to a common purpose – were skills that I guarantee stood every single one of us in good stead for later life, whatever path we subsequently took.

At that stage I had no thought of becoming a professional actor. Reading this book you would be forgiven for thinking that every step along the way had the measure of inevitability but that wasn't the case. My passion may have been theatre but I was still playing under the piano, tentatively peeking out; throughout my teens I was convinced I was going to be a lawyer. In fact, Dad and I had a whimsical idea that he would retire from medicine and we would study for the bar together, no doubt in some rickety Dickensian attic, by candlelight.

During the holidays in my teens I used to go and sit in the law courts. I liked watching Lord Denning in particular. The Master of the Rolls as he then was had a Hampshire burr and sometimes employed a homespun manner when summing up, no doubt exaggerated for effect. In drawing together the threads of one particularly complicated tax avoidance case he began something like, "So, if a man were to take his cattle to market and in the square was there to tether his cows while he himself settled in a tavern awhile with a draft of ale; and in that tavern were a transaction to take place in which . . ." and so on, transporting me to the legal world that Justice Shallow reminisces over in *Henry IV Part 2*. It was, of course, the theatre of it all that attracted me. The gowns and wigs, the minutiae of court procedure, the bowing and the language, the tension and tedium, the circumlocutions and the cross-examinations, sweaty witnesses and precise prosecutors, the Court of Appeal as mesmerising to me as Court No. 1 of the Old Bailey.

I spent a couple of days shadowing Bruce Mauleverer QC. He talked me through the barrister's typical day (there isn't one) and he explained some of the strange rituals and etiquette of the inns of court. I followed him to court as he explained details of the brief. He took me to lunch in Inner Temple, the inn to which he belonged. To become a barrister you have to join one of the four inns: Gray's Inn, Lincoln's Inn, Inner Temple or Middle Temple. Part of the process is to sign up for a number of "qualifying sessions," dining in the inn to which you are applying. After two days with Bruce I was hooked.

"Will you sign me up for the dinners?"

"No." He was smiling but he was firm.

I was crestfallen. "But why not? I want to be a barrister!"

"You're not yet eighteen. Go to university. Spend three years discovering what you really want to do with your life."

"But . . . but . . ."

"And after that come and see me. If the law is still for you, then we'll talk."

Thank you, Bruce, for your wisdom. At that age I had no idea that I could do what I loved for a living.

8

The Old Man in the Blue Coat

A new teacher blew into my school like a breath of fresh air. Paul Carling swept the cobwebs off theology, made it come alive, and as a result four of us took it up for A Level. Through his enthusiasm for the subject I became obsessed with the Synoptic Problem – the similarities and differences between the gospels of Matthew, Mark and Luke – and by the time I got to applying for university I found myself gravitating towards theology rather than law. I figured that I might as well do three years of something I really enjoyed before switching to a lifetime of weighty tomes and legal process.

I was never a great academic but I worked hard enough and after A Levels and an interview got a place at Corpus Christi College, Cambridge. With my place assured I was encouraged to let rip in the entrance paper and so I opened up about a dotty hypothesis I had been developing about the southern tribes of the Sudan being related to the ancient tribes of Israel. If the Israelites had fled into Egypt, as described in the Old Testament, who's to say some didn't migrate even further south once there and influence or be influenced by forebears of native tribes such as the Nuer, the Shilluk and the Dinka? I got an Exhibition of £40 per year as a result and a travel grant of £100 from my school to go off and further explore the idea. To earn money for my travels I cleaned toilets in a law firm in Marylebone for a few weeks but hit my stride working in a wine bar off the Brompton Road. The clientele were mainly unattractive men looking for attractive women and unattractive women looking for attractive men. Both subsets were destined to disappointment but after a bottle or two they were more than happy to lower their sights. None of them had a clue about wine, anyway. "I'll have a sweet dry wine, please" was a favourite. There was one regular, a really entertaining Irishman, who drove both a Rolls-Royce and a Citroën 2CV, either of which might be parked outside. I once asked him the significance of the number plates, 1MMM and 1MMM2.

"Oi Make Moy Monney," he replied with a wink. "And Oi Make Moy Monney Tyoo."

After a few months working as many shifts as I could get I had saved up enough to book my flight to Cairo. From there I set off up the Nile to Luxor, crossing over Lake Nasser, and boarded a train at Wadi Halfa that chugged for thirty-six hours across the desert to Khartoum. Then a boat south to Juba, talking to tall, striking tribesmen whenever I encountered them. I eventually wrote up my hypothesis but by then I was more interested in the simmering tensions between Islam, the Christian Missionary tradition and indigenous tribes than whether or not the body markings and dietary laws of the last overlapped with those of the ancient Israelites.

I played Romeo in my first term at Cambridge and we toured round Europe in a coach, playing a variety of sports halls and theatres, even a nuclear bunker in Zurich. During the tomb scene in this strangest of locations, Jo Unwin as Juliet, suffering from a tummy bug that day, rose from the dead a second time and dashed off stage to be sick.

We played a US military base in Giessen, Germany. After the show we were billeted in pairs to stay with US army personnel. Dominic Dromgoole (Benvolio) and I duly climbed into the Praisemobile, a VW camper van covered in biblical quotations. Over a late dinner our hosts, a colonel and his wife, explained that their children were on a sleepover at the base's chapel, "digging into the Holy Spirit." As I climbed into bed I picked up a mini comic book of religious stories from the bedside table and leafed through it. The Devil wore a CND badge. At breakfast next morning, as the colonel poured coffee, I pressed him on how he reconciled his Christian faith with being in charge of a bunch of weapons that could extinguish mankind in a matter of minutes. His kindly smile never left his lips as he explained that in the Old Testament God often had to use force to ensure that right prevailed. Pancakes, bacon, maple syrup. Delicious. I asked how far we were from the Russian border.

"About a half hour in the Praisemobile, Hugh," he said cheerily. "That's about thirty seconds by missile."

I acted in a lot of plays in my three years at Cambridge and was not what you might call a focused theologian. In fact, I once attended a fluid mechanics lecture with my roommate Andrew, an engineer, as I thought it might be more fun than the one I was due to attend on Origen's theory of atonement. Mind you, I did enjoy my Supervisions on Early Church History with Dr. Rowan Williams, who went on to be Archbishop of Canterbury. He had a spectacular beard, which I studied closely, its configuration shifting and twitching with each gentle word uttered by its master's voice. I sometimes wondered if birds nested in there – a place of tranquil meditation, if a little itchy. The truth was I spent more time in the rehearsal room than ever I did in the lecture theatre.

I wrote a terrible sketch for the Cambridge Footlights but I never performed with them. I nearly did. Nick Hancock and Steve Punt auditioned me for the Footlights Summer Show but by the time they told me I had been successful I had already agreed to produce *Coriolanus* at the ADC Theatre.

In the spring vacation of my second year I confessed to my parents that I wanted to give acting a go professionally and was going to try for drama school. It was something that had been bubbling under the surface for so long now, half-hidden, and felt as seismic to me as coming out of the closet was for some of my friends. Mum and Dad were cautiously supportive. Had they told me not to be so ridiculous I wonder if I would have had the courage to run off and join the circus. With or without their blessing I would no doubt fail. It was a profession about which I knew next to nothing and for which the stats for success didn't stack up well. But I would rather try and fail than spend forty years in a suit wondering what might have been. I gave myself three years to get an Equity Card. If I didn't achieve that, I told myself, then Someone was trying to tell me something and I would reverse out of the whole thing and get a Proper Job.

My director of studies, Dr. Horbury, a New Testament scholar, was incredibly tolerant but as more and more reports of sub-standard essays came his way he tried to put his foot down. I agreed I would rein in the theatre stuff and focus on my academic work.

As a urologist working mainly in the NHS at three London urology hospitals, St. Peter's, St. Paul's and St. Philip's – affectionately known as the Pissing Apostles – and with consulting rooms at 147 Harley Street, my father had an eclectic list of patients. Problems in the waterworks department know no social boundaries. He looked after a production line worker from the car plant in Dagenham as well as a wealthy merchant seaman called Mr. Grindley, who was extremely grateful to Dad for "sorting him out downstairs." I never met Mr. Grindley but he expressed his thanks regularly. Amazing sparkly watches would arrive, indelibly inscribed "To JP with eternal gratitude," which meant my big idea of flogging them on as new to the jeweller's in Lewisham High Street fell at the first hurdle. The same was true of a gold carriage clock my parents didn't need: "To JP, with my undying thanks . . ." So, no resale value whatsoever, dammit. Why couldn't he just send a wodge of cash with a note saying, "To Hugh, son of JP, as a mark of my affection?"

In fact, a gift from one of my father's grateful patients of far longer-lasting value came one Christmas in the form of lunch.

I was in my last year at Cambridge when Mum asked if I'd like to go with them to Mr. Evans's lunch party. The idea of hanging around with my parents at some stuffy do with a bunch of people I didn't know filled me with dread, so I mumbled something about revising for Finals and declined. But when the day came it was snowing quite hard and there wasn't much in the fridge, so I grudgingly put on a tie and got in the car.

Laurie and Mary Evans held parties every summer and winter at their beautiful home in West Sussex, Chesworth House, a Tudor estate where Catherine Howard grew up, before she had her head first turned and later chopped off by Henry VIII.

As we pulled up I could see through the leaded windows that the party was well under way. We got out of the car and headed for the front door, the snow falling more softly now and crunchy underfoot. Just ahead of us, moving slowly, was a frail figure in a dark blue overcoat, walking with the aid of a stick, a nurse shadowing him in case further help was required. But the gentleman was determined to make his entrance unaided. As he reached the front step he lifted his arm towards the doorbell. Realising that this might be a stretch too far, I nipped in front of him and pulled the handle. A bell rang somewhere inside. I turned and smiled at the diminutive old man.

"Thank you," he said, and put out his hand to shake mine, adding by way of introduction, "Olivier."

My father's former patient, Laurie Evans, the host of the party, was a theatrical agent, now in his seventies. He'd co-founded International Creative Management (ICM), one of the most prominent of London agencies in the post-war era, representing at various times the likes of John Gielgud, Noel Coward, Peggy Ashcroft, Rex Harrison and Alec Guinness. However, Laurie's closest professional relationship down the years, as I now discovered, was with Laurence Olivier.

It was a relaxed buffet and I soon lost Mum and Dad in the crowd. Lord Olivier and Laurie had parked themselves at the head of the kitchen table, around which there was room for about eight other people. Telling myself that I'd never get the chance again as long as I lived, I plonked myself down opposite the two septuagenarians. Needless to say, I was hypnotised; probably in shock.

I was too young to have seen Olivier on stage but every actor, even of my generation, had their Larry impersonation and I'd read most contemporary accounts of his legendary performances. The critic Kenneth Tynan, in particular, wrote so vividly about them that sometimes I felt as though I had actually witnessed Olivier's Oedipus, or his Chebutykin in *Three Sisters*. His Henry V, Hamlet, Richard III and Othello were all there on celluloid, and his Shylock and Big Daddy and Lear had been recorded on television tape, but nothing would match seeing him in the flesh, albeit at a kitchen table just outside Horsham.

Towards the end of the meal, with the room packed with ogling well-wishers and me with the best seat in the house, Laurie and Larry started singing music hall ditties, finishing with a rendition of "Two Gigolos" that was met with cheers and whistles from the groundlings. Olivier's son Richard was next to me by then. To him it was just Dad having a laugh with his old friend. To me it was as if I'd died and been sped through the Pearly Gates for a one-off performance.

*

The Marlowe Society production at the end of the summer term was one of the staples of Cambridge University's theatrical calendar. The budget allowed for a professional director, often a Cambridge graduate, to sprinkle some magic dust from the real world over our self-indulgent amateur theatricals.

In my final year a director called Peter Stevenson took on *A Midsummer Night's Dream*. He cast me as Oberon. Two principal memories have stayed with me about the production. First is the fact that I had to keep it a secret from Dr. Horbury and my parents. I had assured them that, having got a Third in my Part Ones the year before, I wouldn't do another play until after Finals; I really was going to knuckle down. Well, that went out of the window as soon as the "Auditions" poster went up. The second thing I remember is the director's tennis ball.

Apart from looking worryingly like the Yorkshire Ripper, and sounding like he could be too, Peter was quite a spiritual person and was very much in touch with his inner something or other. In fact, the whole production was to be based on his inner something or other, so we did a lot of breathing (always useful) and hours and hours of t'ai chi. Barefoot and costumed in burgundy silk ruched pantaloons, I did my best to float around the rehearsal room being mysterious and wafty. In reality, I resembled nothing so much as a bull that had been speared by Carlos Arruza and was crashing into the side boarding of Las Ventas bullring in Madrid; or bearing in mind our supposedly eastern aesthetic, a bull in a china shop. A friend from Corpus, Caroline Loncq, played Titania, wild-haired and with fabulous eye shadow.

One afternoon I was early for rehearsal and found the Erasmus Room in Queens College empty apart from Peter's script, a Tupperware sandwich box and a tennis ball. To while away the time I picked up the ball and started bouncing it against the wall, like Steve McQueen in *The Great Escape*, neither going over my lines nor revising for Finals. After a few minutes the door opened. There was a strange silence. I glanced round, mid-bounce. There stood the Yorkshire Ripper's double, not looking too happy.

"What do you think you're doing, Hugh?" he asked, his voice strangely quiet and menacing.

"Nothing," I said, immediately guilty of some unknown crime.

"Can I have me ball back, please?"

"Well, I'm only—"

"Hugh," he interrupted, his dark eyes growing smaller and beadier, "that ball is for me anal retention."

I looked at the ball that I had been fondling for the last five minutes, then at Peter, at the ball again, and then gingerly handed it over, as cautiously as a bomb disposal expert. Peter snatched the ball, placed it on the parquet floor, sat down hard on it, closed his eyes and started chanting angrily.

Our relationship never really recovered after that. During one particularly spiky notes session he told me that my Oberon was ridiculously middle class and totally predictable.

Gaby Chiappe was really good as Puck and unknowingly alleviated my recurring lumbar pain every time she hurled herself on to my back – a foray into physical theatre of our own invention, suggesting our characters' corporeal and metaphysical connection. Demetrius got off with Moth at the last-night party.

9

Foot in the Door

Having arrived at the Webber Douglas Academy of Dramatic Art in the autumn term of 1985 I did some basic maths. There were about twenty students in my year on the postgraduate course. There were maybe another thirty students in the final year of the three-year programme. We would all be graduating the following July and beginning our hunt for a job and the all-important Equity Card.

In those days, when union membership was the only route to employment in theatre, there were two ways of getting a provisional Equity Card. One was to build up a number of contracts from one-off gigs in pubs and clubs around the country. The other was via the rep system. Each repertory theatre in the country had a quota of two cards to give away to newcomers each year. It didn't take a maths genius to work out that the odds of getting one of these treasured provisional union tickets was going to be vastly diminished come July, when through the doors of drama schools across the nation would prance hundreds if not thousands of leotarded students, pirouetting into the world, hungry for employment and an Equity Card. My chances of getting a Card were going to be greatly improved,

I figured, if I got out into the market place sooner rather than later. So, as soon as I arrived at Webber Douglas I started trying to leave.

One evening during my first term I was in a pub in Clapham with a classmate. He wasn't a chirpy soul at the best of times. He stared into his pint.

"As far as I can tell and from the beginning of fucking time, in this profession it's not what you know, it's who you know," he said, and swigged glumly. "If you haven't got any contacts, don't bother."

I slumped into a dark mood with him. I didn't really know anyone in the industry I had set my heart on joining. Michael Bates was dead. My dad had met a rather odd impresario who invited me to his office above a theatre in the Strand. But once he had twigged I genuinely wasn't interested in anything he might have to offer other than an introduction to the world of acting, the conversation petered out somewhat. I had recently read about a Hollywood legend getting his first break by smashing up an audition room; he'd taken the bull by the horns and Gone For It. Maybe that should be my approach.

As an actor, Derek Nimmo had found television fame in *All Gas and Gaiters,* defining the character of "English vicar" for an entire generation. He was also a producer who had cornered a niche market, doing after-dinner theatre abroad for ex-pats, notably in the Middle East. An acquaintance of mine had done a couple of these and somehow got me an audition for a production of *Outside Edge*. Derek Nimmo opened the door of his posh house in West London dressed in a tracksuit. I suppose I had expected him to be wearing a dog collar. I read for him and he expressed a degree of interest. However, he said, in all likelihood the ship for the next Middle East tour had sailed, figuratively at least. The director of the show, Roger Redfarn, had all but secured his cast and anyway he was running the theatre in Plymouth and was a busy man.

I may have had no contacts but hell I had talent, determination and a map. I wasn't taking no for an answer and I set off for Plymouth in my Vauxhall Astra.

The stage door keeper looked at me blankly. I had no appointment and besides, the artistic director was out getting his laundry, so would I please leave. I said I'd wait. She tried to get rid of me several times that morning but I was in an audition-room-trashing mood and refused to budge. When Roger Redfarn finally appeared two hours later I announced that I'd driven two hundred miles to give him the chance of auditioning me for a role I was born to play. Wearily he took me into his office. "Sit down," he said. He leaned his elbows on the desk, ran his hands through his hair and groaned. "Look, I cast that part a week ago. Why on earth didn't you ring and find out before driving all that way?"

"I was taking the bull by the, er, y'know, by the horns," I said, dredging some chair-kicking confidence from the depths. But I took his point. Seizing an opportunity is one thing, doing due diligence to work out if there even *is* an opportunity is quite another.

Next day I bought my first copy of *Contacts,* the entertainment industry directory of agents, producers, casting directors, theatres, costumiers, armourers, fight directors, choreographers ... you could probably find a plumber in there too. The pink cover of my 1985/86 edition has long since faded. Portrait photographers' adverts provide a snapshot of contemporary hairstyles: Bucks Fizz for the women, Simon Le Bon for the men. And there's a woman clutching an alligator. There are also the ghosts of the two hundred plus addresses I culled from its pages in order to write to agents and theatre companies, announcing the arrival of the best thing since sliced bread, namely ME. I took pains to make each letter personal ("I've often dreamed of performing in Leatherhead ...") and was scrupulous about spelling, punctuation and the correct form of address. To the agent Lou Coulson, for example, I wrote "Dear Mr. Coulson." Strangely, she never replied.

However, about a hundred and fifty others did reply, informing me via photocopy that they would keep my details "on file" and I would be invited to audition when they were next casting or when hell froze over, whichever was the later. For years I kept these rejection letters on a bit of string tied to the toilet roll dispenser in my bathroom – a gesture that combined two-fingered defiance with a nod to recycling before it became The Done Thing. As time went by my wad of spare loo paper diminished. I think the Churchill Theatre Bromley was the last to go down the pan.

Out of the two hundred and fifty letters I was invited to two auditions.

On the day of my meeting for Chichester Festival Theatre I was staying with my sister. Unfortunately, my adrenalin that morning was such that, having made her a cup of tea, I didn't so much walk up the stairs to her attic bedroom as bounce and in doing so smacked my head against the beam under the eaves. There was blood but nothing major, I said to Clare, and certainly nothing to hinder my interview. I mopped up the tea and took an aspirin, but by the time I got on to the stage of the Garrick Theatre to deliver my audition speech my head was thumping and I didn't know up from down. From the stalls, the director suggested that I stop and perhaps come back another time. I waved vaguely in agreement, found a loo backstage and threw up.

My birth certificate reads Hugh Richard Bonniwell Williams. In my teens Dad told me we were probably Huguenots (after a millisecond of research I discovered we weren't) and that my third name would have been Bonneville, or maybe even *de* Bonneville. So, for a time I went round signing everything *de Bonneville-Williams,* reinventing myself as some ponce in a novel by Dumas.

When it came to my audition for Regent's Park, at the artistic director's house in South London, David Conville – at first sight a ferocious figure who as an actor must have played umpteen brigadiers and generals in his time – saw my name and spent the first twenty minutes of the interview banging on about how Hugh Williams and his wife Margaret wrote "very serviceable" plays in the fifties. He'd known them personally and was keen to ascertain if I was in any way related to them. If I was it would be a marvellous thing and I must send Hugh's widow my regards.

"No, no relation."

"You sure?"

"Quite sure."

"Pity. But you know Sam Williams, his son. The actor."

"No. I'm afraid I don't know Sam."

"He was in *Upstairs Downstairs.*"

"Oh, do you mean *Simon* Williams?"

"Yes, Sam."

"He's called Sam?"

"Yes. Of course he is for heaven's sake. Everyone who knows him knows he's called Sam."

"But I don't know him, you see."

"Well there you are then. He's got a brother. Hugo."

"And what's he called, then?"

"What d'you mean 'what's he called'? He's called Hugo. He's a writer."

"A bit like his father, then, Hugh."

"Who?"

"You said his father was a writer."

"Well yes, but Hugh was an actor, too."

"Ah I see, like his son."

"Hugo? No, Hugo's a writer."

"Simon."

"You mean Sam."

David looked at me like I was deranged, which indeed I was beginning to feel.

"And you're called Hugh Williams . . ."

"Yes."

"But you're not related."

"No. Not related."

"Could get confusing. In this profession."

"I think maybe I should use my middle names instead."

"What are they?"

"Richard Bonny . . . er, Bonniw . . . Richard *Bonneville,*" I suddenly asserted with confidence.

"Well that's not going to confuse anyone is it? Unless you run into a member of the chocolate family."

"I think that's Bournville."

So, for the next ten years I went by the name of Richard, a name I had never associated with myself, ever. I eventually dropped the Richard after going to a party at which my host, a friend from school, didn't know by which name to introduce me and so didn't introduce me to anyone. I often wonder if Eric Blair's or Gordon Sumner's pals were ever equally flummoxed.

I got a recall the following week to meet Declan Donnellan, who was directing *Romeo and Juliet* that season, with Ralph Fiennes and Sarah Woodward in the title roles.

As soon as I was in the room, I launched into my Oberon, full of voice and semaphore. I was booming on about oxlips and nodding violets, waving my arms around as if trying to tell a plane where to park, when Declan interrupted me, pointing out that I was not on stage at the King's Theatre Glasgow with a need to impress the Upper Circle, but in a cosy sitting room in Putney playing to an audience of one – him – who was all of three feet away. He told me to start again.

Breaks come when Luck allows you to put your indisputably talented self in the right place, at the right time and in front of the right person. Just don't shout.

PART TWO

Curtain Up

10

Biting My Thumb

It was spring 1986, and I was on my way to Scotland for a holiday with friends. We'd stopped off for the night at a mate's house near Oban. There was a message for me to ring home.

"Mr. Conville from Regent's Park Theatre called," said my mother, in a tone laden with nosiness while trying not to sound nosy. "He wants you to telephone him."

I dialled. Through the study window I could see a ewe and her lamb chewing away on the scrubby moor some distance from the house. The sky was bright but cloudy.

"Ah, yes," boomed David Conville, once I'd announced myself. "Now look here, it's perfectly simple. The offer is Play as Cast. Three plays. Understudying, Acting ASM and what have you. And you'll get your provisional Equity Card. Think about it."

I didn't need to think. Aged twenty-two, this was one of those crossroads moments in life.

"Oh Mr. Conville," I gushed. "Thank you. Thank you!"

"It's not a question of thanks, this is business. You'll get a hundred and ten pounds a week and three pounds extra if you go on for your principal."

"Thank you! Oh my goodness, thank you!"

"Yes, now stop that. Rehearsals start last week in April."

Click.

Through the window the lamb started suckling its mother, its tail twirling like a helicopter.

David Conville's stern vocal authority and martial manner were quite terrifying. He had glowering eyes, fantastically bushy brows and a face in repose that looked like thunder. You'd cast him as one of those dour men who'd had a bad war and now ran the family pile in the Home Counties as a prep school, meting out punishment for his own ghastly childhood by way of a cane on boys' bottoms.

David directed Shakespeare with rigid efficiency, wearing a Panama hat with an MCC ribbon round it, and at first he scared the living daylights out of me. However, over the thirty-plus years since he gave me my first job I not only remained grateful to him for giving me my Equity Card, I also became extremely fond of him. Even in that first summer I began to glimpse the sweeter side of his nature, popping out like streaks of sunshine between lowering clouds. Everyone tried their impersonation of David – the stentorian tone and the furrowed brow, as if anything anyone ever said was an irritant to him, intent on contradicting whatever incontrovertible truth he had just laid down. "I mean, look here. Shakespeare *wrote* this play. I'm *directing* it – I *think* – frankly I don't understand your *point*." But when one of the established members of the company imitated him to his face, his features would crumple into a fit of giggling, shoulders shaking, and suddenly you could see the boy of eight years old, in long shorts, growing up in India, being naughty for Nanny and hiding from Pater, who was something severe in the Colonial Service.

I wasn't even a Fairy in *The Dream*, I just sat at the back of the stage and bashed a cymbal under the sozzled tutelage of Nick the musical director, a worryingly thin, multi-talented musician who seemed to play best when completely arseholed, which as far as I could make out was absolutely all of the time.

Ralph Fiennes was cast as Lysander but because he was also playing Romeo in the opening production of the season and *The Dream* was to open soon afterwards, with the two shows rehearsing in tandem, I would occasionally rehearse as Lysander in his place, while he was off doing serious balcony work with Sarah Woodward. As a reward, I was to be given several matinees and three evening performances as Lysander, guaranteed, instead of just lurking in the shadows, hoping Ralph might get laryngitis. This was a pretty good deal, as it gave me the chance to invite agents to see me play a decent role – they weren't going to glean much about my potential by watching me hang about at the back of the stage waiting to break the fall of a drunken lute player.

David Conville had directed several productions of *The Dream* and prided himself on knowing about comic business, so in his wisdom he decided that he would oversee the Mechanicals scenes and leave his assistant, a young graduate from Bristol University called Emma Freud, to handle what I suspect he considered to be the boring stuff, namely the quartet of lovers. So, under Emma's eye I often got to rehearse the Lysander/Hermia scenes opposite a fantastic bundle of Brummie energy called Beverly, who had changed her surname from Williams to Hills (I still can't quite believe she actually chose to do that).

A Midsummer Night's Dream is a beautiful play, funny and touching and magical, even though the interjections of the "nobility" in the penultimate scene, taking the mick out of the well-meaning but theatrically unpolished working men's playlet, are unfunny, irritating and a great advert for wiping out the aristocracy.

I remember that summer of my first professional job in crystal-clear detail, perhaps because I knew it was the start of something precarious yet valuable to me and therefore to be treasured, but mainly because I still couldn't quite believe I was being paid more than a hundred quid a week to do something that up until then I had willingly done for free.

Apart from understudying, other duties for the acting assistant stage manager involved checking that all the props were in place before each show. My partner in crime was another newbie, David O'Hara. Under the supervision of the deputy stage manager we'd go through the *Dream*'s props list on the half (thirty-five minutes before curtain up), like pilots doing pre-flight checks: "two thrones – check; two goblets – check; Fairy wand – check; Snug's business cards – check . . ." Then we'd head back to the dressing room, David to get dressed as Cobweb, me to dress as – well, as the bloke who thumped the cymbal whenever the Queen of the Fairies paraded up and down.

For some reason *Romeo and Juliet* was scheduled to play on several Mondays during that season. Let's face it, no one looks forward to Mondays in whatever profession. David, as Tybalt, had quite a lot of fighting and dying to do in *Romeo,* while I mainly carried a big white bass drum and had one line, as Abram the servant, biting my thumb at thee. As it was a Declan Donnellan production, whose company Cheek By Jowl had recently taken the theatre scene by storm with its director-led ensemble style, there was a lot of sitting on stage watching the action and being supportive of your fellow actors. So David and I created a superstition. We decided that, once we'd checked all the props, if we sat in Oberon and Titania's thrones (parked to one side for their night off) until the quarter hour call and didn't move an inch, the show would be rained off and we could all go to the bar. Miraculously, we achieved this for about six or seven Mondays in a row during the course of that summer and I developed a taste for Rioja (discount price for company members).

Whenever it rains during an open-air production, a Dunkirk spirit prevails, especially at Regent's Park – it's part of the fun. Drizzle is ignored, that's par for the course, that's just England, but when the drizz turns to droplets, the brollies go up, the forestage starts to puddle and for a while the cast splash on heroically, until the stage manager pokes their head out of the booth at the top of the raked auditorium, does something scientific like stick a finger in the air, decides that it's wet, and calls a halt to proceedings. Then comes a collective good-natured groan from the audience, the cast scatter into the wings (or in our case into the bushes upstage), spectators scurry to the bar, and everyone waits in their respective holding pens for the rain to pass. When it does, the performance resumes to rapturous applause. Come the curtain call, cast and spectators give each other standing ovations, knowing they've survived something remarkable and bonding, like the battle of Agincourt, and we happy few disperse into the night (or the bar again) uplifted by a unique shared experience. In fact, the audience is usually so giddy about the whole thing that by the time they hit the pillow they've completely forgotten that they've just spent a small fortune on the pleasure of getting trench foot and a cold at the top end of Baker Street.

One of the giants of that season, quite literally, was Bernard Bresslaw. I had grown up watching his gormless features in the *Carry On* films. These were a staple of my childhood cinematic experience but nowadays are probably considered, at best, a bargain basement series of end-of-the pier comedies, with perky music, painful double entendres, appalling attitudes to pretty much everything and over-the-top acting. They were as much a part of the 1960s and 1970s for me as flares, space hoppers and *The Banana Splits*.

Standing at about 6ft 6in, Bernard had terrible eyesight. I looked through his glasses once – it was like squinting through the bottom of a wine bottle – and so when he acted without them, which was most of the time, he couldn't see a thing ... and therefore appeared to the world at large as totally vacant. As a result of this physical shortcoming, he played lots of really dim characters. In fact he was very smart, extremely well read, and was a terrifically instinctive actor; he'd won the Gold Medal at RADA. His was the best Bottom I've ever seen (as Kenneth

Williams might have minced in *Carry On Shakespeare* ... now *that's* a film they should've made).

His deep baritone voice had a timbre that sounded as if it had been created by mooing into an empty wooden cask of madeira, warm and rounded but with an intrinsic echo of melancholy. He was very, very funny and the Mechanicals' hopeless production of *Pyramus and Thisbe* was full of brilliant gags, Bernard's death as Bottom being a lesson in over-indulgence which went on for hours. It still makes me chuckle. Karl James as Snug the Joiner, a cute and timid soul, gleefully handed out business cards to his well-heeled on-stage spectators and won the hearts of the theatre audience too, often eliciting a sympathetic "aaaah" when expressing nervousness about learning lines. Sentiment on stage was something director David Conville couldn't stand.

"Now look, Karl," he boomed during one notes session, "your performance ... I mean, it's getting ridiculous. You're not in a Walt Disney film, for God's sake."

During matinees actors' voices would compete with aeroplanes stacking over London for landing at Heathrow and cheers from Lord's cricket ground, and then as the sun set during the evening performances, blankets (or brollies) would come out and distant sirens would shriek through the rustling trees. Backstage between shows or sometimes after them we played poker. Not just Holdem but any number of variants to keep things interesting: Irrawaddy, Blasphemy, Fiery Cross. Some of these I learned from Sarah Woodward (poker name: Princess) and Karl "the Mouth" James, some from a regular school I was part of in Cambridge, our final session lasting twenty hours through the night after Finals, a last hurrah to the unreality of being students, knowing it was all about to end.

For meals on matinee days we would head to the café in the park, passing Peter Whitbread's yellow Ford Cortina estate that was parked up near the admin block. He lived in Norfolk, so for the nights when he was playing Egeus or Capulet, he'd sleep in his car. It even had little curtains.

My parents had always been supportive of me when I acted in plays at school and I don't think they missed a single show when I was with the National Youth Theatre. Supportive, yes, demonstrative, no. They weren't the kind of people who would turn up at the stage door with flowers and showers of approbation. Instead theirs was more the tone of Farmer Hoggett at the end of *Babe* (and if that movie isn't in your top ten, then I'm afraid we can never be friends), when he looks down at his porcine protégé and says with understated pride, "That'll do, pig. That'll do." However, in the company of others I think my parents' pride megaphone was often deployed as well as a certain amount of Chinese whispers. That summer of my first professional gig, playing the bass drum in *Romeo and Juliet,* the cymbal in *Midsummer Night's Dream* and an Officer in Shaw's *Arms and the Man* – grand total of lines uttered: five – I was hardly setting the stage alight; sweeping it maybe. One afternoon I ran into my godfather in the Marylebone Road, who said, "Congratulations. Your parents tell me you're playing Romeo at Regent's Park."

"Well, not exactly. I'm playing *in Romeo* at Regent's Park."

11

Shane

With my handful of matinees and three evening performances as Lysander in *The Dream* guaranteed, I was able to set about inviting agents to come and find out what they had been missing. A couple said they'd come, I booked them tickets, and then they didn't show up. Wankers. Shane Collins, however, did come along, as promised. He had recently left the agent Susan Angel to set up on his own. Shane had himself trained at Guildhall and loved a bit of glitz and glamour. I honestly think if I'd given my all as King Lear for three hours, he would have come backstage and said, "Darling, what *does* Mrs. Dreary Leary think she's wearing?!" Having been to one of my precious performances as Lysander he invited me for a chat in his first-floor office in Berwick Street, where the noise of the bustling market outside rattled the big sash window. It was a modest set-up, just Shane and a typewriter and on the wall above his desk a rogues gallery of his clients, a handful of 10×8 photos stuck on with Blu Tack. After a chat about what we expected of each other, I became the next headshot to go up, and very proud I was too. I had a job, at least for the next few months, and now an agent. And I adored Shane. While his screaming down the phone like a hyperactive drag queen about some ghastly show he'd had to endure the night before would leave me in stitches, he was also kind to this new boy and didn't pretend he had all the answers. From the outset he reminded me of something important: "I might be able to help get you an audition and I can negotiate the contract but I cannot get you the job." The requirements inherent in being self-employed were drummed into me early on. The thick skin to cope with rejection, the thin skin to show your talent. But it's down to you. An agent might get you a foot in the door but it's you and your abilities that have to nudge it open. And one other thing I always say to aspiring actors: if and when you get an agent, never forget who is employing whom.

Come the end of the summer, plans were in place to tour *The Dream* round Europe. Phil Bowen had decided to hang up his codpiece as the Fairy King and so Ralph Fiennes took over as Oberon and I took over from him as Lysander, full time.

When you're on tour, the days are strange pockets of time in which to explore your surroundings. I was struck by Munich's mix of architecture: the older, muscular oom-pah-pah jostling with the modernism of post-war reconstruction. A lunch, an art gallery maybe, then before you know it, it's time to head to the theatre for the evening show. We would congregate backstage during the half to get changed and chitter chatter about the day. Donna, Nick and Rob had "done" Marienplatz and volunteered a restaurant recommendation; Ben, Beverly and Carolyn had ticked off a couple of museums. But each day during that week of performances in the capital of Bavaria, one or two people would not join in the pre-show tourist chat because where they had been that day had knocked the wind out of them, leaving them reflective, even tearful.

Dachau, the site of Germany's first concentration camp, is situated about ten miles north-west of the city. The simplicity of the memorial and museum that remain as a testament to the atrocities committed by my fellow human beings merely adds to the extraordinary emotional impact of visiting. No birds sang, at least not on the day I was there. One of the most vivid images of that summer is of the gentle giant, Bernard Bresslaw, sitting on a chair in a backstage corridor at the theatre in Munich: stockinged feet, half dressed as Bottom, in an open calico shirt, braces holding up his britches, with Paul Raffield applying the clown-white make-up to his bald head, as he did every night. But on that particular Thursday evening, instead of the banter that usually ricocheted between them, Bernie said, "Just going to be quiet tonight, luv, if y'don't mind."

I have been asked many times what I consider to be my Big Break. (I've also had the comment "You must have been so relieved when *Downton* came along," as if the preceding twenty-five years of my career had been one long, painful slide towards hell.) Aside from the obvious first break of getting my Equity Card, a British director deciding to go on holiday to Italy in the autumn of 1986 has to be a pretty close second.

Standing in the queue for customs at Florence airport on the next leg of our European tour, I looked across at the neighbouring line and saw two of my fellow cast members talking to a curly-haired man in his forties whom I recognised from the telly. He evidently accepted their invitation to see the show because a couple of nights later, on the way back to the hotel after the performance, Beverly Hills said, "By the way, Jonathan Lynn thought you were good. He said so. You should write to him at the National."

I had no idea that the actor I had recognised from shows like *Doctor in the House* and *The Liver Birds* and who had then struck gold as the co-writer of *Yes, Minister* was now directing plays at the National Theatre. I gave him a few days to get over his mini-break and then wrote to him via the stage door of the National. To my amazement he wrote back saying yes, he had indeed enjoyed me in the show and would pass on my name to the National's casting director, recommending me for an audition.

Among the two hundred plus letters I had written the previous year, one of course had been sent to the casting department of the National. A second letter had winged its way to the South Bank earlier that summer, inviting anyone with a pulse – or their cousin – to come and see me in *The Dream* at Regent's Park. On both occasions I received a letter in return, saying that my interest had been noted and that my details were "on file." By now I had learned a thing or two about the business and had taken to saying "You're on file" to every biscuit wrapper and apple core I tossed in the bin.

But the word from Jonathan Lynn did the trick.

12

Pierre Le Pied

Throughout much of the 1980s Gillian Diamond was head of casting at the National Theatre. She was famously intimidating, with short Jean Seberg hair and strong lips. She wouldn't have looked out of place wearing a beret and smoking Gitanes while overseeing a printing press during a run of angry revolutionary pamphlets.

Jonathan Lynn had recently had successes directing *A Little Hotel on the Side* at the National, as well as *Jacobowsky and the Colonel,* and was, at the time I wrote to him, in rehearsals for *Three Men on a Horse*. Thanks entirely to his recommendation, I was invited to meet Gillian Diamond and Di Trevis.

Di was to direct two plays, *School for Wives* starring David Ryall in the Lyttelton Theatre, followed by *Yerma* with Juliet Stevenson in the Cottesloe. Aside from her two leading players she was looking to create a single group of actors to populate the two productions.

Di had dark frizzy hair, a sharp nose and slightly pursed lips that made her look focused and intense in repose. She was as serious-minded as she was smart but when she laughed she threw her head back and all the lights shone.

Molière's *School for Wives* is a comedy about a neurotic old git grooming his young ward to be so innocent that when he marries her she will be too naive ever to notice another man. It all goes wrong, of course, and a suitor, Horatio, breaches the walls of her ignorance. Lorca's *Yerma* is an achingly poignant poem-play about a barren wife yearning for family and fulfilment. I was auditioning to understudy Neil Dudgeon as the rakish young buck in the French comedy and God knows what in the Spanish tragedy – my agent, Shane, had said, "Read the plays and just go along and chat, dear. You'll be fine."

"Two very different plays," said Di, as we sat down in the windowless rehearsal room somewhere near the top of the concrete maze of the National.

"You could say that!" I laughed, trying a little too hard to be liked, perhaps. Gillian Diamond scribbled something on her notepad – probably "Tries too hard to be liked."

"But if there is a link," continued Di, "I suppose both explore the role of women within a patriarchal society."

"Absolutely," I agreed. "Also, one's funny and the other isn't."

Di's expression faltered for a moment. Gillian began to show interest in a fly on the ceiling.

"But no, in terms of a connection," I waded on, through ever-thickening mud, "then I would say definitely the patriarch, the patriarchal, y'know, definitely. The link."

Gillian sighed at the fly. But Di wasn't giving up on me so easily.

"I want to create an ensemble. In *School for Wives*, for instance, I want to see a vibrant world on stage, the town in which Arnolphe lives coming to life in between scenes. So even though on paper you're an understudy, I wouldn't have you sitting in the dressing room."

"No?" The mud was receding. Things were looking up.

"Far from it," said Di. "I want everyone to be involved throughout rehearsals. We'll be exploring commedia dell'arte, doing a lot of improv."

This was music to my ears. The idea of a theatre troupe being shaped organically over seven weeks of rehearsals (a luxury of the subsidised theatre), discovering and honing performance skills along the way – this was what I had dreamed drama school would be about (except I hadn't hung around long enough to find out). The National Theatre would be my training ground and Di was going to be team coach.

"Thank you, Di!" I blurted, my mind racing ahead to a world in which I had actually been offered the job.

Di hesitated, before changing tack to the other play. "And in *Yerma* you'd be the flamenco dancer with—"

"Ha!" I spat-vomited a short laugh, stopping her mid-sentence. The more serious side to her personality instantly crossed her face. Realising she might not in fact have been joking, I tried to match it. "Flamenco. Yup." I nodded gravely.

"Yes," she continued cautiously, not entirely sure we were on the same page, "as the story reaches its climax? When the villagers congregate?"

"Oh yes, that bit, I remember," I said, not remembering.

"A gypsy man and woman dance flamenco. It's a celebration of fertility. The air charged with an intense sexual energy."

"Right. Fertility, I see. And this 'intense sexual energy' you, er, mentioned?" I asked, in the casual tone of a rookie policeman taking notes at his first crime scene.

"Yes, that would be you," said Di firmly.

At this point Gillian sneezed. I think it was a sneeze. Might have been a snort.

"You and Celia Imrie."

"Christ alive."

"Sorry?"

Becoming part of the National Theatre Company as an understudy and spear bearer (all right, flamenco dancer) meant the world to me. I still have my first Staff card. As the new kid on the block it was time to be scared all over again. We gathered for the readthrough of *School for Wives* in a windowless rehearsal room near the backstage canteen. (Yes, another windowless rehearsal room. Theatre architects have a lot to answer for.) The dozen or so members of the cast, assorted stage managers, designers, the composer, assistant director, Janey from casting. A room full of grown-ups, all with way more experience than me, all intimidating. As I hovered by the tea urn, pretending to focus my attention on a tea bag, a woman murmured in my ear . . .

"Isn't this ab-so-lutely terrifying?"

I looked up. A beautiful, smiling face with striking cheekbones, short reddish hair. It was Celia Imrie. If an actor of Celia's calibre was admitting to first-day wobbles then I guessed it was OK for me to be nervous too. I had an ally. Celia was already on her way to becoming a national treasure as one of the brilliantly funny troupe in *Acorn Antiques*, a soap parody segment on Victoria Wood's TV show. That day she became my mentor, taking me under her wing. She had been at Regent's Park early on in her career too, so we had David Conville stories to share. Kind and funny, I adored her from day one. "Do It Now," she always told me whenever I asked her advice about pretty much anything. A woman of endlessly supportive energy.

After the readthrough we viewed a model of the set: a lumpy volcanic hillside, not the urban backdrop I had anticipated at all. Then it was time to roll up our sleeves and get stuck into rehearsals. I was excited at the prospect of all the theatre games we were going to play, the new skills I was going to acquire, while being paid at the same time. What could be better? For the early part of that first week we engaged in various theatre exercises, developing confidence in each other, starting to create our characters, particularly for the sequences of local life Di imagined linking the scenes together. But not everyone was entirely enthusiastic.

David Ryall had thinning white hair, beady eyes and a beaky nose. He looked older than his fifty-something years. He had an easy wit but there was also a weary, guarded quality to him. He had been a drinker in his time and was now, apparently, doing well on the dry slopes. Overall it gave him a slightly hooded demeanour, vulnerable and cautious. If you were to conclude, therefore, that he might not be one to share our director's interest in exploring the foothills of commedia dell'arte, then you would be right. He hated it. Here was Di Trevis fizzing with ideas about how to make the play come alive, in direct contrast to her leading man who was, in essence, scared and just wanted to get on with it.

It came to a head at the end of the first week, with an exercise involving groups of three. Two truculent servants were to serve breakfast and the morning newspaper to their grumpy master as clumsily as possible, revealing to the audience their disdain for him without ever being caught out by the boss. I formed a trio with two of my fellow understudies and we set about creating a sequence of slapstick moments.

"That's it, Tony," said Di from across the rehearsal room, encouraging Tony Trent, playing one of the servants, as he approached David Ryall – sitting as if at his breakfast table – and dropped a newspaper at his feet, supposedly by accident. On picking it up Tony allowed the inside pages to scatter to the floor, provoking his tetchy master even more.

"Now pick up the papers, David. And while he's doing that, Celia, in you come with the teapot."

The other servant, Celia, sloshed imaginary tea all over David, while keeping a straight face.

"Oh, I'm terribly sorry, sir."

Celia started mopping his lap with a cloth, fussing around him like a wasp. Enough to drive anyone mad, particularly a character like Arnolphe . . . or a human being like David.

"Yes, and now pick up the rest of the papers, David."

But David didn't budge. He was sitting stock still, staring at the bits of newspaper.

"The papers, David? . . . David?"

Suddenly he stood up. "When you've finished all this farting about I'll be in the canteen." And he stormed out.

The silence was deafening. For a moment Di stood rooted to the spot, stunned. Then she exited in pursuit of David. In unison the rest of us turned expectantly to Irina Brown, the assistant director.

"Let's take five," she said, before exiting in pursuit of Di.

There followed huddles round the tea urn, vague chat about Doing Anything Nice This Weekend?, everyone studiously avoiding the topic of the elephant that had just stampeded out of the room.

Twenty minutes later, Irina returned alone.

"Right. Um. We're going to break there for the day. Have a great weekend." Silence. "See you all ten a.m. on Monday!" she added brightly, with a single clap of the hands as a full stop and a Please Don't Ask Me Any Questions Or I Might Cry.

I came into rehearsals on the Monday morning to find that the production had shifted on its axis. Script in hand, Di began blocking Act One Scene One with David Ryall and Roger Lloyd Pack . . . then Julia Ford joined, then enter Neil Dudgeon. We understudies sat to one side, noting our principals' moves in pencil, eraser at the ready for when readjustment was required. All energy, sparkle and invention had evaporated from the rehearsal room. From then on the whole thing became, for me, what the director Peter Brook called Deadly Theatre, lacking in invention or contemporary nuance, merely a regurgitation of tried and tested tropes.

I sat in the backstage canteen that lunchtime with a soup and a bread roll. I slurped on my own and eavesdropped. A few spaces further along the central table sat the pert, crop-haired figure of Anna Massey, opposite the elderly, sonorous and patrician Basil Henson, tweed jacket and open-necked checked shirt. *King Lear* starring Anthony Hopkins was in previews. Anna was playing Goneril and Basil, Oswald.

"How did it go for you on Saturday, Basil?" asked Anna, navigating a salad.

"Not too bad, I suppose. It's a matter of trains, really." Basil drew on his cigarette and stirred his tea.

"Trains?"

"You see, if I stay for the curtain call I can only get one train. Which is altogether too tight. What if I miss it? So I'm thinking of asking David [Hare, the director] if I can go after I die. That way I can get two trains. And if I miss the first . . . you understand."

"Yes. Yes, indeed."

"I expect he'll be difficult about it. But if I can go after I die it will completely alter my life."

Back in the gloomy rehearsal room, the one sliver of light was that the entr'actes were to be retained, so some of the work we had done the previous week hadn't been in vain and I would actually get to go on stage rather than loiter in the dressing rooms which is the fate of most traditional understudies. In one of these exercises I had discovered my character, the village cobbler no less, and Pierre Le Pied was my name. As rehearsals progressed, while my fellow understudies did things with washing and wheelbarrows or whatever, Pierre was to enter from stage left and navigate the peculiar lava flow of the set towards Monsieur Arnolphe's front door where Celia, as the servant Georgette, would hand him some shoes for repair. I'd pop them in my cobbler's basket and head off up the mountainside trying not to twist my ankle before exiting stage right. Then, between Acts Two and Three the igneous village community would come to life once again and I'd return the now-repaired shoes. It was hardly *A Tale of Two Cities* but it was a little narrative arc I had constructed and I was extremely proud of it. The big, cumbersome basket and I became acquainted early on in rehearsals. Gradually other elements were accrued from the props department. I had a belt with a hammer and awl attached to it and a cobbler's last dangling from the buckle. As far as I was concerned, I was now a fully paid-up shoe mender. The design department had other ideas.

About five weeks into rehearsals Sonia Friedman, one of the assistant stage managers, escorted me from the rehearsal room down flights of stairs and along myriad corridors to the props workshop. Here I was introduced to Tom, one of the props makers, whose workstation was an impressive array of books, drawings, worn tools, offcuts, loads of sawdust and unwashed mugs. A mad professor type, he had round wire glasses and wore a welder's mask atop a mass of frizzy hair, the whole picture finished off with a generous sprinkling of iron filings.

"Welcome to where the magic happens!" he beamed.

Like a conjuror revealing a rabbit from beneath a silk hanky, he whisked a sheet of A3 paper from a pile of tea-stained drawings and with a flourish presented me with a detailed technical sketch of what looked to me like a calliper.

"Ah, you're not far wrong," he said, grinning, his index finger wagging to indicate I'd made a good stab at an answer, but no. "No, it's a replica of an eighteenth-century French cobbler's last, you see." He moved aside a plate of biscuit crumbs to show me a dusty tome. "Here he is sitting on his stool with the metal frame either side of his leg, held in place at the bottom by his foot. Attached to the top of it is the wooden last, see? So, we're making you one."

"You're what?"

He pointed to some metal tubing, already cut into rough lengths. And there next to his Thermos flask was a wooden last, in the shape of a foot.

"But I'm not on stage long enough to actually sit down and start hammering away at a shoe. I'm Pierre Le Pied, en passant, so to speak."

"Come again?"

"It's great that the designer got you to research it but I wasn't aware this was happening and I could have told her that ... I mean I could've ..."

A squall of disappointment blew across Tom's face. He lived for this stuff, for the delving into hidden corners of invention, the tinkering of re-creation over a mug of tea and a Digestive.

"But, yes, wonderful!" I U-turned.

Instantly Tom was back to full beam and a tape measure was produced, sizing up the distance between my knee and the ground, in order for the calliper element of the contraption to fit me just-so.

Rehearsals continued without incident. I studied Neil Dudgeon as he developed his performance, diligently noting his moves in my script and learning his lines, so that by the time it came to the final run-throughs in the rehearsal room I could mouth along to his performance like an irritating groupie.

The get-in to the theatre and the technical rehearsals are the lumpy bit of any production, when any creativity that may have been spun into gold during rehearsals is reduced to base metal, as issues to do with the technical reality of putting on a play lurch into view. Several prefabricated metal frames were manoeuvred into position and bolted together, the undulating jet-black landscape of the set beginning to take shape. Rows of lighting bars were lowered from the flies, lamps adjusted, refocused, then hoisted aloft once again. In the middle of the stalls was the production desk – wide boards straddling a couple of rows of seats, laden with computer screens, headsets, notepads and polystyrene cups. Gradually, on stage, actors in costume drifted into view, designer Pamela Howard's attention shifting from doors on the set that wouldn't open to pointing out necessary nips and tucks to the wardrobe supervisor, who in turn passed on instructions to tailors and seamstresses. With sound cues checked and Dominic Muldowney's music finalised, the first dress rehearsal could begin. On time.

Back in my dressing room I listened on the tannoy as scene

one rumbled on. The deputy stage manager's voice, low and calm, a notch above a whisper, inviting Mr. Bonneville and my fellow Misters and Misses to stand by for the first entr'acte, surnames being a backstage tradition when it comes to rehearsal notice-boards and calls to the stage.

Pierre, fully dressed in his pre-revolutionary cobbler's outfit, belt and tools in place, set off to stage left. I quietly entered through the air-lock doors into the silent penumbra of the wings. There on stage were David Ryall and Roger Lloyd Pack coming towards the end of the first scene. An ASM pointed out my big shoe basket, underneath the props table. I was about to reach for it when there was a commotion behind me. The air-lock door burst open and there was the sawdusty figure of Tom the props maker, his eyes barely visible behind the debris that caked his little round spectacles.

"Here y'go!" he beamed, whispering hoarsely, thrusting the cobbler's contraption at me.

I tried to hide the fact, I like to think successfully, that I had completely forgotten about this particular prop. "Oh, wow," I whispered, speed-mining enthusiasm. It was almost dark back there, so I'm pretty sure my smile was convincing enough.

"Stand by," hushed the ASM, as the cue light on the rear of the upstage flat came on, glowing red.

Tom exhaled a triumphant sigh of relief and nodded a Good Luck. I put the calliper in among the shoes and picked up the basket with two hands. Unfortunately, the basket was shallow and the calliper thing immediately toppled out and clattered to the floor. I put the basket down and gathered up the unwieldy prop. On stage, the scene ended, the lighting state shifted, the entr'acte music began and in the wings cue lights turned from red to green.

Thrusting my arm through the two metal struts of the calliper with the intention of hitching it on to my shoulder, I picked up my shoe basket once more and tottered on to the bumpy incline of the Lyttelton stage. Sadly, the struts of the calliper were narrow and there was no way this thing was going to sit happily on my shoulder. Instead, it slid down my arm, coming to rest in the crook of my elbow, and swung there like a pendulum as I tried to steer myself and my big basket up and down the humps of the stage towards Celia Imrie, who was way over there, waiting by Monsieur Arnolphe's front door. As I neared centre stage, the swinging calliper thumped against a hillock to my right, knocking off a huge wodge of the volcano, revealing wisps of white fibreglass beneath; maybe we could get away with calling it snow, I thought.

"Stop. STOP!" A voice from the darkness of the stalls. The director, Di Trevis. The music cue died. The traffic of the stage ground to a halt. "What on earth is that?"

Eyes turned to me.

"Oh, hello, Di, you mean this? Well, you see, it's a replica of an eighteenth-century cobbler's last. It's a sort of anvil he would have used to—"

"CUT IT!" she interrupted, irritated, no time to lose. "Re-set, please. Let's go again from the end of the scene into the change. Sorry David, sorry Rog."

I believe passionately in the importance of subsidising the arts but the fiasco of this contraption gave me pause for thought. A complete waste of time, energy and money. In the commercial theatre that prop wouldn't even have made it to the drawing board. But perhaps more importantly to me, as we took off our costumes after the dress rehearsal I pictured poor props maker Tom, staring up at his bedroom ceiling that night, an empty bottle of whisky in one drooping, paint-flecked hand.

13

Cinderella

Juliet Stevenson would whirlwind into *Yerma* rehearsals clutching piles of research books and a handbag – more of a carpet bag really – that spilled an array of household items on to the floor when she plonked it down. "Sorry I'm late. Am I late?" She wasn't, but there was a breathless energy to her that made you double-check your watch as she swept a tumble of chestnut hair across her strong face, eyes quick and darting, reading the room, the mood, processing everything with impressive speed.

I had first seen Juliet on stage in, of all places, our school sports hall in 1980. She was playing Lady Percy in a touring production of *Henry IV Parts 1 & 2* with the Royal Shakespeare Company. To have the RSC in Sherborne, setting up their portable auditorium in our gym, felt like a coup. They were in town for four nights. Not only did I sign up straight away to see the two shows but on the afternoon between those performances I attended a workshop laid on by the assistant director and some of the company. Watching them work on scenes together was intoxicating and I stuck my hand up for each and every acting exercise that required volunteers. I suppose, therefore, I could say I once played Prince Hal for the RSC. At a pinch.

Over two nights I watched the two plays, loving Alfred Marks as Falstaff and marvelling at Stuart Wilson's dangerously dim Hotspur. He played it like a slightly deaf Eeyore, an ass, slow on the uptake, at one point even chewing on a carrot. He was electric. Opposite him, Juliet shone in the one scene wonder role of his wife. The assistant director had noted my over-the-top enthusiasm during the workshop and spotted me hovering around the box office desk on the Thursday night, hoping that a ticket might be returned for the sold-out show. "Come with me," he said, and led me past the ushers into the hall, up the staircase of bleacher seats, and pointed to his own seat in the corner of the top row, next to the lighting desk. "You sit there, I'll watch from down below." I was so excited to have been given this quite literally lofty position. I smiled and waved at anyone and everyone who approached up the stairs, sidling closer and closer to the lighting operator as if it might make people think I was actually a member of the RSC. The lights went down and I became absorbed in the script the lighting guy was following, a little clip light casting a soft beam over the page, a web of asterisks and arrows. At one point I turned a couple of pages to look for Hotspur's next entrance and received an audible smack on the wrist. Understandably the LX operator was fed up with the irritating sixteen-year-old wannabe who kept encroaching on his personal space.

After the last performance, the school laid on farewell drinks in the adjacent dining hall. Wannabe was back in action, of course, this time handing round canapés, or rather, it being the Sherborne School catering department, small chunks of pork pie. Patti Love was playing Lady Mortimer. She had also been involved in the workshop I had attended and since I had pretty much lit the production myself the night before, as far as I was concerned we were now best friends. She was standing to one side of the hall talking to Bob Hoskins, who had been to see the show that night. They had appeared together in the film *The*

Long Good Friday and were enjoying a private catch-up. However, WannabeMe wasn't reading any such signal. I stood there for a moment, waiting to be noticed. I wasn't noticed. Perhaps intentionally. Refusing to be ignored, I lifted the plate closer to Bob Hoskins' face.

"Canapé, sir?"

Mr. Hoskins gave me a polite smile that said both No Thanks and Fuck Off, I'm Talking to My Friend. But WannaHugh was keen to bathe in the post-show glow with his fellow actors and continued to linger.

"Did you enjoy the show? I did," I asked and answered.

"Yeah. Yeah I did very much. Thanks."

There was another Go Away in Bob's thanks, but I didn't hear it.

"Good," I said, in a tone that reassured him he would remain on my Christmas card list after all.

There was a pause. Three friends hanging out. Another pause.

"I'm playing Azdak in *The Caucasian Chalk Circle* next term," I added, attempting to insert a morsel of credibility in the gap between a sixth former, two professional actors and some pork pies.

"Azdak? Yeah, I played that a while back. Fun part," said Mr. Hoskins, again with an air of finality, to which I remained oblivious.

"Fun? FUN?!" I spluttered. "I really don't think I can agree. It's a very, very hard part, you see."

"Listen, son. Would you mind?"

"Mind what?"

At this point my English teacher, Mr. Wellby, appeared from nowhere and, taking me by the elbow, deftly steered me towards the Abbey House matron, who turned out to be quite partial to processed meat.

In the seven years since then, Juliet Stevenson had worked her way up through the ranks of the RSC to play the leading classical female roles, and here she was stepping across the river from the Barbican to the South Bank to try her hand at Lorca. The performance she created in the Cottesloe was passionate, searing and memorable. Opposite her, Roger Lloyd Pack played Yerma's hard-working, stolid husband Juan, a man of toil and the soil. A number of actors from the *School for Wives* cast, as well as some newcomers to the company, filled out the supporting roles.

Now it was time for Celia Imrie and me to unleash our inner flamenco. Celia, I should add, originally trained as a dancer. If I had had any training whatsoever it was in my imagination, and even that had taken place at Madame Flatfoot's Academy for Incompetents. However, Jane Gibson liked a challenge. She taught at LAMDA and was the National's go-to choreographer and movement director. Her salt-and-pepper hair, cut short, with a flick over one eyebrow, made her red lipstick pop out in bright contrast. She didn't tolerate larking about or self-doubt; only hard work and sweat would be rewarded with a smile and sometimes a laugh, so it was worth putting in the hours.

Rehearsal space at the National was always at a premium, and the security guards who rotated protectorship of the keys to the handful of spare rooms that could conceivably be used for the purpose worshipped at the altar of No. One afternoon, despite Jane having booked the tiniest of rooms for a one-hour session, the amount of teeth-sucking from the man with the jangling bunch indicated that this dancing business simply wasn't going to happen, at least not on his watch. We weren't in the book, see.

"Fine," said Jane, "FINE. We'll rehearse in the bloody stairwell, then."

"Right you are," said the security man, who presumably had failed his interview as a Professional Torturer and was going to play out the rest of his working life making things difficult for anyone lame enough to be involved in theatre.

The National is not a pretty building and backstage is even uglier. The staircases are stone and echoey, and the ceilings on each floor are low, with removable square roof panels that conceal miles of girders, pipes and wires.

With actors and admin staff passing us up and down the stairs, shuttling between the canteen level below and the dressing rooms and offices above, we started to rehearse. The flamenco music from Jane's ghetto blaster ricocheted around the stairwell, now sounding like a tinny arrangement for Spanish guitar and Nightmare. It was really quite hard to re-create the sensual spirit of Lorca's duende with Monica from Touring Admin squeezing past while munching a limp white bread sandwich, but we did our best. Clapping along vigorously to the rhythm, Jane spurred us on, Celia swishing her rehearsal skirt this way and that, her torso still, her feet clattering like a machine gun on the hard stone floor; me circling her, the bull with his eyes locked on hers, heels rapidly rising and falling to the pulse of the music.

"Good, good. Keep the tension, straighten your back, eyes only on each other, that's it. The passion. The spirit. And here it comes. Ready . . . ready . . . and, ARMS!"

Symbolising the thrust of a bull's horns, my arms shot straight up and crashed through the ceiling tile, bruising my knuckles on a pipe in the process and bringing a confetti of wires and debris down onto Celia and me.

With both shows having taken their place in the repertoire, it meant a day or two off each week, sometimes longer. During one such break in July my girlfriend and I went to stay with her parents in Suffolk. We had been sitting in the garden with her mother, drinking tea. I hadn't checked my messages for a few days and so while I boiled the kettle again I dialled into the answerphone at my flat in London.

"It's Janey from the National." Janey Fothergill from Casting played Good Cop to Gillian Diamond's Bloody Scary Cop. "Could you, er, could you phone me back, please? As soon as possible. Really as soon as you can would be, would be ... if you could."

I dialled. No wonder Janey had sounded flustered. Roger Lloyd Pack had been involved in a car crash. He was going to be fine but he would be in hospital for several weeks. The Cottesloe Theatre carried no understudies because the economics didn't stack up, so would I learn the part and step into Roger's shoes for our next performance in six days' time? I'm not sure if the phrase Janey used was "would you be interested in" or "would you be prepared to," or whether it was simply "for Christ's sake, please just save our fucking bacon." In any event, I wasn't exactly going to turn down the opportunity.

Juliet and Di Trevis were extremely generous to me in that hurried rehearsal week, presumably praying each night that I would at least feed Juliet her cues. It was thrilling to be pushed out of my comfort zone and into the world of the unexpected. I went on and did OK and with each performance I grew in confidence.

The production was in the round and one night, during an intense scene between Yerma and Juan, a woman got up and walked across the stage between us. Juliet and I carried on the bitter back-and-forth for several more minutes. Long enough anyway for the woman to return and, during a moment in which you could hear a pin drop, as Yerma pleaded in anguished silence for her husband's understanding, walk back across the stage right between us once again to her seat. Well, when you gotta go, you gotta go.

Roger recovered, and after a couple of months in the limelight, Cinderella went back to the kitchen.

14

The Great Gambon

The dressing rooms at the National are on several floors, built around four sides of a rectangle open to the sky, with big windows facing each other across the void, the wig department on the top floor getting the most light. The long sides of this rising funnel hold dressing rooms for up to six people, the short sides reserved for pairs, or for single stars. Unless the blinds are drawn, everyone knows everyone else's business – who's in, who's late, who's lost a button. I used to track the progress of the wig team as they knocked on each dressing room door and entered, like hospital doctors checking up on their patients, listening to woes and gossip and new bad jokes while trying to complete their rounds before the call for Act One Beginners. In the summer months there were occasional water pistol fights during the half – King Lear taking on Ting Tang Mine – and severe tellings-off from the wardrobe department for putting costumes in the line of fire.

If it was a Michael Gambon day there was usually an added playfulness in the dressing room block. He'd pick some pretend argument with someone in another dressing room on another floor and generally entertain the troops by yelling out of the window.

Each evening: three companies of actors, preparing for shows in three different theatres, with three different audiences. I was in a great big dressing-up box and even though I barely featured in the stories being told, I loved being part of it all.

At 6:40 p.m. the first of the evening's tannoy announcements would be broadcast backstage. "Olivier Theatre. Good evening, ladies and gentlemen of the *King Lear/Small Family Business/ Antony and Cleopatra* company, this is your half-hour call. Half an hour please, thank you." Followed fifteen minutes later by "Cottesloe Theatre. Good evening, ladies and gentlemen . . ." and then at 7:10 p.m., "Lyttelton Theatre. Good evening . . ."

With each theatre's Quarter, Five and Beginners calls singing out as the clock counted down, the sense of mounting anticipation was palpable – three ships preparing to leave harbour.

7:15 p.m., the hushed tones of the DSM: "Olivier Theatre. Lights up on Act One."

7:30 p.m.: "Cottesloe Theatre. Lights up . . ."

7:45 p.m.: "Lyttelton Theatre . . ."

And off they'd sail on a cruise to distant lands of the imagination. Docking a few hours later, the passengers would disembark and the crews would gather in the backstage bar to swap stories of that particular voyage's adventures and mishaps.

As I had loads of time off in my two shows, I would chat with the other actors in my dressing room as they dashed in and out to change costumes for *King Lear* or *Antony and Cleopatra*. Or I'd tune in to one of the three theatres via the tannoy system, Michael Simkins' long, chilling yell of "Edddddddie Carrrrrrrbone!" in the Cottesloe telling you *A View from the Bridge* was reaching its shattering climax. Or I'd sneak into the wings of the Lyttelton, or into the Olivier vom (vomitorium) – an entrance from within the auditorium but out of sight of the audience – and watch the shows unfold, each production different, each audience bringing its own flavour of the day to season the evening's experience. Learning by osmosis.

Along one side of the building, just above the stage door, is the staff canteen. On one of my first days with the company I'd seen Michael Gambon and Tony Hopkins, one getting a coffee from the servery, the other with his lunchtime tray, looking for a place to sit. Some twenty years before, they had shared a dressing room at the Old Vic when they themselves were spear bearers at the National under Olivier.

"Awright, Tone?" called Gambon, in a fractured, high-pitched cockney voice.

"Not bad, son, not bad," came Hopkins' cheery reply as the duo fell into banter, adopting the personae of two old wheezing geezers, nattering about personal ailments.

It was funny and ordinary and a quick lunchtime gag, to them. To a youngster like me it was like catching crumbs from the table of giants.

After a period away from the stage, Anthony Hopkins had bounded back into the theatrical limelight in *Pravda*, a searing satire about a monstrous newspaper tycoon, a hybrid of Maxwell and Murdoch. I marvelled at how his head seemed to inflate out of his shoulders, his whole body pivoting forward, energy thrusting out of his husky anorak as he pointed with a balled fist at his nervous employees and seethed venomously, "You are weak people. Because you do not know what you belieeeeeve." Now he was leading the company again in *King Lear* and *Antony and Cleopatra*.

Gambon I had come to revere in recent months as I watched him from the wings, stealing moments during my slow evenings to watch the three quite different roles he was playing in the repertoire. He was in Alan Ayckbourn's company within the National Theatre company. The shows had struck gold.

In *Tons of Money*, a daft 1920s comedy set in a country house, he played Sprules the butler and Diane Bull played Simpson the maid. Their pairing was a masterclass in stage comedy. As characters, Simpson's dotty devotion to the ageing

Sprules was as touching as it was hilarious. As actors, Michael and Diane goaded each other on to giddier heights of silliness. The butler's tailcoat that seemed way too small accentuated Michael's big frame, so that his arms appeared to protrude to an impossible length like an orangutan's as he ushered people in and out of the drawing room. That was in the Lyttelton, where on other nights we were playing *School for Wives* on our volcanic hillside.

Some evenings the pair could be seen in the Olivier Theatre, in Alan Ayckbourn's new play *A Small Family Business*, which he had written specifically for the cast. This I used to watch night after night from the vom. The opening scene sees Jack McCracken coming home after work on his birthday, feeling a bit frisky. As he searches the darkened house for his wife, he gradually undresses. Finally, he throws open the door to the living room, trousers round his ankles, the lights come on, and there are his family and friends gathered for a surprise party. The audience is in on the joke and it was always the first belter of a laugh each performance. Having recovered his trousers and his dignity, Jack thanks the surprise guests and the story kicks into gear. Gambon planted himself downstage with his back to the stalls and delivered his next speech upstage to the rest of the cast, who were facing the audience. Although I couldn't see his face, I could tell just by watching Diane's whether Michael was being naughty; more often than not, she'd crack. Corpsing (laughing out of character) is officially frowned upon. Audiences have paid good money to come and see actors deliver of their best, runs the mantra, how dare you be so disrespectful as to cheapen the experience with such behaviour? But Gambon, completely in control himself, could mangle a word or change an inflection just enough to set the others off.

In *A View from the Bridge* by Arthur Miller, Gambon played longshoreman Eddie Carbone, whose dark secret fuels the tortured climax of the play. The cast had an inkling that they might be on to something after one of the last run-throughs in the rehearsal room, when usually expressionless technical bods – more interested in seeing how their lighting rig is going to be deployed, or how on earth they're going to shift that bit of furniture on and off – were actually dabbing their eyes at the end. At the first preview performance the cast were back in their dressing rooms before they realised the applause in the auditorium was still going on. The stage manager came over the tannoy, calling them back to the stage Immediately, Please. The standing ovation that greeted them when they reappeared, blinking under the stage lights, went on for a long, long time.

Watching Gambon as the Italian-born titan of a dockhand, at the start of the play confident, swaggering, master of his domestic kingdom, leaning back on a kitchen chair like a rearing horse, transform into a shamed and disgraced apology of a man was to watch acting and direction of the highest quality. Arthur Miller saw the show and told Ayckbourn afterwards that it was not only the "finest production I've seen but the fastest. By six minutes."

To have been able to watch Gambon from the wings giving three entirely different performances night after night was an education. Some who worked with him adored the man but not the actor, finding that his restlessness after just a few weeks of a run could turn into something self-destructive. Having delivered a towering, lauded performance he would, time and again, turn on the very thing he had created, opting for making his colleagues corpse, as if acting wasn't a proper job for a man like him, whose real passion was engines and mechanics, which he considered to be more real, valuable. Tangible. Acting, after all, is make-believe.

I would often see him in the Green Room having a coffee before a matinee but I was always too in awe to say hello. Thirty years later I finally got to work with him on film, in *Viceroy's*

House, and although he was now frustrated by his failing ability to commit lines to memory, his charisma was as vivid as when I had first witnessed it from the soft glow of the vom at the Olivier Theatre.

15

Biggus Dickus

The memorial for Sir Peter Hall was held in Westminster Abbey in the autumn of 2018. He had co-founded the Royal Shakespeare Company, had been artistic director of the National Theatre when I first worked there, was an acclaimed opera director, and a thorn in the side of any government minister who shied away from supporting the arts. The service was, unsurprisingly, impeccably stage-managed. The tributes were perfectly pitched, the hymns stirring and the choral music eye-prickingly tender. Dame Judi Dench spoke Cleopatra's words about Antony as if they had just occurred to her and as if iambic pentameters were quite the natural or rather the only way in which to express her thoughts. That is her genius, and that was Peter Hall's obsession: the rhythm and pulse and forward momentum of the verse. In fact he had written about it, and lo, there on every seat in the abbey was a copy of his creed – a hard-backed treatise, Sir Peter's face looming out of the front cover, on how Shakespeare's language should be handled. Not how it should be performed – every generation and every actor must interpret works of art for themselves – but the building blocks, the architecture of the language, he was convinced, are a given, and are essential to the fundamental workings of the plays; ignore them at your peril. Break up the form and the musicality of the verbal structures, and meaning, too, disappears, along with the sheer aesthetic pleasure of the pulsing heartbeat of the metre.

As Judi's words echoed around the abbey, the congregation drinking in the cracked honey of her voice, I was transported back thirty years to when I worked with Peter and Judi in their production of *Antony and Cleopatra* on the Olivier stage at the National Theatre, with Anthony Hopkins in the other title role. It's not a production I have ever put on my CV, not because it was poor – quite the opposite, it was sumptuous and epic – but because I think crediting myself with having appeared in it, while technically accurate, would be a garish example of what might be called Bigging Yourself Up.

One day, mooching around backstage during a matinee between my entrances in *School for Wives*, I noticed a memo pinned to the "General" noticeboard outside the canteen. *Antony and Cleopatra* was in previews. It had a large supporting cast but evidently not large enough. "Wanted," pronounced the sign, "Army for Act II. If interested and available, please read on."

I was interested, and I did read on. In Act II Scene VI, Octavius sweeps on stage as the tension rises. The threat of battle is in the air, as signified by the massed ranks of his supporting army. However, evidently the ranks looked more missed than massed on the expanse of the Olivier stage and I suspect some titters had been heard in the audience, prompting Peter Hall to nudge his assistant into formulating a Plan B.

The notice asked for those interested to report to the wardrobe department the following day for a fitting as a Roman Soldier, followed by an on-stage rehearsal in the afternoon with the assistant director, before going on for that night's performance. Given that the army's three-minute appearance occurred at roughly 8:05 p.m., I calculated that on *School for Wives* nights in between entrances I had plenty of time to change from one costume into another and back again; on the nights we were performing *Yerma* it would be a tighter timescale but with practice and a loyal dresser by my side, still doable. I signed up, thrilled that as well as getting to appear in the Olivier I would be better off by several pounds sterling per appearance.

Next morning I went up to wardrobe and joined the queue of other supernumeraries who were being kitted out in a dark red tunic, leather legionnaire's skirt, breastplate and head gear. Having been recruited, dressed and presented for final inspection (I was half expecting a medical), I was nodded through by the wardrobe supervisor. I glanced in the long mirror. Staring back at me was one of those knobbly-knee'd centurions straight out of *Asterix and Cleopatra,* complete with slightly oversized helmet slipping down over his eyes.

That afternoon I had a matinee and so wasn't able to attend the on-stage rehearsal because the timing clashed with one of my entrances in the Lyttelton. That evening the curtain went up on *Yerma* in the Cottesloe and at the appointed moment my dresser helped me get out of my Spanish villager's outfit and into the chunky Roman garb, one of my dressing room mates, Patrick Brennan, who was in *Antony and Cleo,* pointing out how to wear the sword belt properly.

As I made my way up to the Olivier, somewhere I had never been before, I started to get nervous. "I'm about to go on stage in the Olivier Theatre," I sweated to myself.

I reached the top of the echoing concrete stairs, the bland eastern bloc strip lights flickering above, and pulled open the pass door marked Olivier Stage Right. I shut it behind me and, as in an air lock, opened the darkened inner door that led into the wings. Immediately, I stepped into a dark, chaotic world that was like a sketch from Monty Python's *Life of Brian.* There were what seemed like dozens of clueless Roman soldiers all squished into a corner of the wings, being shushed by assistant stage managers, while a props master handed out a variety of spears and

SPQR banners to the jostling troops. A man with a beard and a clipboard squinted at me in the darkness. I recognised him as the staff director, Alan Cohen.

"Who are you?" he asked.

I told him. The red light of the standby button glowed threateningly as he scoured his list and checked off my name.

"Take this," he said, grabbing a spear and thrusting it into my hand. "You know what to do."

"Actually, I'm afraid I don't."

"What do you mean, you don't? We rehearsed it this afternoon."

"But I wasn't at the rehearsal" – instinctively I almost added "sir" as I suddenly felt like a schoolboy whose dog really had eaten his homework – "I was doing a matinee."

Somewhere on stage, trumpets started blaring. *Pampara! Pampara-para!*

Alan now talking louder above the din: "Follow these guys, stay in line. Stop when—"

Now the drums kicked in. *Boom ba da-da bom. Boom ba da-da bom.*

"Stop when what?"

And the trumpets went up a notch: *pam-paa, PARAM-PAPAA!*

"Stop when they stop!"

"RIGHTY-HO!"

And now the dry ice started pumping from just behind my arse. Great clouds of the stuff billowing through my flapping skirt across the wings and out on to the stage.

"THEN WHAT?"

TANTARAA! BOM-BODDY-BOM! TANTARA-TARAAAA!

"THEN MOVE OFF WHEN THEY MOVE OFF!"

The cue light changed colour, illuminating my face with an eerie emerald glow. The soldiers at the front of the melee started to move.

"NOW GO!"

"WHAT – YOU MEAN NOW?"

"JUST FUCKING MARCH!"

The guy next to me was already off. I studied his feet and did a quick step-ball-change in order to match his stride. The dry ice was by now a fog, a complete pea souper. It was everywhere, mainly down my throat. I coughed. But I kept marching into the void.

TANTARAA-PA-PAMM! BOM-BODDY-BOM!

"Twats!" snarled an amused voice from the darkness of the down right wing as we marched past. It was Enobarbus, Michael Bryant, one of the pillars of the company.

Left right, left right, left right. The music reached a final *BA-DOM!* and the marching soldiers came to an abrupt halt. I did so half a moment later. *Da-bom.*

Somewhere off to my right, miles away downstage, Tim Pigott-Smith and David Schofield, as Octavius and Pompey, started having a go at each other. Slowly the fog cleared and it began to dawn on me that I was actually on the stage of this famous theatre. Incredible.

However, the moment was short-lived because, as the mist finally rolled away, I realised that I was staring at the ear of the soldier in front of me. What I hadn't taken on board, because of the poor visibility, was that when they had come to a halt, all the other soldiers had done an abrupt right turn so that they were facing downstage. I was the only soldier still facing the opposite wing and was therefore at right angles to the rest of my platoon.

I had three choices, really. The first was to do nothing and pretend I was the soldier whose job it was to keep a look out eastwards, while the rest of the cohort faced south. Option two would be to make a sudden right turn with military confidence, thus signalling my arrival and possibly upstaging whatever my senior officers were up to way downstage over there. Instead, I plumped for option three. Ever so slowly I began to turn, like a figure atop a mechanical musical box, feet appearing not to move while veeerrrry carefully shifting the position of my body, not to mention the spear. By my calculation, if I effected this manoeuvre slowly enough, no one would notice and after about five minutes all would be well. However, after only thirty seconds there was a sudden piercing *TARANDA-DAAA!* and the bloody trumpets and drums kicked off again. The soldiers all did a sudden left turn in which I was immediately swept up, all thoughts of facing front now abandoned, and off we marched again, into the darkness of the prompt side wings. There, spears, flags and halberds were grabbed from us and, like a ship's crew making for the life rafts, we were ushered at speed through the doors out into the corridor.

"I've just been on the Olivier stage!" I boasted to my dresser, who frankly couldn't have given a toss about my landmark experience and had far more pressing things on his mind.

"We've got less than a minute," he said, grabbing my Roman helmet and handing me the rough linen shirt for *Yerma*.

I bounced off down the staircase, half hopping, pulling off Roman stockings with each step and pulling on Spanish socks, throwing aside my russet tunic and pogoing into peasant britches. Down at ground level now, through swing doors, run along a corridor, more swing doors, tucking the shirt in, ruffling the hair, into the Cottesloe scene dock – mouthing "Made it!" to the ASM as she pulled open the pass door as quietly as possible. A flurry of chords on the guitar and Jenny Galloway began to narrate the dance.

"In the mountain river, the woman comes to bathe . . ."

And there was Celia Imrie across the other side of the stage, hoicking up her skirt, locking eyes with mine as we started our steamy, foot-stamping encounter. Looking back, possibly the two most unlikely flamenco dancers in the history of terpsichorean expression.

16

A Count with an "O" in it

David Edgar's *Entertaining Strangers*, originally written as a community play for the town of Dorchester, was about the cholera epidemic in the middle of the nineteenth century. For the new production in the Cottesloe in 1987 the cast was smaller but still large by NT standards and most of the ensemble played a number of roles. As well as a tattooed man at a funfair, I was to be a sergeant at arms and a couple of other townsfolk. A scaffolding mock-up of the set was assembled in Rehearsal Room 1: a raked hillside, on which some of the audience would stand or sit, up close and personal with the actors, promenade style. The play was directed by Sir Peter Hall and the two leads were Tim Pigott-Smith and Judi Dench. It was my first proper encounter with any of them and I was awestruck.

It was the day of my first solo rehearsal with Judi. Peter Hall plonked his chair at the bottom of the slanted hillside, his script on a stool beside him and a cigar in his mouth. From the side of the rehearsal platform, I watched a scene unfold between Tim and Judi, ready for my first entrance as George Loder a few pages later.

Tim played the pastor who saw God's plan in all things, even in the suffering that cholera brought with it. Judi was Sarah Eldridge, a pragmatic publican who tolerated the Lord just so long as the bills got paid. Their scene was progressing, my entrance was coming up. My pulse quickened. Tim finished his speech, a slight bow as he put on his parson's hat, taking his leave of Judi and exiting stage right. Now it was my turn to enter, stage left.

"Oh bloody hell shit it's Judy Dench," my Unhelpful Self started wibbling, "and I'm about to do a scene with her, and that man with the cigar founded the Royal Shakespeare Company, oh shitting fuck I'm going to wet myself."

Practical Self chipped in: "Left foot goes in front of the right, idiot. It's called walking. And it's Judi Dench. With an 'i.' If you're that scared, imagine her on the loo. And picture Peter Hall naked."

"Why is he in the bathroom with her? That's horrible. I feel sick now."

"Just get on the stage, you wazzock."

Judi looked across at me as I inched robotically on to the platform, script in hand. Had she heard all this, or detected a twitch, or spotted a bead of sweat? Maybe I was dribbling? She'd noticed something, certainly, something that amplified the cacophony of nerves that were jangling inside me because she suddenly did something I shall never forget. From her position centre stage she made a single, decisive move all the way downstage to the lip of the platform, near where Peter Hall was sitting. She then turned her back to him and to where the audience would be, thus inviting me to take up what had been her central position, making me the focus of the scene.

She literally gave me the stage.

It was about the most generous gesture a senior actor could make to a nervous newcomer.

Michael Byrne played Judi's soak of a husband. I still have the first night card he gave us all, itself a photocopy of a hand-written card Laurence Olivier had given him when he had taken over from Ian McKellen as Claudio in the National's 1965 production of *Much Ado* at the Old Vic. In it Olivier advised the younger actor to "Keep your neck back . . . Don't make little gestures . . . Keep a sense of legato . . . He's a young Count with an O in it remember." I liked the sense of stage tips (and jokes) being passed on from generation to generation.

The last scene of the play took place in a graveyard as the snow fell, the two central characters reflecting on the epidemic that had devastated the community and on a God that had allowed it to happen. Judi's final speech was mesmerising, performance after performance. The heartfelt simplicity of her delivery, of what she and her family had endured, never failed to move me, or the audience. After three weeks of the run I plucked up the courage to bump into her in the scene dock after the curtain call.

"Judi?"

"Hello!" she said brightly, taking off her black bonnet as we travelled at speed through the workshops towards the dressing rooms. "Good one tonight, wasn't it?"

"Yes, can I just . . . that last speech . . . every night it's just . . . it's so . . . it's riveting and so moving. Just wanted to say."

"Oh, thank you! That's very kind of you." She stopped in her tracks, one hand clutching her bonnet and hair grips, the other taking me conspiratorially by the arm as she whispered, "Have you any idea what it means?"

Being a promenade production, the cast got to glimpse members of the audience at closer quarters than it would in the more traditional setting of a proscenium arch, or a thrust stage. While some of the spectators were seated in the galleries above, a third of the audience experienced the show from the hillside below, among the actors. One night Judi spotted the director Howard Davies seated on the mound among the on-stage promenaders. She hurriedly scribbled a note in pencil – "Fancy a shag?" – scrunched it up and, as she entered the scene, dropped it in his lap, her skirt brushing his shoulder as she passed. Towards the end of the scene she glanced across to enjoy his reaction to her billet-doux. But far from grinning up at her he was staring, bewildered, at the tatty bit of paper. Whoever the man was, she realised, he was not Howard Davies.

17

Striking Matches on the Anaglypta

Michael Winter, artistic director of the Colchester Mercury Theatre in the 1980s, was so muscular he was more of a gym bunny who ran a theatre on the side. Square jaw, brown hair cropped tight like an American GI, an impressive physique and a voice of light sandpaper, rasping but soft. The plays he was casting for the summer of 1988 were Ayckbourn's *Taking Steps, The Circle* by Somerset Maugham, Shakespeare's *Taming of the Shrew* and *Look Back in Anger* by John Osborne. When my agent called to tell me that my audition had been successful I wasn't sure which of the plays I was to be in.

"All of them, dear," said Shane. "You're through cast."

My dream of working on a variety of plays with the same company of actors was finally becoming a reality. But I was wrong. It turned out I was the only actor to be "through cast," all the others came and went after a play or two. Still, I at least was to get a decent run of things and a nineteen-week contract at £150 per week.

I could have stayed on at the National Theatre, I had been offered small parts in "The Late Shakespeares" that Peter Hall was mounting, but one of the actors with whom I shared a dressing room said, "Stay here playing small parts and they'll love you for ever. You'll also be playing small parts for ever. Go off, do rep, play bigger parts, then you can come back and play bigger parts."

I had spent several weeks at Leicester Haymarket doing Rattigan's *French Without Tears* and now, as I was going to be in Colchester for many months, I wanted to get the right digs. In any profession, securing accommodation is the Russian roulette element of being away from home for any length of time. However, it is especially true in theatre, where living allowances are meagre. Some of the landlords and landladies of yesteryear were legendary, particularly on the touring circuit, when companies on the road would tell each other where and where not to stay in any given town, usually via a hurried chat on a station platform at Crewe as they changed trains on a Sunday. Mrs. Lansdown in Malvern who charged for soap; the couple in Bradford who would be only too happy to consider payment In Kind if the gentleman or lady was a bit short that week. The actor Roy Barraclough told me he was fond of old Mrs. Kinleigh of Harrogate. On one of his visits she opened the door and said, "Oh, Mr. Barraclough, what a relief to see you. Couldn't wait to see the back of them Romanian acrobats last week," adding with a roll of her eyes and a tut, "striking their matches on me anaglypta."

So, with these images in mind I inspected the Colchester digs list. Too many unknowns and no messages of recommendation in a dead letter box on the platform at Crewe, or indeed on the Ipswich line. I then remembered that my Cambridge roommate had an aunt who lived on the marshes outside Colchester. He gave me Jilly's number and I rang her to ask if I might stay a couple of nights while I checked out digs in town. I turned up with my bag on the Sunday . . . and left six months later, by which time Jilly had become a second mother to me and a lifelong heroine.

Despite the casts at Colchester changing between productions and so not really being a cohesive company, it was still about the best training a young theatre actor could have asked for as the traditional rep system was coming to an end. In *Taking Steps* I played a tongue-tied solicitor, a dream of a comedic role; in *The Circle*, Teddy was an Anyone for Tennis type; in *The Shrew* I played Petruchio, the ultimate alpha male (I was originally cast as Lucentio – someone must have dropped out); while Cliff in *Look Back in Anger* was passive and sensitive, deftly defusing the verbal bombshells of Osborne's explosive creation, Jimmy Porter, played with viperish invective by Ben Stevens. With a variety of directors at the helm I learned a lot about playwrights and stagecraft. The productions were well received and the quality of the actors, from old school to young bucks, was consistently high.

Just as we were putting *Look Back in Anger* through its final paces in the rehearsal room, Michael Winter took me aside and asked me if I would like to do the next show at Colchester. I racked my brains. There wasn't anything else in the season, apart from the Christmas show, and surely he wasn't going to suggest—

"I'd like you to play the Dame in *Dick Whittington*."

It may have been an unlikely piece of casting – a twenty-four-year-old who had just played Petruchio showing up as Sarah the Cook – but it turned out to be fantastically instructive as well as knackering. The tradition of a show in which the lead male is played by a girl and the matriarch by a man in a frock leaves overseas visitors somewhat baffled but it is ingrained in our culture and I have always loved it, regularly hiring a charabanc to take friends and family to see the annual Christmas offering at Windsor Theatre Royal. For my first entrance here in Colchester I sailed on in a big blue gingham dress.

"Hello boys and girls, my name's Sarah the Cook. But you can call me anytime."

I love that line. Then I reached for my sore hip.

"Ooh. All day I've had this pain down my side. All day this pain."

From the oversized pocket in my dress I pulled out a sheet of glass and chucked it into the wings. *Smash!*

"Pane's gone now."

The panto was the most fulfilling experience of my career to date for the simple reason that kids tell it like it is. Beware the line "Hello boys and girls, are we enjoying ourselves?" because they will tell you if they aren't. If you can keep several hundred children happy twice a day for eight weeks, or if you can bear the sweet wrappers, sweets, slings and arrows they are all too willing to hurl at you if you don't deliver, you can put up with a slow Saturday night on a West End stage . . . and even then – especially then - ask yourself if it might be You and not Them.

Towards the end of the run I went to interview for *The Bill*, the cop show that had become a regular fixture in the ITV schedule over the previous few years as an hour-long procedural, told from the perspective of the police. My audition was for the role of a university graduate who was being fast-tracked through the system and into the police force. So, this meeting called for a suit – remember that detail – something I rarely wore in my working life. Back in the days of weekly rep it was standard that the jobbing actor would provide his own dinner jacket, as the chances were that at least one show in the repertoire would require the wearing of black tie. But I had hardly worn a suit since school. I dusted it down and was amazed to find it fitted well enough.

"Please, sit down," said the producer, smiling.

I was one side of the trestle table, the producer, a writer and the casting director on the other. The conversation flowed. I had read an episode and liked it, and I liked it even more when the producer told me how they saw the character developing and taking his place in the show. As the graduate new boy, he was smart but not streetwise. How would that play out with the diehards who had come up through the ranks? He'd be sidelined, bullied even, but he'd prove his worth and the dinosaurs would come round in the end. No, of course I didn't mind reading a scene with the casting director. All was going swimmingly. They were looking at me with That Look. The Look that says We Like You. The Look that says Welcome to the Family.

There are two rules of thumb worth remembering about interviews, in whatever walk of life they take place. Don't promise something you can't actually deliver and, while never succumbing to sycophancy, at least try and maintain a positive attitude until you've left the building.

"Could we have a look at your showreel?"

"My showreel?"

"You have got a showreel, haven't you? I mean because—"

"Of course I have!" I said too quickly and loudly.

"—it's not a problem if you haven't."

Our lines were overlapping now. "A showreel of course I have." I ploughed on regardless of sense or dignity. "My agent has the showreel and he will send it to you at once forthwith."

The only thing resembling a showreel that I could think of consisted of a six-minute short of an eighteen-year-old Joseph Fiennes pretending to throw himself into the Thames the morning after the Great Storm of 1987. And I didn't even appear in it. I was the director, and we had made the story up as we went along.

"Great. We'll be in touch with Shane, then."

"Yes you will be in touch with Shane you will yes."

"One other thing," said the producer, his pen down now, leaning back in his chair thoughtfully. "The one-hour format – well, forty-eight minutes plus adverts – we're looking at shifting to half-hour episodes. What do you think?"

Since I had now pretty much got the job, despite the minor hiccup with the showreel, I thought it best to be completely honest with my new buddies.

"I think that is an absolutely terrible idea. You'll lose your audience overnight, the stories will become rushed and trite, and the characters indistinguishable, with no room to breathe and develop. It would be a disaster. Don't do it."

There was what you might call a silence in the room before the casting director stood and stuck out her hand. I shook it, beaming.

"We'll be in touch," she said.

Following the audition, I had some time to kill before getting the train back to Colchester, so on a whim I popped into the National for a cup of tea in the backstage canteen with Paul Greaves, one of the stage management team. He'd never seen me in a suit either. Afterwards, on my way back down the echoey stairwell to the stage door, I happened to pass the director Peter Gill, who was on his way up.

"Hello." He sounded rather startled. He looked me up and down. "The suit. I've never seen you in a suit."

Me in anything other than jeans and a T-shirt was clearly becoming headline news. Peter's eyes narrowed and he crooked a finger against his pursed lips.

"What are you up to at the moment?" he asked with a hint of mystery.

I told him.

"Will you come and see me when you've finished at Colchester? Might have something for you. Nice suit."

It wasn't particularly but I took the compliment, a few weeks later the meeting, and subsequently my next contract at the National. I will be forever indebted to Lady Luck for that stairwell encounter and to Marks & Spencer for the two-piece.

In the end *The Bill* went in a different direction. Can't think why. The show did indeed change to the shorter format and ran for another twenty years, winning multiple awards and regularly topping the ratings.

18

The Part with the Suit

The part with the suit, as I came to call it, was Charles Bentham in *Juno and the Paycock*, Sean O'Casey's painful and painfully funny play about a troubled Ireland before North and South were divided.

Had I not had a couple of hours to spare that day after *The Bill* audition and decided to call in at the National . . . had I not been heading down that particular staircase as Peter Gill was walking up it . . . had a butterfly not flapped its wings in the rainforest . . . Every moment in a person's life appears, with hindsight, to be connected. Had Jonathan Lynn not chosen Florence for a long weekend in the autumn of 1986 would I have played Charles Bentham three years later, or Henry Brown in the *Paddington* films twenty-five years after that? Or been asked to write this book? When I am questioned about how one makes a start in the business, or how one catches a lucky break, I answer that the industry owes you nothing, but putting yourself in Luck's way is a helpful start. You have a better chance of nearing the job you crave if you at least hover in its orbit. The whizzing atoms that coalesce into a moment called Opportunity are more likely to occur if you are working in a box office or selling ice creams in the interval than if you are sitting at home staring angrily at the phone, or working in a carpet factory in Kidderminster.

Having made his mark directing adaptations of D. H. Lawrence at the Royal Court in the 1960s, Peter Gill went on to found the Riverside Studios in Hammersmith and then in the 1980s established the National Theatre Studio as a place for writers, actors and designers to try stuff out. Located in the old NT workshops next to the Old Vic before they moved to the South Bank, the Studio became a hangout for the younger generation of theatre makers, many of whom looked on Peter as something of a guru.

If Sir Peter Hall up the road in the main building was Prospero, Peter Gill, in the grubbier marshlands of the Studio, cast himself as Caliban, earthily anti-establishment and faintly subversive. He had a flop of greying hair and dark eyebrows, a strong nose and full lips. The leather jacket he often wore seemed slightly incongruous against his soft voice, its Welshness barely detectable. He would hold court on all things theatrical and aesthetic, delighting in withering commentaries on shows that had opened, directors who had flopped, who was au courant, who was passé. He loved being surrounded by assistant directors and fledgling actors, coffee mugs in hand, whom he would entertain with his wry assessments of what constituted the best of contemporary theatre. He gestured continually, his fingers dancing up in front of his face like a panhandler sifting the air for words and ideas, leaning forward in conversation with eyes that demanded your attention, his lips almost permanently poised in a pout, often with the phrase "D'do, do you see?" ending a sentence. He had an obsession with Oxbridge and teased anyone with a university education with faux admiration. While addressing a group of acolytes he would rest a hand on my shoulder as if about to parade me round the Circus Maximus and say with a wry smile, "Now take this oh-so-clever Cambridge boy for example . . ."

Given his preferred status as the outsider, stirring potions in the Studio or in the cauldron of the Cottesloe, Peter directing *Juno and the Paycock* in the Lyttelton was perhaps an unusual departure. With Tony Haygarth as Captain Boyle and Linda Bassett as his long-suffering wife Juno, the cast was rounded out by Irish actors like Tom Hickey and Pauline Delaney and new talents in the shape of Linus Roache and Aidan Gillen. Peter's style of directing was something I had not come across before. His approach was that the only truly valid element of a performance was in the acting space itself. Ros Bennett was playing Mary Boyle, daughter of the house. With his characteristic curled grin he told me he had "caught Linda and Ros talking about what their characters had been up to off stage. They don't exist off stage!" he exclaimed. For him, actors creating back stories for themselves was a fundamental and peculiar error. Personally, I think each to his own; whatever helps you get to the point of being comfortable on stage. He also had a very particular attitude to text. He would never give a line reading – that is, *tell* you how to say it – but he would not let a line go by until he felt the actor had discovered the correct intonation for him or herself.

One Tuesday afternoon I crept into the rehearsal room for my 4:30 p.m. call and took a seat to one side of the marked-up floor. Pauline Delaney as Mrs. Tancred was rehearsing the scene in which she shares her anguish with Juno, her Republican "Die-hard" son having just been killed.

"O Blessed Virgin, where were you when me darlin' son was riddled with bullets? When me darlin' son was riddled with bullets!"

Pauline, script in hand, delivered the line with quiet intensity. Peter was on his feet. He cocked his head towards her, listening, rubbing a thumb and forefinger together as if trying to tease the correct inflection out of the air.

"When my darling son was – what?"

"Riddled with bullets," explained Pauline.

"Again. When he . . ." Peter had this weird smile on his face, as if the correct answer was hidden behind an invisible door to which he held the key. It would open eventually but only when Pauline had landed on exactly the right tone.

"When me darlin' son was riddled—"

"When who . . . ?"

"When me darlin' son was riddled with bull—"

"When he was . . . what?"

Peter's expression was now that of a safe-cracker, ear pressed against the door of the vault, listening for the correct click of cogs that would Open Sesame.

"When me darlin' son was riddled with bullets, when me darl—"

"Riddled with what?"

Tim Supple, the assistant director, tiptoed over to me and whispered that I could probably call it a day as this was likely to go on for some time and I should phone in later to get my call for the following morning.

I headed home along the river to my flat in Vauxhall, stopping at Sainsbury's to pick up some beanshoots to add to the stir-fry I had in mind. I made a cup of tea, watched the early evening news, checked my watch – 6 p.m., rehearsals would have just ended. I phoned the stage door and got my call time. Cooked supper. Phoned an old mate, read the *Evening Standard*. Went to bed. Next morning I had the luxury of a lie-in. I got up at a leisurely pace, showered, watched Frank Bough on *Breakfast Time* over coffee and toast, then cycled along the South Bank to the National. It was about 11:30 when I quietly inched open the door to Rehearsal Room 2.

"And again. He was what?"

"Riddled with—"

"What was he?"

Quite how Pauline hadn't by now thrown the tea urn at Peter was beyond me. She deserved a medal.

Dining at the big house. Lunch break during the first season of *Downton Abbey*, Highclere Castle, 2010.

L-R: Brendan Coyle, Jessica Brown Findlay, Rose Leslie, Sophie McShera, Thomas Howes, Joanne Froggatt, Dan Stevens, Laura Carmichael, Allen Leech.

With director John Landis and my brother, Nigel. In between set-ups on the set of *Burke & Hare*, 2010.

Hollywood legend Shirley MacLaine comes to play at *Downton Abbey*, 2012.

Courtesy of Carnival Film & Television Ltd Photographer: Nick Briggs

Bill Murray adjusting Paddington's clothes. Berlin, 2014.

Paddington got to hang out with *The Monuments Men* at the Berlin Film Festival, 2014. L-R: Bob Balaban, HB, Jean Dujardin, John Goodman, Dimitri Leonidas, Matt Damon, George Clooney.

As Myfanwy the cleaner in *Paddington*, 2013.

Director Paul King, Paddington's creator Michael Bond, Maddie Harris (Judy) and Sam Joslin (Jonathan) – night shoot at Charing Cross underground station – *Paddington*, 2013. The scene was eventually cut, so Michael's cameo appearance was re-shot. In the finished film he can be seen in a pavement café, raising a glass to his creation as Paddington passes by in a taxi.

Paddington really did get about in 2014. Here he is with Ralph Fiennes, whom I was interviewing for a documentary about *A Midsummer Night's Dream* for Sky Arts, at the Open Air Theatre Regent's Park.

Forgetting my table manners as my stomach ulcer burst in the final season of *Downton Abbey*. The flowers were strategically placed to allow a good landing strip for the bloody eruption. Highclere Castle, 2015.

Courtesy of Carnival Film & Television Ltd © Carnival Film & Television Ltd. All rights reserved. Photographer: Nick Briggs

As *Downton Abbey* became more popular, marshalling onlookers and paparazzi when filming on location became a full-time job. Bampton, 2015.

Courtesy of Carnival Film & Television Ltd © Carnival Film & Television Ltd. All rights reserved. Photographer: Nick Briggs

Richard E. Grant having a drink with a friend, *Downton Abbey* Season 5, Highclere Castle, 2014.

A hot night filming *Viceroy's House*, about the partition of India in 1947, in which I finally got to work with Michael Gambon, on the left of the picture – with David Hayman, Gillian Anderson and myself. Jodhpur, India, 2015.

With my darling Dad, summer 2017.

After he'd tried to light a bonfire at 3 a.m. we put an "exit alarm" on the front door.

It's all happening in Frankie Howerd.

John Morton directing Ivan Gonzalez, Max Olesker and Jason Watkins on the set of *W1A*, Pinewood Studios, 2017.

With Sally Hawkins. Mr. and Mrs. Brown, back in the day. *Paddington 2,* 2018.

Late-night selfie at Paddington station.

L-R: HB, Julie Walters, Madeline Harris, Sally Hawkins, Samuel Joslin. *Paddington 2,* 2018.

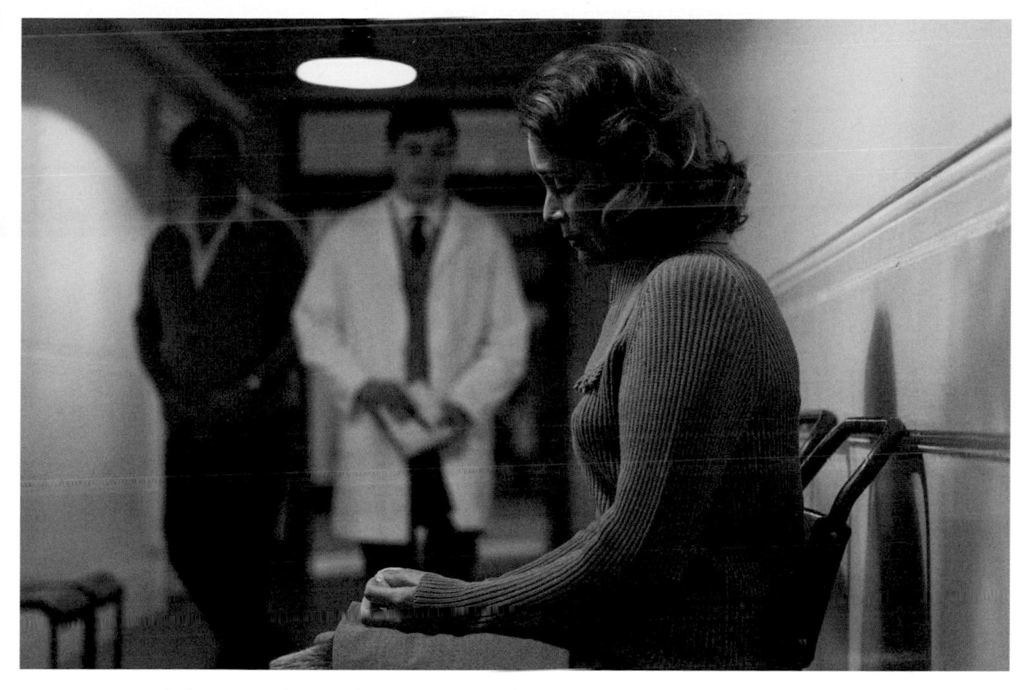

A star-struck hospital doctor (Lewis Spencer) approaches Hollywood actress Patricia Neal (Keeley Hawes), while she and husband Roald Dahl wait anxiously for news of their daughter.

To Olivia, 2019.

Courtesy *To Olivia*.

With Bob "Farmer" Hines at the International Space Station training pool, Johnson Space Center, Houston in 2019. I bet his spacesuit didn't smell as bad as mine did in 1969. Bob went up to the ISS in 2021. We arranged a screening of the second *Downton Abbey* film for the crew while they were in orbit.

Album cover.

L-R: Harry Hadden-Paton, Jonathan Zaccaï, HB, Allen Leech.

The second *Downton Abbey* film – South of France, 2021

Director Simon Curtis either directing Maggie Smith or asking her a question from one of his quizzes. The second *Downton Abbey* film, Highclere Castle, 2021.

19

The Piano String

Peter Wood directed the first ill-fated production of Harold Pinter's *The Birthday Party,* which closed after only eight performances, as well as premieres of no fewer than ten Tom Stoppard plays. By the late 1980s he had had a string of successes at the National Theatre, including celebrated revivals of Restoration plays like *Love for Love, The Provok'd Wife* and *The Rivals,* with Michael Hordern. In 1989 he cast me as Squire Sullen in Farquhar's *The Beaux' Stratagem,* opposite Brenda Blethyn. Now in his sixties, Peter had a mop of wavy grey hair and sometimes it was hard to tell if his broad face was smiling, resembling a crocodile, or in a fixed grimace, like The Joker. His voice had an air of camp languor and he could be a bully, using an actor's inability to deliver a certain line, for example, as a way of putting them down. I had heard that he picked on female actors in particular and would often single one out to be his whipping boy, or rather girl. Waspish.

He was, it has to be said, good on text. The comic structure and rhythm of a scene, the verbal dexterity required within a complicated sentence. I was standing behind one of the scenery flats at the side of the rehearsal room floor as he had yet another go at Jane Gurnett about her phrasing.

"Stop, Jane, stop! Where oh where is an actor who can actually breathe properly and deliver Farquhar's words through to the end of the line?"

"I'm here," I said, stepping into view. Whether it was true or not it did at least take him by surprise and stop him picking on my fellow actor, for a while.

The show started to bubble up. Brenda Blethyn's comic timing was sublime and the company was beginning to gel. We were at the stage of running the play all the way through, but on the day we rehearsed the curtain call dance my life turned upside down.

The dance was a polka, energetic half steps and vigorous turns. My partner was Matyelock "Puck" Gibbs. Because we were performing on a rake, with the set tipped towards the audience, it was important that we got used to the angle by rehearsing the dance in the shoes we would be wearing in the show, in my case the Squire's riding boots. At the piano Dominic Muldowney started to play the intro and off we set, Puck and I galloping and spinning like tops. Suddenly, one of the strings on the piano made a loud *thwunk* noise as it snapped. The next thing I knew I was on the floor, my leg outstretched. Faces looking down at me. I wasn't in pain – shock, maybe – but I knew instinctively I couldn't get up. The assistant stage manager knelt down and lifted my left leg, about to pull my boot off. I jabbed a finger of warning at him.

"You touch that boot, John, and I swear you will never have children."

It hadn't been a piano string I had heard, it was the sound of my Achilles tendon snapping. Heavy-duty cutters were commandeered from the workshop and the boot was cut away. I was levered to the vertical and I tried to walk. Sure enough, while my right foot could rise and fall, the left was resolutely floppy. In the Second World War, Allied POWs were sometimes handicapped on purpose in this way by their Japanese guards: you couldn't get far as an escapee with your Achilles tendon hanging like a limp drawstring on a Venetian blind.

The half-mile journey from the National to St. Thomas' Hospital took nearly an hour in the early evening traffic; I could have hopped there more quickly. But within a few hours the wayward tendon had been fixed on to its original anchor point.

It was lying there that night, pumping fifty-pence pieces into the hospital's portable telephone system – a money-guzzling defibrillator on wheels – that I heard stories about the illustrious company I was in. How when Tony Sher snapped his Achilles while playing the Fool to Gambon's King Lear he got a message of commiseration from Judi Dench, who had snapped hers shortly before the opening of *Cats*, forcing her to be replaced as Grizabella by Elaine Paige. Squire Sullen was hardly at the iconic heights of the Fool or the long-running musical about furry creatures but I felt strangely comforted that I was in a good company of tendon snappers and by the end of that first night in hospital, with my leg in a lightweight fibreglass plaster, a plan was formulating in my mind.

"When can I get back on stage?" I asked the surgeon next morning.

"You're going to be in plaster for eight weeks."

"When can I put weight on it, though?"

He told me I would be able to use crutches in a couple of days and walk in ten days, albeit with the foot set rigid. My mood lifted immediately. Everything was going to work out fine. My understudy, Geoffrey Church, could open the show and, thanks to the new technology of the lightweight plaster, I could return to the stage in a couple of weeks. Squire Sullen could have gout and therefore a limp. Genius. The consultant left and I lay there buzzing with excitement.

Then the phone rang. It was Serena Hill, the new head of casting at the National. "How are you?" she asked gravely. Serena always had a sweet smile and had impossibly long mousy hair, which she tossed to great effect. She was affectionately known by some as "Miss Cast," because when younger actors in the company summoned up the courage to knock on her door and suggest themselves for a part in an upcoming show she'd invariably turn on the smile and with a single toss of the head flick her hair back, while through the hundred-watt beam you'd hear the truncated phrase "S'cast." I often worried that her long hair was going to be the end of her, Isadora Duncan style. What if she got in a lift in a hurry and the doors shut? For some reason I pictured her sitting at her desk with her hair already caught in the wheels of her whizzabout chair. I don't know if she had a whizzabout chair up there on the admin floor of the National but for me at that moment, she did. Maybe it was the painkillers.

I told her the good news. She made noises of encouragement and then spoke with silken severity.

"The thing is, we're going to have to replace you."

The bottom fell out of my world.

"Replace me? What? Have you spoken to my surgeon? He said I can be back on stage in a fortnight. I can play it with a boot. Squire Sullen has gout, whatever."

"I'm so sorry."

"Have you spoken to the surgeon, Serena?"

She purred about the impossibility of the situation, how much everyone wanted me to take my time and recover. But I wasn't listening. Had I been in the office with her instead of on the end of the phone, I would at this point have started turning her round and round in her whizzabout chair so that her lengthy mane twisted and tightened like a strudel plait, her head being pulled further and further backwards as she spun faster and faster until she reached an impossible speed, like a figure skater doing one of those dizzying spins. Then all it would take would be a little nudge from my fibreglass boot and the centrifugal force would send her and her chair through the sheet glass window, spinning her off towards the Thames and quite possibly eternity.

I put the phone down.

*

"I'm going to fight it, Shane. That's my role and I'm going to play it."

"Of course you are, dear."

It was later in the afternoon now. I was on the phone to my agent.

"But they've re-cast you. Marc Sinden has agreed to step in and he's already in rehearsals."

Time stood still.

"I mean, they are going to give you a bit of sick pay, so there is that," continued Shane, as if blowing freshly varnished nails.

"Shane. They've fired me within hours of the accident. They can't do that. Are you going to fight this with me, or not?"

"It is the National Theatre, Hugh," said my surgeon that evening, visiting on his rounds. My parents were equally cautious, not wanting me to take on what they perceived as the might of the Establishment.

"You do want to work again, don't you?" said Mum.

I had never felt so alone. I was out of hospital in a day or two and sitting with my union's lawyers a day after that.

A week after the accident I walked, booted and focused, into Serena Hill's office. She looked "startled," I think the word is. If she'd had a panic button under her desk she would have pressed it. I told her that while I realised they were going to honour my replacement's contract over mine and that I wouldn't be allowed back on stage, I was not going to go away and shut up, I was not letting it drop. As I exited I swear I heard a swish of hair.

It was nearly a year before the industrial tribunal was heard. The panel consisted of three members of the Society of London Theatre who were to hear evidence presented on my behalf by Equity and from the National Theatre as presented by David Aukin, its executive director. David, black wavy hair, neat beard, smart demeanour and a smile that revealed nothing, had trained as a lawyer, and it showed. In cross-examining me he didn't look at me once, his eyes searching the walls just above the panel's heads, as if somehow the truth would be revealed by the chipped paintwork of the anonymous meeting room in which we had gathered.

"The accident that befell this young actor was of course deeply upsetting, not only for him but also for us, his colleagues at the National Theatre. We had to react swiftly and efficiently in the best interests of the production, which was to open in a matter of days. To suggest that he was dismissed would imply a degree of animosity against him."

At this, he turned his body if not his eyes towards me.

"Can I ask where you are employed at the moment?"

"At the National Theatre. In *School for Scandal*." If I sounded a bit surprised it was because I was. He knew all this. The panel knew all this. But I was not used to the wiles of the court room and the ability of a good advocate to make red appear yellow and black, white.

"And very good you are in it, too."

A smile. A ripple of laughter. Smug.

"And who," he went on, "is the director of that production?"

"Peter Wood."

"Peter Wood. The same director who cast you in *The Beaux' Stratagem*, is that right?"

"Yes that's right but—"

"During rehearsals for which you sustained the unfortunate injury. The fact—"

"Yes, but the way I was dismissed was—"

"The fact that Peter Wood has re-engaged you so readily – that the National Theatre has re-engaged you – is a mark of the high regard in which we all hold you. A fine young actor, working at the National once again. No animosity. So, what this actor is really here to discuss . . ."

Like a Rebel Alliance pilot banking his intergalactic fighter into an attack run, his in-helmet, visor-mounted laser-guidance system sliding down into his field of vision, rapidly calibrating co-ordinates, range and seconds to engagement, David shifted his gaze from the pipes above the panellists' heads, swept low across each of their three faces before finally swivelling his sights on to me.

"... what he really wants is MONEY."

And *thwer-kang*! From deep within the silo of his thin, cold smile the missile was launched, rapidly accelerating across the room to three trillion miles per hour, shattering my pathetic defences, vaporising my skull, my dignity, credibility, humanity and any other "ity" you can imagine, all in a nanosecond.

In that instant, I turned from someone trying to stand up for the little people into a money-grabbing shit. I take my hat off to David. He was brilliant. Yes, I did get a few thousand pounds in compensation but that had never been the point, for me. It had been about preventing employers firing people on medical grounds before even speaking to a bloody doctor, and it did at least lead to the National changing its dismissal procedure.

20

Don't Mention the Scottish Play

I experienced my first "dry" as a professional actor on the stage of the Olivier Theatre. I was twenty-six. As I replay it in my head my pulse quickens and my throat dries, which is exactly what happened that night when I was standing downstage left, three feet away from Jeremy Northam. It took place in the "screen scene" of *The School for Scandal,* in 1990, my Achilles tendon now happily long healed and out of trouble. Jeremy and I were playing brothers Joseph and Charles Surface. With Lady Teazle and her potential gull of a husband, Sir Peter, hiding in his reception room, the duplicitous Joseph opens the door to his brother and tries to trap him into a confession about fancying Lady Teazle. Instead, Charles begins to expose his brother's hypocrisy and Joseph takes him aside in an attempt to shut him up. The pace of the scene is cranking up by this point and the dialogue ping-pongs between them. Except at this particular performance Jeremy pinged but I failed to pong. Silence echoed across the wide open veldt, in front of a preview audience of around nine hundred people. Jeremy looked at me. I looked at Jeremy. Deep into his eyes, pleading. He was my big brother. Big brothers help little brothers don't they, surely? Big Jeremy was going to help Little Hugh.

"Wok ig ik?" I asked desperately in a rictus grinning whisper, like a terrible ventriloquist.

"D'no," Jeremy gurned back hoarsely, equally stuck. Then again it wasn't his job to know my lines.

In the chasm of awkwardness that was rapidly opening up, time slowed, the cosmos shifted and the space-time continuum took on an entirely new form; embryos were formed, born, grew up, grew old and died; empires rose and fell, entire civilisations came into being and disintegrated, dinosaurs took over the world again before a comet wiped them out, until at long last the ASM spoke painfully loudly from the prompt corner.

"Egad, I'm serious. Don't—"

"Egad, I'm serious. Don't you remember, one day, when I called here . . ."

And on we went.

The production was well enough received but it had been beset with technical problems from the start. Prunella Scales knew why.

"Oh my God, NO!" she shouted as she stepped on stage at the technical rehearsal and took in the set for the first time. "I can't believe it. Can you believe it?" She was gesturing towards the upstage flats, which were emblazoned with printed words and sentences, as if torn from an eighteenth-century gossip pamphlet, the set designed by John Gunter. From a distance the writing was indistinct but close up the word "Macbeth" was all too legible here and there and, moreover, repeated all the way across the set. To many actors, theatre superstitions are very real, none more potent than that of Shakespeare's Scottish play. To name it anywhere in a theatre, to quote lines from it, or even – as in this case – to see the word written would be regarded as a potential catastrophe for the production. In an attempt to neutralise the curse one has to leave the stage, turn round three times, spit, swear, then knock on the door and request to come back in. But even that doesn't guarantee exorcism and the run of any production is potentially doomed. One way of excusing terrible reviews, I suppose. Pru duly marched off through the prompt side door to the scene dock, did the counter-spell and returned.

Maybe the curse could explain our experience with the drum. This was a large circular area of the stage that could not only spin 360°, enabling deft scene changes from either wing or from upstage, but the disc could also split into two and go up and down. Whole new worlds could arise seemingly from the bowels of the earth, creating occasional moments of wonder for the audience. It was an impressive piece of machinery. When it worked.

My first entrance in the show involved me and five of my fellow actors going into the scene dock beneath the Olivier auditorium and taking up positions on the pre-set furniture of a drinking den. On cue, the drum was meant to slowly corkscrew upwards to stage level as we sang a boozy song, glugging away at pewter tankards. There were teething problems during the technical rehearsals. At one point we found ourselves delivering the entire song to a couple of bemused technicians in headsets forty feet below the stage, because the disc up above had failed to split in two and slide open, like the false volcano floor in *You Only Live Twice*. From a technical point of view the previews were a case of two steps forward, one step back. Chairs that should have been placed at point X on the revolve in order to arrive at point Y when the revolve stopped turning ended up all over the alphabet, and on the final preview the drum revolve ground to a halt as my drinking partners and I were only halfway through our ascent. True to the principle of The Show Must Go On we carried on carousing and singing and clonking our tankards in a jolly fashion but sadly only the last three rows of the circle could actually see us. At this point Peter Wood came marching down the aisle to halt the performance before anyone toppled into the abyss. Or, as the *Daily Express* put it: "Playgoers were left open-mouthed last night when a casually dressed stranger interrupted actors John Neville and Denis Quilley at the National

Theatre ... the man turned out to be director Peter Wood. Some of the audience at the Olivier Theatre thought it was a political demonstration as Wood, dressed in an open-necked shirt, ordered: 'Sorry, the play cannot continue.'" I'm not sure the detail of the open-necked shirt was entirely relevant; perhaps it was the tabloid's swipe at how sartorial standards go off a cliff as soon as you subsidise the arts.

Shows when the drum ground to a halt – and there were a few of them as the run progressed – meant an early night for all of us. Tickets were rescheduled for another performance, engineers were called. The final straw came when, a couple of months into the run, it broke down once again. The stage manager appeared from the prompt corner, headset to toe in black, and stopped the show.

"But this is ridiculous," came a voice from the circle. "This happened last time we came. We want to see the play and the actors, not the scenery going up and down!"

Rumour had it that it would cost £40,000 to repair the machinery properly, money the National could ill afford. Next day the show was re-blocked for good, on the flat, and the magic of the drum revolve was consigned to history, certainly for our production anyway.

Sheridan's satire on the gossips and hypocrites of eighteenth-century society has fizzing storylines, vivid characters and some great situations and lines. Within days of starting rehearsals I could see Peter Wood fixing his beady eye on Diana Hardcastle as Lady Teazle, picking her up on everything from phrasing to diction, usually without any cause that I could discern. He tried the same attack on Sally Cookson, who was playing Maria, the innocent ingenue. Peter came from a generation of British directors who operated on the principle of being the ultimate authority, a step just below God. John Dexter was famously another, using his perceived power to demean or flirt, sometimes in the same breath. Derek Jacobi told me about Dexter singling him out as Brother Martin in the National's production of *Saint Joan* with Joan Plowright at the Old Vic, while rehearsing with a worryingly tall cross at the head of a church procession. It was so tall he had to dip it in case it hit the proscenium arch. "Stop! Stop! What does Daisy Jacobi think she's doing? Hmm?"

I could hear Peter Wood enjoying the same sort of vinegary rebuke each time he came to a line with Diana, or Sally. What he hadn't banked on was them teaming up and standing their ground, which soon shut him up. Rehearsals should never be a battleground. Playgrounds for scrapes and development and discovery, sure, but not podiums for egos to belittle or demean. Who or what does that benefit? Certainly not the production. Peter made no secret of his belief that none of us could hold a candle to the generation of actors who were either dead or now fading from active service: Hordern, Gielgud, Redgrave, Olivier, McCowen – he'd directed them all. Yet he airily lobbed these put-downs at us with an enigmatic smile as if, should he ever be called out, he could say, "But my dear boy, surely you could tell I was joking?" I have experienced mercifully few directors from this tradition. They have passed on, never, I hope, to return. The relentless push-me, pull-you, teasing/bullying of rehearsals was tiring, but as we began the final run-throughs it felt as though the production was becoming solid enough and I realised I had learned a lot from Peter, not least about the rhythm and delivery of text.

He used to talk about how in a Restoration coat there was nothing more appealing to an audience than the actor's back, showing the line of the jacket to best effect; how one gesture above shoulder height was worth a dozen below. The aesthetic of the stage picture meant a lot to him but it was a particular view and not by any means shared by everyone. When it came to my hairstyle, for example, we disagreed. I had a thickish head of hair that curled a bit when long but Peter had decreed I was to wear a neat, tight wig, pulled into a stock at the back. The character of Charles was rakish and messy and the pert bun that appeared from the wig department at the beginning of the tech felt to me completely wrong. But Peter was adamant. There was steel in those grey-blue eyes that could fell a young actor at a hundred paces.

"We are not going to fall out over this, are we," he said slowly and quietly, venom on a needle. "The wig remains."

A couple of previews in and we were gathered in the stalls for notes. Peter shut his notepad, drawing the session to a close.

"Anything else?" he concluded, expecting the answer no.

"Yes, in fact there is," piped up Jane Asher.

"Yes, Jane darling?"

"It's about Hugh's hair, actually."

Peter's eyes switched from warm and cuddly bear to snake tight as his focus flicked from Jane to me, to see if I'd put her up to this. I hadn't.

"You see, Peter," she went on, glancing round to include other members of the cast, "we women find the character of Charles quite attractive. But not in that wig. It's Hugh's own hair that helps make it appealing."

There was a pause and, suddenly taken on by one of the grown-ups who was having none of his prissy little power games, Peter said, "Oh I see. Jane would like the wig to go, would she?"

"So would I," chipped in Pru Scales.

"Me too." That was Tacye Nichols. Pooky Quesnel nodded, as did Diana Hardcastle. The female-led cavalry charge was impressive. Tom Hollander rolled his eyes and laughed.

"Democracy is creeping into the production, is it?" said Peter.

Eyes were fixed on him. He was cornered. He swivelled his viper eyes to me and smiled thinly.

"Oh weelllll. Here's what's going to happen. I'll let you try it without the wig tonight but if for ONE SECOND I think it looks out of place . . . Right, off you all go."

I never wore the wig again.

*

By this time I had been with Shane Collins for three and a half years. Young actors are obviously at a disadvantage as they don't yet know the ropes of the profession and inevitably defer to their agent's greater experience when it comes to advice. However, looking up to an agent as a fount of all knowledge, or leaning on them as either a guru or a nanny, is a mistake. Some actors live in fear of their agent, placing them on a pedestal, not daring to trouble them. Pat Marmont was famously tough on any client who called her unnecessarily, particularly for a general natter to see if anything was blowing in the wind, like maybe a job. It sometimes took one friend of mine, a client of hers, days to summon up the courage to call her. I never had any such fear of Shane. Maybe I was lucky. He would happily gossip about anything and everyone. He was never more talkative than when he'd been on hols to Tenerife with casting director Paul de Freitas and had had an outrageous time, or when he was about to go into rehearsals for an amdram Gilbert & Sullivan and was overexcited about the cozzies. But something began to wane with Shane. The more my girlfriend told me about her own agent – calm and focused – the more the noisy clatter of Berwick Street began to pall.

I went to meet Marina Martin in her office in Islington and felt instinctively that a move to a slightly less effervescent environment was the right thing for me. Marina then came to see me in *School for Scandal* and she agreed to take me on. Telling Shane, though, was like the worst sort of relationship break-up possible. We met for lunch, the first half of which involved Diet Coke and loud stories. The second half, after I'd dropped the It's Not You It's Me bomb, involved Shane staring at his napkin, dramatic sniffs and the inevitable question, "Who is it then?" I told him. His lips puckered to lemon and his eyes rolled defensively, dismissively and defiantly all at once.

"Well, what can I say? Good luck. And you can fuckin' pay for lunch."

21

Stratford

Freddie Jones was a big bear of a man, standing at least 6ft 3in, with a ruddy nose, curly white hair, a grey beard and a thirst for a proper pint of bitter. Now in his sixties, he was playing the role of Sir Nicholas Gimcrack in the Royal Shakespeare Company's 1991 production of *The Virtuoso*. Once he was out of the stage door after the evening show and headed in the direction of Stratford's The Dirty Duck it was almost impossible to keep up with him. His stride was huge and his focus on last orders absolute. He was by nature both a poet and a comic but he could also have an air of menace to the point of terrifying – witness his performance as the owner of the freak show in David Lynch's film *The Elephant Man*.

Joining the RSC had been a dream of mine for as long as I could remember. It so happened that the four plays in which I was cast for the 1991 season were all in The Swan, its wooden galleries and seating wrapped around the thrust stage. Next door, sharing a scene dock with The Swan, was the Memorial Theatre, the Main House, a huge barn of a place with traditional proscenium arch stage. Up the road past The Dirty Duck was the RSC's third Stratford theatre, The Other Place, a versatile black box space in a new building, replacing the corrugated tin hut that previously housed unearthed classics and more exploratory work.

The Virtuoso by Thomas Shadwell was written in 1676 and is one of those "forgotten" Restoration plays. More often than not you discover that they have been forgotten for good reason, usually because they're crap. Occasionally, though, the meeting of unloved play and canny director can salvage a piece and make it shine anew; sometimes you really can polish a turd. When I was cast as Sir Samuel Hearty for the RSC production, Phyllida Lloyd, who later directed the stage and film hit *Mamma Mia!*, was already known as a theatre and opera director of vivid imagination, brilliant at turning plays upside down and shaking them by the ankles to see if anything fresh fell out of the pockets. I couldn't wait to see what she had in mind for this dotty satire on the Royal Society, about a madcap inventor and his family's romantic complications. With designer Anthony Ward, Phyllida set about creating a world of high style and high energy. The mood board was like one of those decadent, high-camp Smirnoff vodka ads of the nineties. Using her cast of twenty, Phyllida and movement director Sue Lefton wanted to create a sequence of stage pictures, entr'actes – *School for Wives* all over again – to represent the mess of late seventeenth-century London life: writhing heaps of bodies, slithering around, on top of and through each other. In leotards, or tracksuit bottoms and T-shirts, we set to on the rehearsal room floor.

"Keep moving, people, that's it. Hungry for pleasure. Up the tempo now," said Sue.

Not a lot of our squirming and groaning ended up in the actual show but it was certainly bonding for us as a company and it got us all on the same page. Well, most of us. There was one session when Sue got more than usually excited as she encouraged us to take the whole thing more seriously.

"Good, people, good. And now you're undulating. Good. And

now show me the disease that's spreading. Disease through the streets of London."

I could see out of the corner of my eye that Finbar Lynch, a Dubliner, on first meeting a dark and brooding figure but on better acquaintance a complete delight, was finding it all a bit of a challenge on this particular Tuesday morning.

"And writhe, people, writhe," oozed Sue. "The fever. The illness. The pus. Now you're pus. Think of the pus of London. Show me the pus."

At which point Finbar, sweating in black trackies and vest, silently extracted himself from the orgiastic clump and went and sat on a chair at the side of the rehearsal room.

"Come on, Finbar, come back," said Sue. "Join in with the group. Join in with the pestilence and the pleasure and the shame and the—"

"No, I'm sorry," interrupted Finbar. "I did not join the RSC to be fockin' pus."

We had a couple of bumpy previews to start with, the cracks in the play quickly revealing themselves down the centuries. But Phyllida worried away at it like a dog with a bone and, taken at pace, the production began to show signs of real comedic electricity. But at its heart was one very nervous, fragile performer: Freddie Jones. Having been away from the theatre for a while he'd found learning lines hard, particularly when the style of the show was so fast-paced that the cues were coming at him like a steam train. On about the third preview he had a series of bad "dries." As I knew only too well, the cloak of embarrassment wraps around one for the rest of the performance and is almost impossible to shrug off. That night Freddie didn't go to The Duck after the show but took himself off to his digs in the Ferry House, not far from the church where Shakespeare is buried. Phyllida followed to console him. It took a lot of knocking on the door before he let her in. She later recounted the look of fear on

Freddie's face, the terror of wondering if he was too old to do this any more, his expressions of remorse and guilt for having let the side down. As the senior member of the company he was hugely respected by us younger members but that night he felt he didn't deserve it. He felt he had failed us, the play, Phyllida and himself. The next night he was stronger on the lines and gradually his confidence returned, show by show. By Press Night – that invidious event when the production is supposedly fully primed and ready for dissection by people with pencils and notepads – he was flying and gave a brilliantly funny performance of a truly oddball professor.

Having opened *The Virtuoso* we then moved *Two Gentlemen of Verona*, which we had initially rehearsed simultaneously, from the back burner to the front of the stove. It is a slight, early play in the canon, in which you can sense Shakespeare toying with plots and characters that he would develop with more confidence in later plays such as *Twelfth Night*.

Instead of dismissing its naivety, the director David Thacker embraced it, setting the production in the carefree 1920s, where love is brittle, and hearts are broken and mended in the measure of a Charleston. Blazers and boaters, picnic rugs and jugs of lemonade, gramophones and girls dressed in boys' grey flannels. It's the ending, when Proteus's betrayal of his best friend Valentine is forgiven in the space of two lines, that usually makes critics (and audiences) give up on the play. But David took this beat of the story seriously. As the quartet of lovers, Finbar and I as Proteus and Valentine and Clare Holman and Saskia Reeves as Julia and Silvia played the simple honesty of the moment and the audience – already carried along by the candyfloss mood and by the lugubrious double act of Launce and his dog Crab, played by Richard Moore and a lurcher called Woolly – came with us. It became a huge hit and there was barely an empty seat for the rest of the season.

*

Guy Henry and I had first met at the National the previous year in *The School for Scandal*. He had played Sir Benjamin Backbite but our paths didn't cross until the final scene. I had long been aware of this tall, vulpine character from afar, often holding court in the backstage bar. Charismatic, funny, more than a bit intimidating. We didn't know each other that well. Nevertheless, having both been cast in the 1991 RSC season in the same four plays, playing a double act in two of them, we decided to add insult to injury and share a house together. 184 Clopton Road became our home for the next ten months and we quickly slipped into the rhythm of The Odd Couple. Our house, initially, was something of a Party Central. Once Pam, the legendary landlady of The Dirty Duck, had kicked us out it would be "Back to 184!" and we'd carry on for several more hours with several more bottles and an increasingly diverse array of guests.

After a few months, however, one night Guy and I found ourselves in the kitchen at three in the morning, both searching for a corkscrew.

"Hello, mate. Who are that pair sitting on the floor by the window in there?" I asked.

"Next to the telly?" Guy replied.

"Yes."

"I thought they were friends of yours."

"Never seen them before in my life."

We looked at each other for a moment.

"Do we in fact know any of the people in our front room?" I asked.

Another pause.

"RIGHT," boomed Guy, who can go from sotto to foghorn in a heartbeat, as he flung open the front door, "EVERYBODY OUT. You've had yer fun, off y'go. Come on. Out!"

Our post-show gatherings were more select from thereon.

*

Guy and I played the double act of Bergetto and his faithful servant Poggio in *'Tis Pity She's a Whore,* John Ford's fantastically bloody play about incest, murder and revenge. Bergetto is the one comic character and Ford's stroke of dramatic genius is to kill him off halfway through the play. In a case of mistaken identity, he is fatally stabbed – a swift blow as a shadowy figure runs past and off into the night. Bergetto doesn't realise he's been wounded, it was surely just an accidental bumpy encounter in a darkened alley. He feels his clothing . . . it's damp.

"I am sure I cannot piss forward and backward, and yet I am wet before and behind."

This always got an uncomfortable titter from the audience as they – like Bergetto himself – couldn't quite work out what was happening. Next thing, Bergetto collapses on the floor in agony and a few seconds later, he's dead. It's a great piece of drama and effectively signals to the audience that now we've killed off the funny guy, things are going to get serious.

By Act V, when Giovanni enters the banquet with his beloved sister Annabella's heart skewered on his dagger, the audience was feeling pretty queasy. Because of the shape of The Swan Theatre, in which the audience is wrapped round the performance space, if something on stage caused someone to faint on one side of the stalls, the person diametrically in line with the incident and the fainter on the opposite side of the auditorium would often keel over too. One night the stage manager's voice came over the backstage tannoy giving us the running times of the show as usual but adding, "Tonight there were two faints, one vomit and an ambulance. Your call for tomorrow is the half at twelve fifty-five, for a one-thirty matinee. Thank you and goodnight." All in a day's work.

At the height of that summer we started rehearsing *The Alchemist,* Ben Jonson's satire on gullibility and greed. With a plot driven by two wily conmen, Face and Subtle, and their hussy of a partner in crime, Doll Common, it skewers the lust, avarice and pathetic hopes of an array of characters who willingly part with their money on the promise of riches and a life of luxury. In the Stratford production, directed by Sam Mendes, I played Kastril, a roaring boy up from the shires to learn how to quarrel like a man. Jonathan Hyde and David Bradley played Face and Subtle and Philip Voss, with his silken bass drum of a voice, played the gloriously repellent hedonist Sir Epicure Mammon.

I love the play and had been in it at school, playing Surly, the sole sceptic of the characters. Some of us in the cast went up to London to see it at the Aldwych towards the end of 1977, with Ian McKellen as Face and John Woodvine as Subtle. The plague has hit London, and Lovewit has quit town, leaving his trusted servant in charge of his house. The servant, Face, is thus free to run amok, playing host and, along with his scheming colleagues, conning clients left, right and centre. By Act V the coiled spring of the farce has been wound tight and is then released, with increasingly rapid exits and entrances, quick changes, and an abundance of door slamming. At the performance we saw of the McKellen production, as the temperature rose in the final scene, he strode in through the front door and slammed it shut, unfortunately breaking part of the latch, so that for the rest of the act the door would swing open at inopportune moments. This was especially tricky when the baying mob outside was supposed to be banging on the door, finding it impossible to get in. The audience, of course, in on the joke that the bloody door was meant to be shut but wasn't, found it hilarious. McKellen wedged his foot against it when he could, Woodvine would take over when necessary; even the angry mob did their best to keep the artifice alive. They got through the rest of the show, largely without corpsing.

At the end of the play Face addresses the audience, conceding that while things might have wobbled as far as his scheming went, he has got away with it. At this performance he said: "My part fell a little in this last scene . . . (so did the door's)."

It brought the house down. As it were.

*

The week came in late August 1991 when, for the first time, we did all four plays in The Swan back to back. Thursday night, *The Alchemist*; Friday night, *Two Gents*; Saturday matinee, *The Virtuoso*; Saturday night, *'Tis Pity*. I found it exhilarating. All those months of work finally up and running and, thankfully for the four shows I was in, well received.

It was my dream job, being in a semi-permanent troupe, acknowledging each other's strengths, supporting each other through the ups and downs of the season, developing a shorthand of how to work with each other.

Meanwhile, the production of *Romeo and Juliet* in the Main House, starring Michael Maloney and Clare Holman, had an infamously difficult birth. They began the tech just as news emerged from Russia of an attempted coup. Over the following days tension mounted. The Kremlin went into crisis mode. Yeltsin and his advisers took to the streets, climbed on to a tank, asserted the authority of the Politburo and finally brought stability back to Russia and, by extension, the world stage. Meanwhile, in Stratford, they still hadn't tech'd the tomb scene.

I felt I'd found a home at the RSC. Indeed, when towards the end of my contract artistic director Adrian Noble urged me to turn down an offer from the National Theatre and remain as a member of the "core company" that he had in mind, I did so. I was buoyed up and had visions of spending several years playing all sorts of roles in a semi-permanent troupe. Then, when it came to casting the following season, I was offered . . . absolutely nothing. I designed a badge of an apple, rotten to its core, and handed it out to the half dozen of my fellow actors who had, like me, hoped to return as part of the core company. Showbiz.

22

Robert De Niro's Leg

They say if you want to get something done, ask a busy person. As we gathered to start work on *Hamlet* at the RSC rehearsal rooms in Clapham in the autumn of 1992, Kenneth Branagh had just completed a radio version of *Romeo and Juliet* with his company, Renaissance. He was editing the film of *Much Ado About Nothing* and was also in the early stages of producing *Frankenstein*, which he was also to direct and star in. So, I guess chucking a full-length *Hamlet* in the mix wasn't much to ask. He was under pressure from many sides but he never showed it in rehearsal, certainly not to his fellow actors, nor to the director Adrian Noble, with whom he had previously worked on *Henry V* to great acclaim.

I was playing Laertes, sometimes considered a thankless part. Early on in the play you have your ear bent by your pedantic father, launch into an enormous speech saying goodbye to your sister, then go off to Paris for a bit of a gap year and several hours in the dressing room. Then, having discovered that your father's been killed, you storm on at fever pitch, full of grief-stricken fury. But you're still only in first gear. You then learn that Dad's been murdered by the Prince (furious grief goes up a gear), and your sister's losing the plot and chucking flowers about (revving up into third). Next, the King winds you up to revenge, Sis drowns (up through fourth into fifth), and Princey boy jumps in her grave, which *really* pisses you off (have you got a sixth gear? Course you have), so you challenge him to a duel (up into seventh). Out with the sword, slish slash, swish swash – aaaaargh – and then you die along with everybody else. I mean it's not Hamlet, sure, but Laertes has a lot on his plate, bless him.

Bob Crowley's design was dominated by a huge grey curtain that traversed the stage. It could divide and swirl, hide and reveal. Blacks and whites and greys was the colour palette, bursting into royal reds from time to time. As we moved from the tech into the dress rehearsals I noticed how calm and unflappable Ken remained. The mechanism that manoeuvred the big grey curtain kept breaking down and during one early performance the show ground to a halt in the second scene. By now, anyone would have forgiven the leading man for throwing a toy or two out of the pram. But in the wings, while the stage manager paced up and down, one hand on the mic bar of his headset, the other adjusting the volume of the radio clipped to his hip to mask his twitching, there was Ken perched on a box by the fly ropes, chatting quietly to John Shrapnel (Claudius).

With only three or four words being cut from this full version of the New Cambridge Shakespeare edition, the production was billed as running for over four hours. After about an hour and a half there was a "pause" in the show, so the audience could stretch legs, rustle sweets and dash to the loo, followed by a full interval an hour or so later. It was a long evening of theatre but it rarely felt like it. The main reason for this was Ken's astonishing verbal dexterity. All through rehearsals, as his performance developed, the lines began to flow more swiftly and easily. Through the dress rehearsals, too, he grew in confidence, trying out new intonations and rhythms within the structure of the lines. In my scenes with him I began to see more clearly how his brain worked, show by show. However, at the first preview he did something extraordinary. His performance changed so significantly that in the interval I marched to his dressing room and rapped on the door.

"You bastard!" I yelled as Ken opened the door in his shirtsleeves, looking bewildered.

"What have I done?"

"You could have fucking warned me you were going to do that!"

I was smiling, I hasten to add. In front of that very first audience Ken had moved his performance up into a completely new gear. The lighter tones were funnier, the heartache plumbed more deeply, the speed of his delivery astonishing. Not only was his diction deft but his celerity of thought meant the lines pinged out at pace without ever dropping the sense. It was as if he had hit some hidden button labelled Supercharge and off he had sped, leaving the rest of us – me at any rate – looking like dozy amateurs.

On the morning of the third Barbican preview, a Saturday matinee, I woke up with a toothache. A real humdinger, with a swelling in my lower jaw. As I signed in at the stage door and headed down to meet Ken backstage for the sword fight rehearsal, I could feel my temperature rising and sweat beginning to pop out on my brow.

"You OK?" Ken asked.

"Fine, mate, fine. En garde."

With only two shows down we were still a bit wobbly on the sword moves but I was particularly hazy that day and went off to my dressing room feeling queasy. By the time the show went up my shirt was dripping and I felt terrible. I stood almost motionless during my first scene, trying to focus on David Bradley as Polonius and then trying to deliver pearls of wisdom to Joanne Pearce as Ophelia. She looked at me quizzically, interested by my new approach to the text, which had shifted from earnest brother to bloke trying to get through life while sucking in pooled saliva every other line.

I came off into the wings and whispered my predicament to the stage manager. I needed to get the tooth checked out, pronto.

"But we're up and running."

"And I now have nearly fwee hours off," I burbled. "I knee da hee a den-hist."

In the split second that the stage manager had to make a decision, there were suddenly two things about the production in my favour: with barely a line cut there would just about be time to get to the London Hospital, see a duty dentist and get back in time for my next entrance of furious grief; and secondly, the production was set in the Edwardian era, so although I might look a bit old-fashioned, I didn't even have to change out of my costume.

Three minutes later I was in a cab. Explaining to a mystified A&E receptionist that my problem was time-sensitive proved tricky, what with the dribbling and the onset of blurred vision, but we got there.

"Oooh yes, quite an ... ooh yes indeed, *quite* an abscess you've got there," said the inappropriately cheerful dentist. "What I'm going to do is put in a bit of something just to numb it and we'll get it sorted."

I explained that putting in a bit of something wasn't an option, what with me requiring use of my tongue in a professional capacity in about an hour – correction, less than an hour. There was some chin scratching and probing, then poking, pain and pus, followed by a lot of cloves and another cab. The pressure on the tooth was at least gone and the sweating had subsided thanks to the paracetamol but by the time I hurled myself on to the Barbican stage and alighted on the bottom step of the Grief and Fury escalator, going up, I had little idea what was happening, frankly. I mumbled my way through the final sequences of the play in a quiet monotone and the sword fight couldn't come soon enough. I flailed my sword around like a handbag, longing for death.

Back in my dressing room the stage manager took my

temperature. It was 101°F. The decision was made there and then for my understudy, David Birrell, to do the evening show. It was a horrible feeling, letting Ken and the team down like this, especially when the production was only in previews and we were only now beginning to find our feet (or sword fight).

I was just packing up when there was a knock on the dressing room door. Unbeknown to me my friend Tom Hollander had been watching the matinée. Tom perched on a chair and looked me straight in the eye.

"Hugh. I've seen you in lots of shows but that ... *that* was the finest performance I have *ever* seen you give. You were so still, so controlled. Every emotion was held in, restrained, Laertes' pain was buried beneath the surface. In*cred*ibly moving. Well done, pal."

I was in bed by 7 p.m. and slept for fourteen hours. Root canal and Press Night were the two highlights of the following week.

The advertised running time may have been over four hours but during previews and the first few weeks of the run the show got quicker as Ken found a pace that suited him, eventually settling at about three hours forty minutes. However, one night during the subsequent Stratford run – Monday 29 March 1993, to be precise – I was struck by how fast the scenes were flying by. At the curtain call, Ken took only one personal bow before sprinting off through the wings, stripping off his fencing jacket as he went and leaping into a waiting car, which sped off into the night. There were apparently some raised eyebrows from "upstairs" when the stage manager's show report was read, indicating that a further twenty minutes had been lopped off the average running time. But from Ken's point of view, at least he got back to London in time to join the Oscar viewing party friends had arranged for him. And at least he got to watch – live – his then wife, Emma Thompson, win the Academy Award for Best Actress for her performance in *Howard's End*.

We had by this point in the run got into a routine. At 6 p.m., Ken and I would convene in the Ashcroft Room, the airy rehearsal space under the eaves of The Swan Theatre, gossip about the day's adventures and then rehearse the fight sequence; 12 p.m. on matinee days. Monday evening was my favourite catch-up day because Ken's Sundays were rather more unusual than mine. We would each sit on one of the stackable tables, legs swinging, an ASM with the epees nearby, like a second in a duel, only reading the paper. As on other Mondays Ken asked me what I had got up to that weekend.

"It was riveting, Ken. Saturday night after the show I went to The Duck. Pam had a lock-in, so we drank until about three. Sunday I got up about eleven and read the papers. Guy Henry cooked a roast, I did the potatoes. We drank a bottle of nasty red and watched three episodes of the *Wogan* show that Guy insists on taping and replaying to anyone who comes round. Today, did a bit of scribbling, had a nap. What about you?"

Ken often adopted an alternative persona when describing aspects of his daily life, so surreal were they becoming even to him. Camp, self-mocking, deadpan.

"Well, dar-ling. Mrs. Hamlet sheds her frock Saturday night, legs it to London. Sunday morning it's Concorde to JFK. Frankie Ford Poppola picks me up in her stretch, doesn't she. We head into town, collect Bobby De Niro on the way, head to the restaurant for a quick brunch to try and persuade him to do *Frankenstein*. We order omelettes. Chat chat chat. JFK, and home by midnight. This morning I'm in the grade for *Much Ado* at nine, then on the road back to Sally Stratford. Shall we?" he concluded brightly, hopping off the table and reaching for his epee.

One day in the middle of the Stratford run I found myself walking along Waterside with him, heading past The Dirty Duck to the stage door before a matinee. It was mid-April, the blossom was out, and the sun was smiling on the two theatres as we approached. At this point I had really only ever done theatre. It was what made me tick and I felt strangely protective of it. It had been Ken's first playground, too.

"You're the lead in a colossal hit," I said. "Look, you can see the queue for returns from here. You're passionate about Shakespeare, why leave all that behind for films, for heaven's sake?"

He smiled and said, "We do *Hamlet* on stage for, what, a hundred performances or so? A thousand seats a show. Maybe a hundred thousand punters, which is amazing. Some of the audience are seeing the play for the first time and maybe it inspires a percentage of them to seek out more Shakespeare."

"Exactly," I said, resting my case.

"Do the same thing on film and you can affect not thousands but millions of people, over time. All around the world."

I didn't know it but he was planning to film *Hamlet* after he had finished *Frankenstein*. On 70mm, too, bringing a truly big-screen dimension to the play, with several of our RSC cast on board.

A few days later he invited me to an afternoon screening of *Much Ado* in Leamington Spa. The film was nearing completion but he hadn't yet seen it on a big screen and didn't want to flog to London and back in a day, what with the evening show to do. I loved it, and the score remains one of my favourites, particularly the climax of the opening sequence when, amid the frenetic energy of the household preparing for the soldiers' return, the men on horseback finally appear over the brow of a hill and the giddy music surges, quick steps releasing into long strides. Goosebumps. I worked with the composer Patrick Doyle a few years later and asked him how this exquisite moment had developed.

"I was having real trouble finding it," he told me. "The images were cutting here and there around the busy household and then suddenly there they are, these stunning men on horseback.

Couldn't get it. Then one day I was by a lake and the wind got up and these waves started forming, with white crests. Rising and breaking, rising and breaking, and suddenly I realised it was the same rhythm as the rising and falling of the horses' hooves in slow motion. And that got me going."

Listen to that opening movement. When the moment comes you can sense absolutely both the waves and the horses.

As we met for one of our last fight rehearsals in the Ashcroft Room, Ken asked me what the scribbling was that I had mentioned. I told him about a John Buchan novel I was toying with adapting for the screen. I didn't really know anything about screenwriting but was having a bash. Ken asked to read the treatment and a week later he commissioned my first screenplay. I couldn't believe it.

Well after the run of *Hamlet* had ended and Ken was in pre-production for *Frankenstein*, I went for a Buchan script meeting at Shepperton. He had warned me he was under strict orders from his execs to focus solely on *Frankenstein* when at the office. I guess they knew of his tendency to spin a number of plates at the same time and, since they were paying him to produce, direct and star in their expensive movie, they perhaps understandably wanted him to focus on the matter in hand. This meant that once our script meeting got under way, every time there was a knock at the door he hurriedly shoved my script in his desk drawer, shouted "Come in!" and switched seamlessly to talking me through drawings of Tim Harvey's set designs.

At the end of the meeting he asked if I had done much film. I hadn't. None.

"Well, if we're going to do the Buchan it would be useful for you to see how a film set works. Leave it with me."

My family had by now developed a joke acronym that referred to the things I would do with my pay cheque AMFF – After My First Film. "I might buy a plane AMFF." In other words, it was never going to happen. As far as I was concerned, I was a Theatre actor and Film was a foreign country. It was what Americans did well, said the rule of thumb that I'd invented from thin air; we Brits may be better at theatre, the classical repertoire anyway. Occasionally we would have a breakout hit film – *Tom Jones, Oliver!, Gandhi, Chariots of Fire* – that travelled the world over but let's face it they were as rare as hens' teeth. By extension, went my clumsy argument, acting on screen was something we British-trained theatre types weren't very good at, compared to those loose, more naturalistic Americans.

That August the casting director sent me the script of *Frankenstein*. The role was Schiller, "hero of the sports field." It was to be My First Film. One line, but I wasn't complaining. Schiller was one of the gang of medical students, pals of Victor Frankenstein, so he would be loitering around a bit before becoming, as I claimed, a quarter of De Niro's performance. That's how I described the fact that after dying in the cholera epidemic, my heroically athletic leg got sawn off by Branagh's Frankenstein and stitched on to De Niro's Creature.

Being on set for the first time is a revelation to anyone but after the first hour most people find it incredibly boring.

"What do you mean you're doing the scene again? You've already done it eight times."

I found it instantly fascinating, from the scale of the set – huge walls of the town of Ingolstadt, a hundred feet long and fifty feet high, definitely ten feet thick, but take a peek round the back and they're just cleverly painted bits of ply – to the cables and camera equipment, the sound trolley, the cranes, the lights, the quiet bustle of time-is-money, the chain of command, the jargon.

"Is the woman with the clipboard the script supervisor or the continuity person?"

"They're one and the same."

The organised chaos.

One scene involved Victor Frankenstein and a group of medical students inoculating citizens against the outbreak of disease that's sweeping through the town. Among those dragged in to be vaccinated is a vagrant with a wooden leg. He picks a fight with the senior doctor, insisting that there's poison in them there needles and he's damned if he's going to have an injection. The argument escalates, the vagrant whips out a knife and stabs the doctor, wounding him fatally. The vagrant flees. Outraged townsfolk give chase, he's captured and hanged for his crime. It's this one-legged corpse that Frankenstein cuts down from the gibbet and uses as the basis for his Creature.

There were about five or six of us medical students called early in the morning for a rehearsal on an interior set at Shepperton, a large room of grey stone, serving as a rudimentary surgery. Playing the senior doctor was John Cleese, positioned behind a table. The vagrant would be played by Robert De Niro, but for now here was his stand-in, lank-haired in a hooded towelling robe.

Ken suggested some basic blocking for us background boys, giving us various jobs to do at tables dotted around the room. I noticed Towelling Robe Stand-In Man hovering quietly in the corner, very still. When he spoke, it was barely above a whisper, so quietly in fact that Ken had to come in close to hear him. The pair of them then huddled with John Cleese and talked through the dialogue. They parted, and Towelling Robe Stand-In Man pulled his hood back as he took up his position to start rehearsing the scene. It wasn't a stand-in at all, it was Robert bloody De Niro. I was three feet away from Robert Godniro. I had no lines, all I had to do in the rehearsal was make an imaginary scratch on an imaginary extra's arm, but I suddenly felt my heart racing. I was properly starstruck.

With rehearsals for the scene complete, the crew moved in and set to work. Lighting, camera tracks, props. Tin dishes and bloodied cloths, microphones Black Tac'd to the side of tables. The extras gathered, maybe fifty "citizens" crowding into the room for the wide shot.

"Action!"

The camera tracked through the noisy room as medics worked hurriedly with patients, none of them more reluctant than De Niro's character, unkempt, one-legged, seething with suspicion and resentment. As the scene heated up, De Niro's voice lifted a bit but not much, his distrust of what the doctors were up to delivered as a controlled rasp rather than a roaring rage. He looked at the surgical instrument Cleese was offering up.

"You're not stickin' that in me!" he hissed.

Having got the wide and the close-up shots on De Niro, lunch was called. In the afternoon, the camera turned round on Cleese. Most of the extras would be out of shot and so were stood down. As he would be entirely off camera, I assumed De Niro might be off home too. Most actors would say it's their job to be there for their "reverses" but, y'know, "stars" (rolling eyes emoji). However, not only was Robert De Niro there for John Cleese's close-up, he was also in full costume, with his leg strapped up and the wooden leg in place. That he was there in the whole kit was impressive enough, but then he did something that I often recount to drama students. When the cameras had been on him that morning his performance had been like a bubbling volcano, at the appropriate scale for the screen. Now, in order to help John Cleese's performance, he went absolutely nuts, exploding at him in a tirade of improvised abuse.

"You're not stickin' that fuckin' thing in me! You mother fuckin' doctors! You put fuckin' poison in that fuckin' stuff! YOU'RE NOT STICKIN' THAT FUCKIN' THING IN ME!"

It was as electrifying as it was surprising and it completely flummoxed John Cleese, whose reactions were that of a rational man being confronted by a dangerous lunatic. De Niro was stunning. And generous.

Even though the John Buchan script never got off the ground, Ken did use some of my writing. I was staying at my parents' house in West Sussex. It was early summer, several months after *Frankenstein* had wrapped. I was lying on a rug in the garden when my brand new 121 mobile phone rang. Feeling rather smug at being an early adopter, I flipped it open and pulled up the little plastic aerial. It was Ken. Having done a couple of test screenings of *Frankenstein*, he told me, the consensus was that there were some holes in the story.

- Why did "x" happen when only three scenes before "y" had said "z"?
- Don't understand the motivation for Frankenstein doing "this" rather than "that."

As a result he was to do some pick-up shots the following week with Helena Bonham Carter, Trevyn McDowell and himself, and would I write three new scenes that could help iron out the wrinkles.

I was so thrilled to have been invited to be involved that I didn't ask why me and not Frank Darabont, whose screenplay it was. History relates that Frank – famous for *The Shawshank Redemption* that came out the same year – hated the way Ken had interpreted his script, which he considered the best he had written to date. Perhaps the fallout had already begun and communication between them had dried up, I don't know, but Ken was a man in a hurry and needed the scenes by yesterday. So, I sat down at my laptop.

Having bashed out three scenes I then had to find a way of getting the pages to him. In those days there was no email and no internet, or at least no internet that he and I were connected to. I phoned a neighbour across the valley who had a fax machine and, clutching the nine pages, hopped in the car and drove over. The pages chugged through the machine painfully slowly but eventually it was mission accomplished.

No sooner had I got home than Ken rang. He asked if this beat could be accentuated, that moment trimmed back. So I sat down once again and started typing. Half an hour later I got in the car again, drove across the valley again, watched the chug chug of the fax machine again and drove back home again. This cycle was completed twice more that afternoon until eventually Ken was satisfied.

One and a half of the scenes I wrote ended up in the movie. And with the cash Ken paid me for my hush-hush rush job, I bought my parents a fax machine.

Almost without my realising it, Ken Branagh had taken me from a world of stage managers calling "Beginners Please" and "Curtain Up" over a tannoy and introduced me to a universe in which first assistant directors pressed a button on their walkie-talkies and said, "Roll Sound." I would never stop performing in theatre but new opportunities began to appear on the horizon.

PART THREE

Roll Sound

23

Big Movie, Small Film

"I'm not sure they realise how devoted our audience actually is," said Gareth Neame, one afternoon at Highclere Castle. The executive producer of *Downton Abbey* was referring to the team from Focus Features, financiers and US distributors of the film, who were visiting the set of the first movie that we were now, after a good deal of herding cats, finally shooting in 2018. A couple of the Focus executives admitted to having limited knowledge of the show; after all they were movie people, television wasn't their thing, although one had just started watching the box set. Throughout filming we got the sense that they were nervous about taking this television show and putting it on the big screen. A different market. A big risk.

"Then on Saturday morning," said Allen, "we drive up to Santa Barbara for a Q&A, then back to the Linwood Dunn Theater for another Q&A, then to the Arclight for a meet-and-greet at tea time."

A year on from filming, Allen Leech (Tom Branson in *Downton*) and I, along with some of the cast, were in New York for the US opening of the movie. We were in a restaurant at the Lincoln Center ahead of a Q&A at the cinema next door, and Allen was talking me through our Los Angeles schedule for that weekend, when the film was to open across North America.

"But hang on," I said. "How long's the drive to Santa Barbara?"

"Two hours? More, with traffic," said Allen.

"And the Q&A is how long?"

"Says here half an hour."

"All that way for thirty minutes? But that's crazy!" I exclaimed.

At the next table, Gareth Neame's ears pricked up.

"What is?" he asked.

He was sitting with four of the Focus team, including Peter Kujawski, the chairman. Suddenly I found myself leaning over the table, offering Peter my hand by way of a bet.

"OK, on Friday, how much does the film have to be predicted to gross on its opening weekend for Allen and me to get a helicopter to Santa Barbara?"

I knew this was a daft idea but it would make a good story for the rest of the cast at the end of the evening. How I had finally thrown British modesty and self-deprecation aside and gone full-on diva.

Peter thought for a moment. Realising he was taking my offer of a wager seriously, his colleagues tensed up.

"Well, hey now, Peter, I'm not really sure we can really—" one of them began, chuckling nervously.

"Twenty-five million," said Peter, confident of success. He liked the film very much but was still acutely conscious that he and his team had taken a gamble.

"Done."

I shook on the deal before he had time to reconsider.

The premiere in New York next day went well. For the first time ever the *Downton Abbey* audience, which for years had consisted of individuals, couples or at most small groups in front of a television screen, now consisted of hundreds and hundreds of people sharing the experience as one big . . . well, it felt like family. Allen and I were standing at the back of the auditorium when the credits rolled. As the applause swelled we put an arm round each other's shoulders.

"Let's never forget this," he smiled in the darkness.

Two days later we were in LA and the cast spread out across town doing radio and TV interviews in ones, twos and threes. On the Friday morning, Allen phoned me in my hotel room before breakfast.

"I think it might be on. I just got a call from someone at Focus asking how heavy I am, for the helicopter manifest."

I looked up the trade websites. "*Downton Abbey* to Dominate Box Office Weekend with $30 Million," declared one.

Focus were as good as their word. The helicopter from Van Nuys airport on Saturday morning took us north over the rugged California landscape, circling over the Ronald Reagan Library before sweeping low along the coast to Santa Barbara. It took twenty-five minutes. A car picked us up on the tarmac and drove us to the Riviera Theater for the interview. Afterwards, we had lunch on the terrace of the Belmond El Encanto hotel. We drank Whispering Angel, natch, and at the end of the meal Justin Balsamo, our host from Focus, asked for another bottle of the rosé, to go.

"Is it for your room?" asked the waiter.

"No," replied Jason, "it's for our helicopter."

Yes, the pukiest comment ever made, and we scuttled away, giggling like Tinseltown tossers, to the waiting car.

Downton Abbey topped $31 million that opening weekend and went on to become Focus Features' biggest ever domestic hit, grossing more than $96 million in the US and $194 million worldwide.

Taking off in that helicopter and drinking overpriced rosé at someone else's expense was the most unashamedly glitzy

Hollywood moment of my life, so let's come back down to earth and put things in perspective . . .

Early in 1993, as the RSC Barbican season was drawing to a close, I went to meet Richard, the writer/executive of a low-budget film. The script was very funny and the lead role of Charles was brilliant. Richard came to see *Two Gentlemen of Verona* at the Barbican that same week. He can't have disliked my Valentine too much because a few weeks later I was invited to meet the director, Mike. Having now closed the Barbican shows and moved to Stratford for the run of *Hamlet,* I took the train down to London. The producer, Duncan, was working with Jim Henson's Muppets team at the time and so the auditions were held in their building in North London.

I sat in the waiting room, one eye on the clock and the mid-afternoon train, a large picture of Kermit looking down at me from the wall. If there's a phrase about punctuality being the courtesy of kings, then director Mike would never make it as a member of the royal family. In theatre, being late for The Half is not only frowned upon but can lead, if you have a strict company manager, to the understudy going on in your place, even if you turn up with five minutes to spare.

After forty minutes being looked at by a green frog, I was beginning to bristle. But hey, I thought, this is the movie business, these things happen. Or so I assumed, never having been in a movie before (this was pre-*Frankenstein*).

Eventually the door opened, some chirpy bugger was ushered out, and director Mike welcomed me in. Although I say so myself, it was a great audition. I don't know if I was actually great in it but Mike was great at making me feel great, like I was a talented actor who merited his time and attention. No wonder he was running behind: he took ages with me, suggesting new rhythms of delivering the lines, putting me through my paces. I came out forty-five minutes later feeling like a right chirpy bugger. I got the train back to Stratford for the evening show, aglow.

A week or so later my agent called.

"Mike loved you."

"I loved Mike."

So far so good.

"It's not going to work out for the lead . . ."

I could have told her that. Even I wasn't stupid enough to think that when they said they'd be happy to cast an unknown it would at least need to be a known unknown. I was a completely unknown unknown.

"But they'd like you to go back and read for one of the supporting parts."

"No problem," I said. "Mike loves me, I love Mike. So, yes, of course. And presumably they'll cover my train fare from Stratford to London and back because, you know, it's not cheap and I'm not exactly earning a fortune at the RSC."

"Well, no, they won't," said my agent. "It's a recall, yes, but they're not obliged to, y'know . . ."

"No, right. Aren't they? I see." A pause. "Well, yes of course I'll go. I love Mike."

A few days later I was back in the same waiting room, the role of Tom in my sights. This time Mike My Love kept me waiting a full hour. I tried not to seethe, after all we were courting, although I have to admit that by the time he flung open the door and boomed his welcome my grin was fairly brittle. I went in. Another fabulous audition, with my darling Mike being attentive, full of ideas of how to squeeze every last comedic drop out of the scenes we read together. And I was in there an hour, so who cares about the poor schmuck out there in the waiting room? This was our time, Mike and Hugh time.

Then it was back on the train to Stratford, a hole in my pocket where a hefty percentage of my weekly wage used to be but with an audition experience as pleasurable and educative as this one had been, never mind. Bread on the water and all that.

Several days went by. My agent called.

"It's not going to work out for the role of Tom, but Mike loves you . . ."

"And I love—"

"Yes I know you do. They want you to go back to read for John."

"John? I don't remember a John."

"It's a cameo role."

"You mean tiny and pointless and bound to get cut?" I changed up a gear, from splutter to huff; after all Mike and I were pretty much going out by now. "Look, we've spent hours together. For heaven's sake, Mike knows what I can do. I'm not flogging all the way down from Stratford yet again to read for a cameo. I mean, come on."

The phone line was silent, quietly patient.

"Oh God all right then," I conceded. "But this time they're paying my train fare down from Stratford, right?"

Another silence.

"You have got TO BE JOKING." I was shouting now.

My agent's voice, as always, remained calm. "I did ask. But as the casting director pointed out, this is a low-budget film with very little chance of making its money back. They simply don't have the cash. If you don't want to audition again they'd quite understand but they won't consider you for the role unless you do."

On the train down to London I prepared my speech. "Mike. My soulmate. Light of my life. These auditions have been special times, we both know that, but I have to say something before we part. Actors at my level are the Little People. Directors, producers and casting directors, the Big People like you, the people with power, know damn well that we Little People, especially those of us who have never been in a film, will move heaven and earth, steal cars, sell grannies for the price of a train ticket in order to audition for even the tiniest role. But this is my third audition with you, Mike, my poppet, my third expensive train ticket in a month, and I'm only on the wage of a middle-ranking actor in a subsidised theatre. What you are doing is not only unfair, it's an insult. It sets a bad example and sends a terrible message to people like me who are trying to get a foot in the door. (Cue Elgar.) Because what this is, Mikey, is Exploitation, pure and simple, because you and the Big People know that it is a seller's market and that when you say 'Jump,' we Little People simply ask 'How high?' and of course I'll buy my own train ticket. (Music builds.) But it's wrong, Mickey. You know it's wrong and I know it's wrong. But unlike me you have the power to make it stop. And stop it must, Michael! Right Here, Right Now!" (Crescendo, curtain, applause.)

I may even have said this last bit out loud as the train rattled through Rugby. All in all it was a coherent and watertight argument, rousing without being cheesy, bound to make a grown man cry, and create a shift of cosmic proportions in the British film industry.

This time I sat in the waiting room for more than an hour and a fucking quarter. I was beginning to wonder how much longer I could keep the flame of our love ablaze. In theatre terms not only would the understudy have been sent on by now, he would have moved into my dressing room and redecorated it, assured of having a home for the rest of the run.

Finally the door opened and a fellow Little Person skipped out, beaming. That Mike was cheating on me was something I had got used to by now, but we both knew deep down he only had eyes for me.

"Hugh!"

"Mike!"

"Come in!"

This role was about five lines, so really didn't merit drilling down into that much. But to give him his due, he directed me this way, he directed me that way. I made him laugh. He commended me on my timing. I felt like saying his own was appalling. After twenty minutes we were done.

"That was great, Hugh. Really great. Again. Now, is there anything you want to ask me, anything you want to say, anything at all?"

This was my moment. This was Henry V on St. Crispin's Day, JFK promising a man on the moon, Martin Luther King having a dream. This was the time to Use My Words and make a difference.

"Er, not that I can think of, Mike. Thanks very much for your time."

We shook hands. I got the train back to Stratford, went on stage as Laertes, and got killed by Hamlet again.

And so the Little People went on being exploited. All because I wanted the job.

In explaining why I didn't get even the cameo part of John, the casting director said, "Mike really likes Hugh. I mean *really* likes him. But this is such a tiny weeny budget film, shooting on such a tight schedule, that Mike needs actors who have camera experience, even in the small roles; he just won't have the time to teach them their craft, however much he likes them. And he really likes Hugh."

I didn't think he liked me. I thought he loved me. Such a cruel world. The whole expensive episode proved two things to me: I needed more experience in front of a camera and I should have invested in a discount railcard.

In the end the low-budget film with little chance of making its money back did quite well. It was called *Four Weddings and a Funeral*.

24

Running Over the Bridge

Jonathan Harvey's play *Beautiful Thing*, about two teenage boys growing up in Thamesmead, had been a hit at the tiny Bush Theatre in 1993. For the mid-scale tour the following year I took over the role of Tony from Philip Glenister. It went down a storm wherever we played, culminating in a sell-out run at the Donmar Theatre in Covent Garden, often with standing ovations at the curtain call. There is a headiness that swirls around the company when a show is a stonking success. It can of course tip over into smugness, but when respected and cherished for what it is – transitory – it's the best feeling in the world; the hard work has paid off, the House Full sign is up every night, and people are queueing for returns. I loved *Beautiful Thing*. I loved the goodwill that swept through the audience during each performance as the two lead characters stumbled tentatively along the road of self-discovery, swerving through the chicanes of life on a housing estate as they came to terms with their homosexuality.

At university I had derived as much if not more satisfaction from being involved in the producing of plays as acting in them. One year I was business manager for the European Theatre Group's production of *Twelfth Night* which, like it said on the tin, toured Europe. I also produced a couple of shows at the university's ADC Theatre and at my college's own theatre space, Ted's Passage. I relished the anonymity of pulling a team together and no one feeling obliged to say to me at the end of the performance, "Darling, you were marvellous."

One night, after another standing ovation at the Donmar, I sat in the bar chatting to Hettie Macdonald, the director, about my affection for the play, wistfully observing that it deserved a longer life and a wider audience. Knowing my history of working behind the scenes at Cambridge, she said, "You should produce it in the West End."

"But I wouldn't know where to start," I said.

"Yes you would. And I'm not going to bet you any more than five pounds," said Hettie, "because I know you can do it and I don't want to fleece you."

Next day I phoned Dominic Dromgoole, then artistic director of the Bush Theatre, and negotiated with him to acquire the West End rights. There followed the most intense five months of my theatre career as I learned from a standing start how and how not to capitalise and produce a West End show. I partnered with Howard Panter of the Ambassadors Theatre Group to remount the production with a new cast at the Duke of York's Theatre. Amelda Brown would re-create her brilliant performance as Sandra, the blousy barmaid mum with a heart of gold and steel, but the boys, first played at the Bush by Jonny Lee Miller and Mark Letheren, then on tour by Mark and Shaun Dingwall, would be cast afresh. Rhys Ifans agreed to take over my role and Diane Parish would play Leah, the character memorably created by Sophie Stanton. But first I had to raise £60,000 of the £100,000 needed to get the show on its feet. With the help of Robin Guilleray, a seasoned West End angel, I wrote to every human being I knew, seeking investment.

I was convinced it wouldn't happen and so didn't give up my quest for a day job. I met director Christopher Morahan to discuss playing Dick Dudgeon, the title role in Shaw's *The Devil's Disciple*, in the Olivier Theatre at the National. Weeks went by and, as suspected, the money simply wasn't coming together for *Beautiful Thing*, so Howard Panter and I agreed a deadline of a particular Thursday lunchtime in July. That Thursday morning I still couldn't make the figures work. I called my agent and we decided to accept the offer from the National, which was to start rehearsals in a few weeks. An hour later the morning post landed on my doormat and with it a cheque for the remaining capital required to mount the production of *Beautiful Thing*.

Suddenly, both shows were on.

It made for a stressful autumn. I would rehearse the Shaw play at the National in the morning, then sprint across Waterloo Bridge, weave through Covent Garden to St. Martin's Lane for production meetings at the Duke of York's Theatre, and leg it back to the South Bank for the afternoon session. As with any production process, *Beautiful Thing* was fraught with challenges: arguments with Hettie over budget, and then, once they were resolved, issues of cast availability, questions about the set, could it be delivered on time, was the marketing working, copyright problems to do with the poster.

Meanwhile, over in Rehearsal Room 2 at the National, Helen McCrory and I were navigating our way through Shaw's melodrama, set in the American War of Independence, about a ne'er-do-well rogue who tries to do the right thing. Christopher Morahan, who had a decade earlier directed the legendary TV production of *The Jewel in the Crown*, had a reputation for being fierce and dictatorial. I found him smart, clear in what he wanted from his cast, collaborative to a large degree but potentially irascible. To be honest my thoughts were so often on the other side of the Thames, trying to solve the latest *Beautiful Thing* production conundrum, that I wouldn't have noticed if his tone was bullying or benign; I just got on with it. The third act sees the entrance of a great character, General Burgoyne, who presides over the trial of our anti-hero. The role is wry, intelligent and, in the right hands, very funny. Daniel Massey, laconic and slightly world-weary, stole the show night after night. It was wonderful to watch him at the top of his game. As I stood there in the prisoner's dock on the other side of the Olivier stage, I'd often think to myself, "Blimey, he was Noel Coward's godson and played the boy in *In Which We Serve*." He had great range as an actor: anyone who saw him play Furtwängler in Ronnie Harwood's *Taking Sides* caught a performance of both immense subtlety and raw power, but he had at times feline grace. Then again, having dinner with him one night after the show, I saw him cramming French fries into his mouth with one hand and thumping the tablecloth with the other in hysterics at a story he was recalling, tears running down his face. That night he was no less than Falstaff, full-throated and in love with life and laughter.

With *The Devil's Disciple* in rep at the Olivier, I was able to spend my daytimes at the Duke of York's. *Beautiful Thing* began its technical rehearsal. I was sitting in the stalls watching the team rehearse the change from scene two into three when Sarah from Marketing arrived through the curtain at the side of the stalls, proudly carrying a box of theatre programmes, hot off the press. She plonked herself down next to me and together we flicked through the glossy pages. This may have been for her just another part of the job but for me it was special: my first ever theatre programme as a producer of a show in the West End. I absorbed every word as the shiny paper glinted under the light spilling from the stage. I got to the cast biographies. Thankfully we had made sure the bios were to the point and didn't weave off into star signs and favourite cats. There was Amelda Brown, there was Richard Dormer, there was Rhys Ifan, Diane Parish, Zubin Varla – this terrific new cast who were going to take the play to a whole new—

Hang on, Rhys Ifan?

"Hmm? What?" whispered Sarah.

"Rhys Ifan? Where's the 's'?" I hissed in the darkness of the auditorium. "His name is Rhys Ifans, for fuck's sake. With an 's.'"

"Everythin' all right, Hugh?" asked Rhys, idling on stage while a lighting cue was adjusted.

"All fine, mate, no worries," I assured him.

Even in the penumbra of the stalls I could tell that Sarah had gone white as a sheet.

"Shit," she said.

"Well yes, shit, Sarah, to be honest."

"Do you think he'll notice? Yes of course he'll notice. Oh Christ. Don't tell anyone. I'll get them reprinted but we'll have to use these for the first two previews. Will you tell him or shall I?"

I looked at her.

"No you're right, I'll tell him," she said as she picked up the box of programmes and scuttled off.

"Hang on," I shout-whispered after her. "The cost of reprinting isn't coming out of my fucking budget, Sarah."

"Don't worry, I'll put it against *Rocky Horror*," she whispered back. "It's been in profit for years."

I wasn't able to attend opening night as I was on stage at the National. As soon as the curtain came down I did my by now customary sprint across town and joined the first night party in the theatre bar. I asked Hettie how it had gone.

"Well," she said, "it went well. And thank you for this."

She held up the Good Luck card I had written her and also the £5 note that I'd put inside it. After all, she'd won the bet.

25

Do You Do Sport?

"Hugh, what if I said I was speaking to you from Raquel Welch's bed?"

"I'd say you were lying, chief."

The spring of 1995. I was on the phone to my friend Chris Luscombe. He wasn't lying. They were on tour together in a production of *The Millionairess*. Chris had also been commissioned to help the American icon go over her lines and work through her role in private, sometimes in her room. According to Chris, one hotel in a modest town on the tour was so blown away that a Hollywood legend was coming to visit that they knocked two rooms into one and put in a jacuzzi in order to accommodate her no-doubt overblown demands. Raquel thought it hilarious and wouldn't have cared less if they'd given her a broom cupboard – and no, she didn't avail herself of the jacuzzi.

At the time Chris and I were writing a film together and so I would sometimes go and visit him on the road and we'd spend daytime hours scribbling, before his show in the evening. One night in Malvern I joined the cast at an impromptu party after the performance in someone's digs. I was introduced to the star of *One Million Years B.C.* in the kitchen. She was by the fridge.

I tried to lean casually on the door frame but ended up half perched on the swing bin by the back door. I don't know what age Raquel Welch was in 1995 but it didn't matter, because icons transcend time, space and the ageing process. They just hover in some sort of ethereal infinity, radiating star quality and, in her case, a ludicrous amount of sex appeal. Even here, by a fridge in a kitchen in Worcestershire. She smiled at me and, unless I'm mistaken, actually looked me up and down.

"Do you do sport?"

She actually asked me that. Raquel Welch asked me if I was fit, implying that she thought I might be and that she'd be even happier if I said I was. For the subject of virtually every 1960s and 1970s schoolboy's fantasy even to notice me, one buttock wedged in a trash can, was probably the greatest compliment I have ever been paid.

"Bit of running," I managed, trying to sound husky, full of mystery and athleticism.

"Chris tells me you're gonna do a show in the West End."

"Yes, I'm taking over in *My Night With Reg* at the Criterion."

"I'd like to come see it."

"Really? It's about a bunch of gay guys. Not sure it's necessarily the sort of—"

"Honey, I'm a gay icon. Chris, as soon as the tour's done, we're going."

Oh. My. God.

It was my son who told me Roger Michell had died. Felix only knew him as the director of *Notting Hill*. He forwarded me a link from the BBC website. "V sad," he wrote. He wasn't to know it was the first I'd heard of it, that the stark simplicity of his message would make my eyes smart, nor that memories would flood back of without doubt one of the finest directors with whom I had worked.

We met when he cast me to replace John Sessions as Daniel

in *My Night With Reg*. Jason Watkins, Richard Lintern, Roger Sloman, Scott Ransome and I were the new boys, taking over from the cast led by David Bamber, who had made an award-winning hit of Kevin Elyot's agonising, funny play about a group of men who, it turns out, had all had sex at some point with the Reg of the title, the Reg who died of AIDS and whose legacy lingers over the rest of the group, like the sword of Damocles.

In the harsh reality of the commercial theatre, a take-over cast is sometimes directed into the show within a matter of days by an assistant director, slavishly re-creating the blocking of the original cast without ever really knowing what motivated such moves in the first place. I don't know whether it was producer Bill Kenwright who insisted or Roger Michell himself, but either way we had the privilege of Roger directing us *Reg* newbies for two whole weeks, from scratch, as if discovering the play for the first time. It was a smart move, because it meant we felt valued and fresh and the decisions we made on stage were discovered by us and weren't simply adopted.

"Where's Hugh?" Roger Michell's calm voice called from the half-lit auditorium.

"Here's Hugh," I replied, stepping into view at the window of the set upstage.

"Ah, there's Hugh. Why do you think Daniel exits in that way, with that line?"

I hadn't even thought about it.

"Have a think about it."

There was no remonstration or disappointment in Roger's voice that I hadn't given it thought. Just a pointer. Never imposing, just asking questions, getting the actor to take responsibility for each action and thought behind or within each line.

I was sharing a dressing room with Jason Watkins. A few weeks into the run, as we sat in front of our mirrors, dotting eyeliner and dabbing powder, I dropped a grenade into our ritual pre-show conversation.

"Chris Luscombe's in tonight."

"Oh good. Haven't seen him in ages. That's nice."

"Yeah." Pause. "And he's bringing a friend . . . "

The look on Jason's face when I said who he was bringing with him is something I treasure to this day.

After the show that night we hosted Raquel Welch, the cast crammed into our modest dressing room deep below Piccadilly Circus. She sat in the one low armchair, effortlessly glamorous, like Cleopatra, with Chris cast as the eunuch at her side. For half an hour Raquel had six grown men eating out of her hand, all exuding testosterone, striving to present their heterosexual credentials; at one point I swear I saw Richard Lintern thumping his chest and baring his teeth like a gorilla in the mood. Thereafter, for the rest of the run no one but no one who entered our dressing room was allowed to sit in "Raquel's Throne."

Ken MacDonald was the one member of the original cast to stay on when we took over. He played Benny the bus driver who halfway through the play confides in Guy, in whose flat the story takes place, that he too slept with their friend Reg. Ken would sit on the sofa facing the audience, nervously grab a handful of peanuts from a bowl and munch his way through them as he made his confession. It was a routine he had worked out over the months of the run, popping a nut into his mouth at specific moments in the speech so as not to interrupt the flow, or clog up his diction.

I was in the stage right wing, waiting for my next entrance. Kenny had just embarked on his confessional and – yes, tick – there was the momentary pause as he flicked the first peanut into his mouth. A line or two later, the second peanut went in. My mind drifted for a moment, relaxing into the rhythm of the scene . . . but was instantly wrenched back to reality because

Kenny's next pause – by which you could usually set your watch – was extending way beyond its customary length. Suddenly there was a loud and heavy *thwump*, like a sack of potatoes being dropped from a height. And then Jason Watkins, playing Guy, said, "Is there a doctor in the house?" A ripple of laughter from the audience, followed by a voice from the stalls: "No, but I'm a male nurse." More laughter. Then the curtain dropped like a stone. Roger Sloman burst on to the set. It took my brain an age to realise what was going on. Kenny was unconscious on the floor in front of the sofa. With Jason and the stage manager looking on, Roger knelt down to check Kenny's breathing, then in order to lift him on to the sofa hoicked him upwards from behind and in doing so, either by accident or design, effected the Heimlich manoeuvre. *Plip* – out plopped the peanut that had lodged itself in Kenny's throat.

A glass of water, stage management huddling to discuss next steps, Kenny slowly recovering in the prompt corner. Ten minutes later the curtain went up again and the play resumed.

The next day three members of the audience rang the box office to ask whether or not the bit with the male nurse and the curtain coming down was in the script as there had been heated debate on the way home. The box office manager assured each of them that it had in fact been a genuine medical emergency and not a nod to Brecht's alienation effect.

26

Not Russ Abbot

Any couple that has experienced a miscarriage joins the bereavement club. For some it is almost incidental, a minor inconvenience, and a few months later, bingo, they're back on track. For others, particularly if it is a repeated loss, it is a pain from which recovery seems impossible. For Lulu and me it focused our minds on the preciousness of it all.

We had met as teenagers through mutual friends and local parties in the lee of the South Downs where she was born and to where my parents had recently moved. I invited her to a play at the National Youth Theatre but she was off travelling with her boyfriend (and future husband) who was just beginning to make his mark as a professional polo player. They started to travel the world with his team and we lost touch. Some fifteen years later, now amicably separated from Nick, Lulu was back in West Sussex running a marquee company. My mum rang her to hire some chairs . . .

"Do yaw remember Hyo?" she asked Lulu in her telephone voice.

"Hugh? Yes, of course. Still doing plays?"

"Well, if you turn on ITV right now, he's the one who isn't

Russ Abbot. It's called *Married for Life* and it's not terribly good but I'm sure some theatre will come along soon."

To Mum and Dad, Theatre was legit, Television a thing of dubious parentage.

"Would you like his number?"

Like a clucking Mrs. Bennet from *Pride and Prejudice*, Mum forever took credit for brokering Lulu and me getting back in touch. I knew nothing about polo or horses, Lulu knew nothing about theatre. We gave it three weeks.

Jacobean plots and language tend to be quite dense, and with a running time of about three and a half hours the RSC production of John Webster's *The White Devil* was going to be a test for even the most ardent theatregoer. But when your date that April night in 1996 hasn't been to a play in years and isn't the least bit interested that you know half the cast ... yup, I probably could have chosen better. On the other hand, when I did Sam Mendes' production of *Habeas Corpus* at the Donmar Warehouse that same year with Jim Broadbent, Brenda Blethyn, Celia Imrie and Imelda Staunton, she loved it so much she saw it four times. Phew. She was there for the matinee when the penalty shoot-out in the quarter-finals of Euro 96 caused such a wave of roars through the pubs of WC2 and into the auditorium of the Donmar that Jim Broadbent halted the applause at the curtain call in order to put the audience out of its misery: England had got through. And thankfully, dear reader, she married me.

After the miscarriage and the tests we were given countless tips: potions from the Orient, chants, crystals, no coffee, lots of coffee, sleeping with a bat's wing under the pillow – anything, everything. Nothing. Going up through the gears of stress, the sands of time slipping through the hour glass. Taking temperatures religiously, the command to get home *right now* and make the magic happen ... still nothing. One day, nearly three years on, we presented a carefully annotated temperature chart to the doctor.

"What are we doing wrong?" we asked, holding hands tightly.

"This," he said, nodding at the chart. He tore it up dramatically and tossed the confetti in the bin as we looked on, astonished. "Now go on holiday and forget about it."

Nine months later, Felix arrived. The name means "fortunate." And we are.

27

Colin Bond

The call I had been waiting for finally came: Eon Productions had been in touch, they were casting the new James Bond. Well, to be exact, they were casting for tiddly roles in the eighteenth production of the iconic franchise, exotically titled "Bond 18." I was even going to meet the director, Roger Spottiswoode, so I wasn't quite an extra.

"Towards the end of the movie—"

I've never quite known the difference between a *film* and a *movie* but when the director of "Bond 18" says *movie* it is instantly the better word and way more cool.

"Cool," I interrupted.

"What?" said Roger.

"Nothing."

"Towards the end of the movie there's a sequence in the South China Sea. The Royal Navy is taking on the Chinese fleet. I'm currently casting the British naval officers and crew."

I immediately saw myself flat on my back on a sun lounger in Thailand. Three weeks of relaxation in the Far East, with a tiny bit of work in the middle – what could be better? This sort of cushy gig was exactly what being a film actor was all about. It had been a long time coming but I reckon I'd deserved it.

I got the part.

The following month I turned up for filming . . . two days in a Royal Navy cadet training simulator in fucking Portsmouth, all of thirty-five minutes from my house.

I was cast as Air Warfare Officer (AWO). My bit involved us actors sitting at radar screens, dressed in blue action-station gear with fire-proof hoods and calm-under-pressure voices at the ready. In reality I looked like a Kwik Fit fitter sitting in front of a tumble dryer. Either side of me and dotted between the other actors at other tumble dryers were a dozen naval cadets who did this sort of exercise day in, day out. They were brilliant at it.

"Four point three – oh-sixer-niner – echo two delta forty minutes at fifty degrees then add fabric softener, copy roger over."

That sort of thing.

I was rubbish at it and kept getting my simple but, to be fair, technically quite complicated lines wrong. Of the actors on my watch, Brendan Coyle was Best in Show. He was particularly good at flicking switches and twiddling knobs while talking rapidly about turbine pressure. It is one of cinema's greatest losses that his line didn't make it into the finished film – sorry, movie. One of my two did:

"Sir, AWACs report two waves of land-based MiG-21s inbound. They should be on our screens in two minutes."

Since my character hadn't been dignified with a name, I decided he was called Colin. I don't know if my fellow tiddly part actor colleagues in the *movie* went to similar lengths of creating a back story – I've never asked the likes of Julian Fellowes, Gerard Butler or Jason Watkins – but I'd like to think I was not alone.

At the time I was into tapestry, a hobby I'd failed to mention to Raquel Welch. A few months before my foray into the world of James Bond in 1997 I had started on a rather fetching rose pattern, which I was intending to give to my sister-in-law as a wedding present. As an indication of how much my passion for tatting has diminished, I still haven't finished it and the youngest of her three children recently turned twenty. For a while doing tapestry stopped me smoking, until I found a method of sewing and smoking at the same time. Back at unit base between set-ups, fellow tatter and captain of HMS *Bedford* Pip Torrens and I discussed wool.

It was pretty much my only encounter with the world of James Bond and, by extension, the Secret Service. My only fictional encounter anyway . . .

When you're on holiday thousands of miles away from home and you wake up on the morning of Christmas Eve to see on your mobile two missed calls from your brother you know something's wrong. To be honest, I thought he was going to tell me something had happened to Dad, the scatty and vulnerable one. Mum was always the rock. I had last seen my parents a couple of weeks before. I was hosting a concert at the Albert Hall and had popped out front to see them during the interval. She was frail, her breathing awkward, as it had been for some years now, but there she was, smiling, typically sweet and encouraging. The bell sounded for the second half. That last kiss bye bye, as it proved to be, traces of make-up powder from her cheek transferring to mine, a faint scent . . . frozen, now, in time. Held for ever. A respiratory infection took her in less than a day. The winter of 2014.

It's horrible, being so far away and waiting for a plane to get you home so you can mourn with the rest of the family. Then, once you are all together, everything is lists and practicalities and the general bureaucracy of death that seems designed to keep you so busy that there's no time for grieving. The grief comes later, in peculiar waves that eddy and pool and confuse. There was a sound Mum made when trying to relieve a tickle in her throat, a sound I've never heard from another human. I can only describe it as the oesophageal version of an animal rubbing its back against a tree to relieve an itch. A sort of internal scratching and squawking; akin to the ancient mating call of some exotic bird, perhaps. In the months after her death, remembering this sound that only she could make would one moment cause me to laugh out loud and then, the next time I recalled it, drown me in a bucket of sobs. Bringing to mind that unique sound now I feel emotions rising from deep inside, but at the same time I smile. The ripples still ebb and flow but somehow simultaneously.

When I was about nine, Mum announced that she was going to get a job, working three days a week. This was, of course, the most ridiculous idea I had ever heard in my entire life. It demonstrated extreme selfishness on her part and, if she was indeed being serious, would render me bereft, alone, unwanted and unloved.

When Dad had been out in the Far East doing National Service in the early fifties, just after they married, Mum had travelled out there too. While Dad was serving on board HMS *Alert* and HMS *Unicorn,* Mum took up a desk job in the Foreign Office in Singapore. Now, in the seventies, the call had gone out for former staff who wanted to rejoin the Foreign Office to please get in touch. So she did.

"But what about me?" I wailed, hot tears of martyrdom beginning to lava-flow as I slammed my bedroom door.

For the next ten years or so Mum went to work in an office next to Lambeth North tube station. Dad would drop her off and, if it was school holidays, I would come too, and together he and I would drive on into central London on his rounds, checking up on patients at various hospitals. I would sit in the car, doing my best to keep traffic wardens at bay. Paddington kept a marmalade sandwich under his hat for emergencies; Dad kept a Kit Kat in the glove compartment. He had to re-stock frequently when I was around.

Flash forward to the early years of this century, my parents now both retired. I opened the evening paper one day and was surprised to see a photo of Mum's anonymous office building, a tower block of ugly post-war functionalism. But it was the headline above the image that made my heart miss a beat and then land with a thud. Ka-*thunk*.

MI6 BUILDING TO BE SOLD

I phoned her at once. Dad called her in from the garden, secateurs in hand.

"Hello, darling."

"Mum, that job you did at the Foreign Office, at Century House. Was it with the Secret Service?"

Pause.

"Bloody hell!" I continued. "And you never told me!"

She chuckled, like someone who had not been entirely liberal with the truth being found out at last. "Well, it's not the sort of thing one talks about, is it?"

"You were a spy! How cool is that? My mum was a spy!"

"I wasn't, darling. Just a bit of filing."

After she died, I asked Dad if she'd ever spoken about her work.

"Not once. She went to the office in Lambeth three days a week, came home again. That was that."

Unbeknown to me, permission was sought and granted for her occupation to be acknowledged at her funeral. And so it was that in his eulogy my uncle revealed to a packed congregation something none of them had ever known: that Pat Williams had worked for several years in P Division of MI6.

Several times during the seventies her bosses had asked her to join them full time but she had declined . . . "because she had a young son at home to think about." When I heard these words in church that day, with my mother's wicker coffin a few feet away from me there in the nave, the tears that welled were those of the selfish little shit who was only now, in his fifties, properly appreciating the choices and sacrifices his mum had made for his benefit.

At the wake afterwards my sister whispered that there were no fewer than five members of the Service in the room … and two of them lived in the village. I didn't believe her for a second.

"Her over there," she said, "and him over there."

"What, *Derek?* Don't be ridiculous! Derek was never in the Secret Service. He's about the most anonymous man on the planet!"

My sister rolled her eyes as if to say that's exactly the type of people they recruit, you nitwit, and walked off. A few minutes later I found myself next to Derek.

"Funerals can be full of surprises," I said.

Derek smiled. He knew I knew. "Your mum and I used to enjoy chatting together whenever we got the chance, away from work. After church on Sundays, fundraising committees, local gatherings."

And just then an image popped into my mind: Mum, stuck in a corner at parties with Derek. I had always felt sorry for her, politely doing her duty by some village bore, so I'd swoop in to rescue her with an invented need for her on the other side of the room. But as it turned out, over all those years she and Derek had in fact been having a whale of a time, catching up on the office gossip. Another type of James Bonding.

"Derek, can I ask you something?"

I liked him more now that I knew he and Mum had a shared secret past and that he had confided a flavour of it to my sister and me.

"Of course."

"Mum said she just did a bit of filing …"

"Did she? Did she now."

He paused enigmatically. Then, as he took a sip of wine, with me on tenterhooks, his wife swooped in, rescuing her husband from the bore in the corner.

*

I mentioned this extraordinary side of my ordinary mum on the radio show *Desert Island Discs*. A few days later I got a message via the BBC's security correspondent that a man from River House, the home of MI6, would like to talk to me. I was intrigued.

"Oh Hugh, hello, thanks for calling." The man's voice was bright, confident and trustworthy – could have been an airline pilot. Maybe that's what his neighbours thought he was. After all, I'd always thought Derek was in insurance.

"Hello, Martin. Well, this is a bit strange."

"Yes, well. Is it? Would it help if I tell you a bit about what we do?"

"I think the less I know about MI6 the better."

I had visions of being tied to a chair and my nuts being used for baseball practice while questions were spat in my ear about the goings-on at River House.

"I heard you on the radio," continued Martin, "and wondered if you'd like to come in and perhaps chat to some of the team. These days we're very much about opening things up, you see. Sometimes we can feel a bit hidden away."

"I thought that was the whole point," I snorted jokingly, pleased with my quip.

"Indeed!" Martin tried a chuckle himself, perhaps wondering whether this smart new initiative from upstairs of making the Secret Service more visible was such a good idea after all. "Anyway," he went on, "I'm running a series of lunchtime talks given by people on the, er, on the 'outside,' as it were. As I say, it can get a tad insular here. Introspective."

Martin was beginning to sound like he longed for a bit of extrospection himself. A spot of golf in the Algarve, for starters.

"And you'd like me to come in and give a talk?"

"Sorry?" Martin had just hit a perfect drive down the 12th at San Lorenzo in a balmy 29°C.

"A talk," I repeated.

"Yes, a talk. Would you? About, oh I don't know, people who've inspired you. That sort of thing. We're keen to freshen things up with perspectives from, well, from—"

"Civilians?" I added helpfully.

"I was going to say real people but yes, civilians pretty much hits the nail on the head. Civilians, yes. Did I mention we can sometimes feel a bit cut off?"

"Yes. Yes, you did."

Martin was warm and welcoming, the offices like any other I had visited – most noticeable was the lack of paperwork in C's office – though I suspect they vet the after-hours cleaning staff quite carefully. (Oh yes, it's C by the way, not M.) Then there was the short, chubby man, about my age, who introduced himself as I made my way to the lecture theatre.

"I joined when I was about eighteen. Same department as your mum."

"So, 'just a bit of filing,' then," I quoted.

"Ha! Is that what she said? Bless her!" He laughed. "It was her job to sort the overnight intercepts, assess their status, decide which were priority, which weren't. So, if someone upstairs wanted a spot-check on such-and-such a situation, we could put our hands on it at a moment's notice. So, yeah, 'filing.' In a way."

He could see by my dazed nod that I had learned more about my mother in that single moment than I had in decades.

"But the thing I remember most, Hugh? Her footsteps. Back then us youngsters would be lounging about in our section, doing the crossword or something, and suddenly we'd hear these footsteps – unique – clacking along the lino corridor. 'Quick! It's Pat! Look busy!' And we'd all jump to it!"

I knew exactly the sound he meant and for a split second this man and I were completely connected. By the memory of a sound.

In that lunchtime talk, in the lecture theatre at the home of MI6, with a hundred or so men and women eating their sandwiches, or sipping coffee (or snoozing), and apparently many others watching from overseas (where were the cameras – hidden in the lids of Thermos flasks, perhaps?), I spoke of the people who had nudged me in the directions I had taken along the way to today. I concluded with this:

> I guess all actors, if they're honest, seek applause and approval from an audience. Everyone in this room, almost by definition, is required to avoid any such recognition and maintain anonymity. So, I want to end by applauding you. I don't underestimate the pressure under which you work, nor how isolating the need for discretion can make you feel.
>
> My mum was, at home, a woman of immense compassion, selflessness and energy. In the village where we lived in West Sussex she was affectionately known as the Colonel – the first to welcome newcomers to the area, the first to rope unsuspecting wives into the rota for the church flowers. She was endlessly raising money for charity, the church hall extension, the refurbishment of the village hall; she reached out the hand of friendship when marriages failed, or when bereavement struck.
>
> But she knew stuff and presumably did stuff at work here in the Service that she could not share with anyone, not even with the man she trusted most in the world. She made a difference to the lives of others, certainly within her family and her community, probably within her section at Century House, and therefore possibly even across the world. You do, too. And I thank you for it.

After Mum died I bought my father a Memory Book so he could jot down key moments in his life, something to pass on to my son. It had page headings like What I Did At School and My First Job. Dad made a few entries in it but not many, before his memory started to fade and fuzz. Perhaps that's why

I'm writing this, getting key memories down before mine fogs, too. One in three of us – or is the statistic even more gloomy these days?

It's been the experience of many of my friends affected by dementia that the final move to "God's Waiting Room," as Dad used to call any care home, is an incredibly painful decision for the spouse and/or children, and often involves degrees of deception. It's sometimes triggered by a fall, necessitating a visit to hospital. This gives the family, who very often have been debating for months how to take the next step, the opportunity to tee up the care home, while telling the injured parent that once discharged they're just going somewhere for a few days' holiday to rest up. Those few days turn into a week and the weeks into months, by which time the hope is that the frequency of the question "But when am I going home?" gradually diminishes until the memory of Home becomes so foggy that the struggle for independence and the yearning for the familiarity of what went before is lost. It's a painful half truth to tell for a long-term good and can weigh heavily.

We were lucky. So lucky.

In the days after Mum died, my brother, my sister and I held family summits, with Dad in benign attendance. He took pride in the fact that "I can't even boil an egg, y'know. Pat's such a wonderful cook."

But the wonderful cook was gone now.

"It's all right, old boy, I'll just stick something in the oven, or eat in the pub."

However, when we discovered that he'd put his coffee mug in the washing machine rather than the dishwasher, we realised that leaving him in sole charge of his domestic domain would be a terrible mistake.

For a few years the rota of home carers coped brilliantly. Dad would play piano duets with friends, go off to local village pubs for lunch, even visit Lord's for the cricket; getting him there and back was a logistical nightmare but it was achieved for a couple of cherished summers. However, having dinged the car on one too many bollards and once too often turned across the A286 without looking, frightening his passenger half to death, the gentle mental decline became more noticeable. We lied by telling him that those rotten insurance people wouldn't let him drive any more (I find it incredible that in the UK you can self-certify that you're fit to drive at ninety, even when everyone around you might be screaming that you're not).

He had the most incredibly sweet tooth and loved a pudding. In fact, it's fair to say that main courses were something of an inconvenience, it was dessert he craved.

"Another helping, Dad?"

His eyes would light up, one hand would go to his chest in a gesture of faux resistance. "Really? Well, I don't want to appear piggy, but . . ." And then he'd slide his plate in the direction of the sticky toffee pudding, or apple crumble. He would watch gleefully as another spoonful landed on his plate, which he would drown in cream or custard. "Well, I must say, this little piggy's been to market!"

Dad started to visit a dementia care home twice a week, taking part in its day centre activities. Singing wartime songs, doing quizzes about flowers and looking at pictures of the Royal Family became regular exercises, now that his enthusiasm for piano playing was diminishing; certainly no more duets. The Queen and Prince Philip would be recognised as distant cousins, or perhaps old work colleagues – he knew the faces but couldn't quite place them. Once or twice Dad picked up his stick and went for a stroll along the corridor (the building was circular, so there was no chance of residents getting lost), poking his head into the bedrooms as he passed. "Is this a hotel too?" he would ask.

One of my greatest pleasures was arriving at his flat for morning coffee and pausing outside the living room door just to listen to him playing the piano. Schubert or Mendelssohn or

Brahms or Scott Joplin. If I crept in and sat on the sofa he would inevitably catch me out of the corner of his eye and stop playing immediately.

"My dear old fellow. How lovely! Cup of coffee?"

And that would be that for the day, as far as the piano was concerned. So, sometimes I'd wait outside the room for half an hour or more, just so I could listen. I never wanted that sound to fade. His brain engaging with his fingers and so through to the keys of the piano, resulting in that astonishing hallmark of human evolution: music. When he was at the piano he was focused and present, in touch with the world, not vague and increasingly out of reach. Then one day he declared his hands to be arthritic and that he couldn't play the piano any more, and just a few days after that he announced he wanted to move to Langham Court.

"They have bedrooms there, you know. I like it there."

He volunteered. With his ability and desire to play the piano now diminished, he was ready to move on.

28

The Notting Hill Film

The first thing I thought when I read the script of "The Notting Hill Film," as it was provisionally titled, was that it was bound to be a flop. It had exactly the same group of characters and the same plot as *Four Weddings and a Funeral* and lightning doesn't strike twice.

Having directed me in *My Night With Reg,* I guess I was on Roger Michell's "list" of actors for Bernie. I went in to read on the first day of casting, November 1997. Inevitably, my lower back problem decided to flare up that morning. So I'd hit the painkillers on the way to the Portobello Studios, which was close to Richard Curtis's house – the house with the blue door made famous by the film, as it happens. I sat in the waiting room for the audition feeling quite drifty and by the time I went in to read – with thankfully no hanging around of Mike Newellian proportions this time – I was positively floating. Everybody was lovely, including the pot plant. The reading went fine. But as I got up to leave I realised I could barely move. Roger carefully helped me to my feet, where I remained for a moment at a right angle, before eyeing up the door and launching into as graceful a crab-like exit as possible. If I'd been auditioning for the Hunchback of

Notre Dame I would have been a shoo-in. At the door I turned, announcing to the room, "And, of course, I do my own stunts."

Emma Chambers, Dawn French's adorable sidekick Alice in Richard Curtis's hit TV comedy *The Vicar of Dibley,* was on Richard's list for Honey. He'd written the part for her and in fact had told her as much. But there was a process to go through. She auditioned on the first day of Honeys. I had known Emma a bit at drama school and so we decided to call each other regularly to check on casting progress.

I began work on the second series of a sitcom called *Holding the Baby.* I wasn't in the first series. I was taking over from Nick Hancock, playing a single dad who had been dumped. I had a lot of fun working with Sally Phillips, Lou Gish and Joe Duttine. Carrying the show, I was also carrying too many pounds and so I went on a health drive and lost over a stone. Every Monday I'd get home from rehearsals and ring Emma. Still no news. I started to hear through the grapevine of other actors going up for the film, Sally Phillips included.

Another Monday. Emma. No news.

I think it took about nine or ten weeks before the role of Bernie was finally offered to me, followed by a call from Roger Michell.

"Hello, Hugh. Really excited it's worked out."

"Same here. Thank you."

"But there's a problem."

"Oh?"

"Your weight."

"Roger, honestly, I've been doing my best. I've lost at least sixteen pounds."

"That's just it. You're too thin. There are several references to Bernie being, well, porky."

Indeed, in the script the character is described as "mid-30s-plump-in-a-suit, but looking a mess in it."

"Thing is, Hugh, for the comments to land you really do need a City tummy."

Most of my life my weight has gone up and down like a pair of bellows, usually coming to rest on the inflated side of things. So, I was crestfallen. I begged Roger not to make me put on weight, not when I was doing so well.

"I tell you what," he said, by way of compromise. "We'll get Shuna to measure you up for a prosthetic stomach."

I breathed a sigh of relief and called Emma. She too had finally been cast. When I heard that my friends Gina McKee, from the National Youth Theatre, and Tim McInnerny, from my time at the RSC, not to mention Rhys Ifans (definitely with an "s"), with whom I had shared not only a role but an agent, and Sally Phillips, with whom I was currently working, were filling out the other supporting roles, I began to feel properly excited. Forget Hugh Grant and Julia Roberts, this lot were all the pals I would need to get me through the nerves of my first decent part in a movie.

Rehearsals started in April 1998, in a freezing cold church hall in Portobello. Gas heaters tugged as close as possible to the trestle tables around which we shivered over our scripts. Julia Roberts was arriving in a few days' time but first, Roger Michell, as forensic and measured as he had been during *My Night With Reg,* worked through the script with Hugh Grant and the rest of us, the "gang of friends." The cigarette butts piled up in the ashtrays. Roger's were the ones with the filters torn off. On the morning of Julia's arrival everyone had miraculously given up smoking, assuming, I suppose, that being one of the most famous film stars in the world (playing one of the most famous film stars in the world) she would have it in her contract that she would only breathe smoke-free air and drink tonic water made from yak's pee. She came in wearing black jeans, sneakers, a T-shirt. Shook hands.

"I'm nervous as hell. Anyone got a cigarette?"

And out came four packets.

Sometimes research is handy, other times it's overkill. But

since I barely knew how premium bonds worked I thought it might be a good idea to learn what the hell a stockbroker actually did. I had been at school with Giles Morland who, unlike my character, Bernie, had become a successful one. He introduced me to some of his team, who sat at banks of screens looking at an array of flashing lights and colours. All very pretty and completely mystifying, which was all I really needed to get a handle on the character, who, equally bemused, was quite capable of losing his company millions of pounds a day.

With spring in the air, and filming having begun, it was time to finalise Bernie's outfits. Shuna Harwood the costume designer bound me up in the padded tummy, put me in the messy City suit, and off we went to show Roger Michell, who was on set in Notting Hill shooting what would be the final scene of the movie. On a bench, in a park in the sunshine, Julia was lying on Hugh Grant's lap while he read a book. Observant viewers subsequently noticed that the book is *Captain Corelli's Mandolin*, in fact a nod to Roger's next movie (which in the end he had to pull out of for health reasons).

In a break between shots I proudly presented our work, my City tummy flopping over the belt of my trousers. Roger scratched his chin, thinking, and asked me to walk up and down a bit. He shook his head and said, "Sorry, I just don't believe it's real."

So Shuna and I went back to the wardrobe truck and the drawing board. We fussed and faffed and then suddenly – brainwave! – I came up with another idea. Ten minutes later we were back on set, with me showing off the new look.

"Ah, now that's more like it." Roger was smiling now. "How did you do it?"

I lifted my shirt to reveal that I'd got rid of the padding and was just sticking out my own stomach. Thereafter, not only did Richard Curtis personally offer me sandwiches whenever they appeared on set, which I resisted (on the whole), but often, just as the 1st AD was about to call "Action," I'd hear producer Duncan Kenworthy hiss "Tummy!" as a reminder to stick mine out. A few lines were tweaked – in the finished version Bernie refers to himself as "chubby-cheeked" rather than "fat" – so at least a sense of indulgent lunches was preserved.

The mark of a good director – a good *actors'* director at any rate – is the ability to be able to draw the best performance out of each member of the cast, whatever their personality, or however individual their way of working. Some actors take notes and suggestions willingly, others less so. Some actors dig deep into character and want to stay that way for hours, days even (watch Jean Dujardin in *Call My Agent* – a brilliant parodic example), others put down the crossword as the cameras roll and casually drift on to their mark. Knowing how to bring all the different types of human beings together to play in concert is not a skill every director possesses. Roger had it.

There was a scene that never made it to the final cut. The group of friends, walking abreast through Portobello, saying a line or two each. It lasted about forty-five seconds. After the first take, and as the camera re-set, Roger took off his headphones and came up to each of us individually, quietly giving a fresh perspective on our lines – "Would Bernie ever consider x . . . ?" – in a way that was both personal and collaborative. As we went back to first positions, Emma Chambers said, "How does he do that? He knew exactly what I was thinking and he's just suggested something new to think about next time."

On the third take that afternoon one of the shopkeepers started lobbing eggs at us from his doorstep. He didn't seem in the least bit angry, just having a bit of fun. While the security guys had a quiet word and presumably upped his nuisance fee with a folded banknote, a market stallholder covertly showed me a napkin, autographed by the other Hugh.

"Signed that for my lad, he did. Needn't have, need he? Reckon that Grant's all right."

Another passer-by asked what we were doing. I explained we were making a film.

"What's it called?" he asked.

Richard Curtis looked up, enquiring of the impromptu test audience, "Would you go and see a film called *Notting Hill?*"

"Might do," answered the passer-by. "Depends if it's any good."

Fair enough.

The dinner party sequence had been Richard's starting point for the whole story. After Oxford, he and a group of friends used to meet regularly at a friend's house for dinner. Their host, Piers, was an ambitious but terrible cook, always burning everything. But it didn't matter. Their get-togethers were about friendship. A thought popped into Richard's head: how would my gang react if one night I brought the most famous film star in the world along as my date?

By 2 p.m. one particular Wednesday at Ealing Studios I was all dressed up and prepared to film my first exchange in the dinner party sequence. It may not be the most important scene in cinema history but to me it was a big deal. A one-on-one moment with Julia Roberts, for heaven's sake. I paced up and down my dressing room, which was a slightly awkward exercise given that it was about the size of a bathmat. A three-way is not nearly as exotic or erotic as it might sound. It's a trailer chopped up into three compartments, each usually boasting a modest sofa, maybe a chair and table, often nowhere actually to hang a costume and, if you're lucky, a loo.

"Still a few minutes away," said the runner, apparently interested in some banana peel on the ground outside my hutch, in fact listening intently to a message on her earpiece.

"No problem," I said. "I'll wait. So—"

"Yes, switching to two," said the runner, diverting to a more interesting conversation.

The tiring bit of filming is not the twenty minutes on any given day when the camera is actually on you, it's the eleven or so hours when it's not. The crew continue to work their socks off, while the actors mooch about. Some actors are great at switching off, writing their novel, or catching up with their bookie, or indeed their tapestry, but this scene was, let's say, significant for me and so all that afternoon I felt like a sprinter at the start of a 100m, the starter's gun pointed skywards, alert, permanently in the get set position.

Three o'clock came and went.

More pacing. Told the runner a hilarious story about my time doing Shakespeare from the back of a Vauxhall Astra in my Theatre in Education days. However, as she listened I noticed that her concentration on a thistle growing between concrete slabs was particularly intense, which culminated in an exclamation of "Copy that" and her running off towards the production office.

At five o'clock I was stood down. I had done a thousand paces of my cell, adrenaline bubbling, wittering inanities to anyone in earshot, on edge about doing my first decent dialogue scene in a grown-up movie, with a bona fide Hollywood movie star. And then not doing it.

Next morning we shot the scene.

Having clocked that Julia's character is an actress, Bernie, who is completely unaware to whom he is talking, commiserates with her about the poor wages most jobbing actors receive.

"I mean, last film you did, what did you get paid?"

In an early draft of the script her answer was "Ten million dollars." During rehearsals in that cold church hall it was changed to "Twelve million dollars." It came to her close-up. On the third take, Julia suddenly changed her reply to "Fifteen million dollars."

Once we'd finished the scene I asked her, out of interest, why she'd changed the number again.

"I was kinda tired of low-balling," she winked.

A few weeks later I read in the papers she was to be paid $20 million for her next movie, *Erin Brockovich*.

The circus moved on to a residential square in Bayswater, to film the wedding sequence. The bit where Roger Sloman's mountaineer, hero of the book launch at the beginning of the story, finally makes his feelings known for James Dreyfus, the bookshop assistant, by gently putting his arm round his shoulder as they watch the dancing.

View the movie as often as you like, you won't see either moment. The script was always long and so there were bound to be cuts. All of the group of friends lost major chunks of material but at least some of our stories made it to the screen. Roger isn't in it, nor is Toby Jones's bemused American tourist. Nor will you see Sally Phillips' beautifully crafted performance. She was cast as one of Hugh Grant's potential girlfriends, a hopeless dog trainer. Her wedding gift to the happy couple at the end is a puppy but, inevitably, she can't get it to "sit" on the table that's groaning with presents. It was very funny. But gone. Sally and the others had become victims of what Richard Curtis viewed as just another stage of the writing process.

He and I shared a car to Shepperton Studios one afternoon during the shoot. I asked him if the film was coming to life in the way he had anticipated way back when he was writing it. He said the script we rehearsed in that cold hall was probably the fifth or sixth official draft and at least the seventeenth draft he had written since putting pen to paper. His partner, Emma Freud (the very same Bristol graduate who had been delegated to direct *The Dream*'s lovers in my first job at Regent's Park), was a ruthless editor, coming down hard on anything that gave her a whiff of doubt about a sequence, character trait or line.

"What's initially in my head is what I write down," Richard said, "that's obviously stage one of the film. But then you cast it and you rehearse it and you start to see that you didn't need those ten lines in scene nine because the point's already been made by another character in scene seven. Then when you start shooting it changes shape again because the whole thing becomes three-dimensional and other elements – costume, set, camera – start to tell the story. Then you're into another stage of 'writing,' the editing room. Here you realise that scene seven is unnecessary because the entire content is conveyed by a single look someone gave in scene five. The audience has already got the point, so all you're doing is labouring it. And then there's the length of the whole thing. It's always too long. So you have to cut. And all too often you have to murder your darlings."

The dinner party sequence was where I got my first proper lesson in continuity. The scene culminates in a contest about who deserves the last brownie. Hugh Grant managed to turn his line about "hogging the brownie" into an innuendo that kept me amused all morning and then did a startling impression of a lizard sticking its tongue out which set me off for most of the afternoon, otherwise I don't think I would have managed the "spontaneous laughter" required whenever the 1st AD called "Action."

There is a top tip about how best to eat on camera in scenes that involve a group of people at a table: don't. Back in 1998 I was not only naive and inexperienced, I thought nothing of chomping my way through a couple of chocolate brownies at eight in the morning. The crucial Note to Self is, whatever action you do on the master shot – meaning, usually, the wider shot that becomes the template for the scene around which all the other "coverage" is based – you have to stick to it, time and time again. If on one angle you take a sip of coffee before the line "Well, Mother, there was blood everywhere" but on the second angle you take the sip after the line, you're giving the editor a headache and no choice but to use either one camera angle or the other, unless the editor thinks it helps the story that you appear incredibly thirsty by taking two sips of coffee unfeasibly close together. Commit to an action and stick to it, otherwise after the master has been established you may well have the script supervisor wagging their finger at you, getting inside your head after each take.

"You pick up the brownie with your left hand and take a bite just before your second line, then take a swig of your drink with your right hand on your third line but before you pick up the second brownie, which you also do with your right hand. You bite into it on the word 'useless' not the word 'hopeless.' And by the way, on your first line it's 'wouldn't' not 'shouldn't.'"

Moreover, scenes set around dining tables are rarely completed in one shot, and what I hadn't really taken into account on what shall henceforth be known as The Day of the Brownie was that there followed at least four other camera set-ups in which I was to feature and would have to repeat the action several times from each angle. There was the raking three-shot across Hugh, Emma and me. That's two more brownies right there and maybe four or five takes before Roger Michell was satisfied that he'd got the shot. Then a medium shot. Two more brownies, on each of the three takes. Then my close-up. Two more, times two or three. Not to mention the over-the-shoulder shot on to Julia – I got away with miming on this angle, because it was just the movement of my hand that needed to be consistent. Then there was a wide angle from another corner of the room. From each and every position of the camera, two more brownies landed on my plate. By 7 p.m. I hated the little square bastards. Never again. Except, on wrap that evening I went to a friend's for dinner and yes, you can guess what he served for dessert.

By the time it came to the dozens of dinner scenes in *Downton Abbey* I felt I had not only learned my lesson down the years but had pretty much mastered the art of eating/drinking only rarely and at precise moments of a scene, involving the minimum of fuss and mastication. Dame Maggie ate one green bean in a decade. Of course, it's also about character choice. When Shirley

MacLaine joined us on *Downton Abbey,* she decided that Mrs. Levinson couldn't get enough of the devilled kidneys that were served in one scene. She wolfed down the mushrooms that doubled for kidneys and looked decidedly queasy by lunchtime. And for me, the sausages that Lisa Heathcote the on-set caterer provided were so damn good that, provided the scene was being shot first thing, I'd skip breakfast at unit base and wait to dive into what she'd prepared for the silver dishes in the dining room. The bellows expanded again.

The exterior of Tony's restaurant was in Notting Hill itself but the interior was built at Shepperton Studios. Cost is of course everything on a movie but a major advantage of a studio build versus location is control. On location there are dozens of variables that can conspire to muck up the shot, anything from traffic that doesn't want to wait while you complete the take to passers-by who don't want to not pass by, planes overhead, drills and sirens, trains rumbling, and disgruntled neighbours increasingly fed up with having their lives disrupted for days on end. Or how about not actually being able to fit the camera in the corner of the room? In the studio there are fewer obstacles and you can remove annoying things like walls and stick a camera in their place. As long as the audience believes that the studio build is in fact what exists on the other side of the real-life front door then you're fine.

I did a day on *EastEnders* once. Having walked across the lot at Elstree to the dressing room, I got changed (own suit) and asked the assistant where filming was taking place, as I'd like to go and watch, to get myself in the zone (method acting, or wanting to gawp at some famous people, take your pick).

"In the Queen Vic pub," was the reply.

I knew where that was, I'd passed it on my way in. So back I toddled across the lot of Albert Square and quietly inched open the front door of the pub so as not to interrupt the action. What greeted me, of course, was a web of scaffolding poles and scrubland. Still, at least it proved that you can fool some of the people some of the time.

Idiot.

Through the window of Tony's restaurant in the studio the production team had constructed a brilliantly detailed replica of the junction of Golborne Road and Portobello Road. Shepperton Studios were particularly busy at the time, so the only stage available for this set was way smaller than the design required. The real depth from the window of Tony's restaurant to the buildings across the street, therefore, was impossible to replicate, there simply wasn't room. It had to be foreshortened, so the set beyond the window was an optical illusion. From inside the restaurant, the shops and houses across the street seemed to be at a distance, but in reality they were painted on a backdrop and were only a few feet away. Even the zebra crossing was a trompe l'oeil. The art department did an amazing job. As a consequence of all this shrinkage, the supporting artists had to be similarly According to Scale. No way could a 6ft 5in extra walk through the back of shot, he'd make the supposedly fully grown tree suddenly look like a sprig of parsley. The supporting artists therefore, on those "Tony's Restaurant/Interior" days, were all under five feet tall, on the call sheet billed as "Perspective Crowd." Some of the most fun days on the movie. A small set, small group of people, and smaller people having a laugh. One supporting artist, Mark, kept taking the piss out of Rhys Ifans for being so tall and demanded that he himself sit in Rhys's canvas director's chair. He kept doing pratfalls while failing to climb into it. Mark told me he'd auditioned for *Time Bandits* but sadly nothing came of it.

I am always in awe of stunt men and women. They are highly skilled and usually a little mad. I suppose it goes with the territory. Whatever extraordinarily dangerous moment the writer has come up with, it's up to the stunt co-ordinator to assess its risk and feasibility and then – because he himself is now a leathery sixty and has more metal in him than the Brooklyn Bridge – to delegate which of his nutty team is going to undertake the leap through the plate glass window, or hurl themselves down two flights of stairs. And often it runs in the family. I saw a tear in the eye of one senior stunt man as he talked with pride about his three children, two of whom had followed him into the business. Their fitness, dedication and skill, he said, were astonishing. I nodded approvingly, then asked, "And what about your third child?"

His eyes left mine and looked to a horizon of disappointment, tinged with disgust. "He plays the violin."

I don't think we actually needed a stunt person on *Notting Hill* but Emma Chambers thought we should have, so she cast me in the role of Ronnie the stunt co-ordinator, who specialised in dangerous language. Each morning Ronnie would seek her out in the make-up trailer and talk her through his risk assessment.

"Mornin', Emily."

"Morning, Ronnie."

"Me an' the team 'ave been lookin' frew scene forty-eight."

"Thank you so much."

"S'fairly straightforward this one, Emly, tubby honest wiv you. It's four sentences. Fairly standard, t'be fair."

"Oh well that doesn't sound too bad, Ronnie."

"Yerbud justasay, one of 'em's got a free-syllable word innit."

"Oh dear. Three? Has it?"

"Now, I've walked it frew wiv the team."

"Right."

"We fink it's safe bud I know how you can be wiv polysyllabubs, Emerlee, an' I only want you t'do viss if you feel compleely cumfable. We gonna put a crash mat down, obvyssly, in case you twip over a word, coz there's a few plosives before you aksharlly get to the big one. Or alternativeknee I got Francine on standby – she's licensed to do iambic pentameters and everyfin'. But supda you."

June turned into July and we approached the end of the shoot. What defines a friendship? A shared experience, yes, and chemistry of character. But then you lose touch. Inevitably. Time passes. Weeks, months, years. And then, all of a sudden, by circumstance, there you are again. You bump into each other on another job, a street corner, in the post office. And all it takes is for one of you to quote an in-joke from that once upon a time and you're off again, laughing. You're back there and right here, all at once, dancing in space and time and memory. It's not just soppy nostalgia, it's tighter than that.

Like a ring of bark.

A hug round the tree.

We had that then.

We've got this now.

It's the connection.

My friendship with Emma Chambers was like that. Years would go by and then we'd bump into each other somewhere and she'd ask me how Ronnie the text-conscious stunt man was and so out he'd pop and she'd snap her head back and laugh the Emma way, grabbing my forearm as she giggled. The last time I saw her she was dancing. With Dawn French and Trevor Peacock, as it happens, at the wrap party of the last ever episode of *The Vicar of Dibley*, in which I appeared.

Emma's heart stopped beating at the age of fifty-three. Ridiculous.

There was one last scene in Tony's restaurant still to shoot. In the story it marks the end of an era, things haven't worked out as planned and the restaurant is closing. A mood of gentle melancholia. So, Richard McCabe (Tony) and I rehearsed Roger Michell's favourite Beatles song, "Here, There and Everywhere," as the scene setter. The two of us crooning, warmingly tipsy at the piano. Neither Richard nor I are exactly known as musical performers. He, in fact, is a really good singer but rather shy about it. I, on the other hand, can't sing but refuse to believe it. So, we rehearsed doggedly once a week throughout filming in order to get it right. The night before shooting the scene Duncan Kenworthy rang.

"You and Richard have been doing brilliantly with the Beatles number."

"Thanks, Duncan. Because, between you and me, I'm not really a singer . . ."

"No, I know. I know. No, the thing is we've run into a brick wall over the rights. It's going to cost six figures to record the Beatles track in vision and, great though you two are . . ."

So, next morning we came on set and rapidly learned "Blue Moon." Roger was disappointed but not half as disappointed as Mr. McCartney would have been if he'd heard me ruining his and Mr. Lennon's song.

Ten months later the film had its premiere in London. It went down well and the atmosphere at the party afterwards, held at The Orangery in Kensington Gardens, was buoyant. I was standing with Tim McInnerny, Gina McKee and Emma Chambers when Julia Roberts came over – that smile – to say hello. Cue mutual congratulations and general fandom.

"So," she said, "you guys are coming to the New York premiere next week, right?"

It had never occurred to any of us that this might even be an option. There was a bit of foot shuffling.

"Er, no," said Tim. "It's not really . . . I mean, it hasn't been mentioned, no."

Julia's smile flickered for a moment, then resumed full floodlight.

"Don't go 'way."

And off she went. A few minutes later she reappeared with the executive producer of the film and co-boss of Working Title on her arm. He was visibly chuffed to have the star of the evening single him out for personal attention.

"Hi everyone!"

"Hi Tim!" we chorused.

"Now, Tim," said Julia, cranking up the wattage. "Just so you know. If these guys don't go to New York, I don't go to New York."

She turned her beam fully on to him. Tim Bevan may be a fine producer but he's not perhaps the world's finest actor. At any rate he wasn't that night because he failed miserably at trying to mask his discomfort, which was instantly visible on his face as the cost implications ticker-taped at speed across his frontal lobe, rapidly followed by the consequences of Julia not showing up to the US opening of the film if he said no. He had been well and truly – and elegantly – caught in a trap. The next sounds that came out of his mouth weren't so much words as a sequence of strangulated squawks.

"'Fcourse! D'lighted! Make th'arrangements first thing morning."

Julia gave him a kiss on the cheek, winked at our astonished little group, and steered Tim Bevan off into the throng.

A week later. New York. Julia had invited us Brits to a supper party at her agent's apartment off Central Park. A group of us gathered outside the hotel to hail taxis as they passed, car horns and sirens punctuating the white noise of the evening traffic. Lulu and I were with director Roger Michell. A taxi pulled up. Tim McInnerny, his partner Annie and another couple got in, just as two men were approaching along the pavement, one in his fifties, another handsome and way younger. As the cab pulled off I noticed Tim and Annie pointing frantically in my direction, as if my flies were undone. They weren't.

"Roger!" said the older man. "What are the chances?"

"I can't believe it," smiled Roger, and then, turning to me and introducing the man, "This is my American agent. Hugh, Lulu." Handshakes.

"Great to meet you," replied Roger's agent. "And this is—"

CAR HORN. The name of the younger man was lost in the Manhattan rush hour. No matter. He shook my hand. I noticed he had three books about the history of New York under his arm.

"We've just been kicking some ideas around with Marty," continued the agent.

"Yeah!" said the Young Man brightly, flicking a forelock of boyishly blond hair over his strong and tiringly handsome forehead. "Hey, take a look at this Polaroid. Here's me an'—"

"Christ, that's Martin Scorsese!" I ejaculated, realising that the photo Flop Hair was holding featured one of the most revered movie directors of the last half century.

"Sure it is!" laughed Mop Head. "Just me and him goofin' around! Like, who's got the better 'brows, man?"

Martin Scorsese and the Irritating Wannabe, in front of a costume rail. How *dare* he refer to this Living God of Cinema as if he was a loser in a mono-brow contest? By the time we got in our cab I'd really had enough of the level of – quite frankly – disrespect the Little Shit had shown towards one of the titans of the film industry. And as we sat back in the yellow taxi I said as much to my wife, Roger, the taxi driver and anyone in New York who was prepared to listen through the open window.

"Hugh?" asked Roger, gently.

"WHAT? I mean, *honestly*. Did that boy have *any* idea who he was laughing at? Martin *Scorsese*, for heaven's sake. These young people. Absolutely *no* respect."

Roger's calm voice once again: "Hugh, I don't think you need to worry about Martin being offended by Leonardo DiCaprio."

29

Pussycat Pinter

"I've got the readthrough for this film tomorrow," I said. "What if Harold Pinter says hello to me?"

Summer 1998, and I was having Sunday lunch with the theatre director Joe Harmston at his home in West Sussex. Joe and I had first worked together when he was assistant director on Ronald Harwood's play *The Handyman* at Chichester, in which Frank Finlay played the title role. Joe had recently directed Pinter in his own plays *The Lover* and *The Collection*, at the Donmar in London.

"Harold? Oh, he's a pussycat. Just tell him I tried to poison you with my cooking, chat about cricket and you'll be fine."

The following morning the cast of *Mansfield Park* gathered for the readthrough in a church hall in Hammersmith. It was the familiar ritual of nods and welcomes and looking for your assigned place at one of the trestle tables.

I was at the sanctuary of the urn, pouring hot water over something I pretended I wanted, when I sensed a presence at my shoulder. It was Harold Pinter himself, selecting synthetic equipment for a drink. I introduced myself. With a peremptory grunt he snatched a smile and a plastic teaspoon. Now was my chance. I plunged into cheery.

"That, er, that – ha! – that Joe Harmston tried to poison me at lunch yesterday," I quipped, taking my first sip with confidence. Ow. Too soon, too hot. Ow. *Shit.*

Pinter looked at me, serious. "Why on earth would he do that?" he said, flicking down the black lever on the urn to fill his cup.

There was a menacing pause. I know it was a menacing pause because the man I was trying to engage in conversation pretty much invented them, at least as far as post-war theatre was concerned. But I wasn't giving in and deftly changed tack, to cricket. It was the last day of England against South Africa at Lord's.

"So! Ha-ha . . . I wonder . . . who's going to win the Test then, eh?" I underlined my chuckle with a little rise on to tiptoes and a twitch of the head as I took another sip. *Ach.* Still hot.

Pinter glanced at me again with benign distaste. "How can I *possibly* know that? They're still playing." And off he went to take his seat.

In 1814 *Mansfield Park* became the third of Jane Austen's novels to be published, after *Sense and Sensibility* and *Pride and Prejudice,* and was by far the most popular in her lifetime. Our 1998 film version was the vision of the Canadian film maker Patricia Rozema. The story follows the progress of Fanny Price, who comes to live with her socially superior relatives the Bertrams at Mansfield Park. It starred Frances O'Connor as Fanny and the aforementioned pussycat Harold Pinter as the imposing Sir Thomas Bertram. I played Mr. Rushworth, a small part with a big wig.

Having read the script, I started on the book but gave up trying to track the differences between the two. There comes a point in doing even basic research like reading the original bloody story where you have to shrug your shoulders and admit that if it's not in the script and not worth fighting to include, then you might as well just get on with it. Patricia was directing her own screenplay, which was "freely adapted" from Jane Austen's novel. Through her lens the story was reimagined as a critique on slavery and also explored, for instance, the sexual awakenings of the heroine. I scoured the novel for sapphic titbits but to no avail.

As soon as a contemporary writer, classic novel at their side, cracks their knuckles and boots up their laptop, it's a sure sign that a distortion of the artist's original intentions is about to take place. It is inevitable. As you begin to reassign the story for radio, stage or screen, the source material is by definition altered as it takes on a new shape in a new medium. Shifts of emphasis are magnified by choices to do with design, say. We shot *Mansfield Park* largely at Kirby Hall in Northamptonshire. Several rooms had walls whose plasterwork was stripped back to the brickwork, a level of public decay the successful merchant of the novel Sir Thomas Bertram would not have countenanced. But it suited Patricia's commentary on the fabric of society. She also thought Embeth Davidtz, playing the vivacious Mary Crawford, would look chic in a little black number, despite costume designer Andrea Galer explaining to her that women in Britain at the turn of the eighteenth century wore black when in mourning, not when enjoying the gaiety of a ball.

In any adapter's hands the original text becomes a springboard, an inspiration for an entirely new creative exercise. There are always those who get their knickers in a twist about a stage or screen version not being true to the original – well of course it's not. The original is a book.

Guy Andrews' wonderfully inventive mini-series *Lost in Austen*, in which I played Mr. Bennet, took the intimacy of the relationship between reader and book to a whole new level. Amanda Price is a twenty-first-century girl obsessed with Jane Austen's *Pride and Prejudice*. One night she meets Elizabeth Bennet, the heroine of the novel, in her bathroom. Amanda then steps through a door and into the novel. The story explores the perils of tinkering with a well-structured and much-loved plot.

Before it aired in the autumn of 2008 there were murmurings from the press and the guardians of the Austen flame about the travesty that was going to befall the work of Saint Jane. In fact, Guy's adoration of Austen shone through in the character of his heroine, played with gorgeous wit and warmth by Jemima Rooper. It simply took the game we all play when reading a good novel – I love this world so much I actually want to live in it – to its logical conclusion. He placed a true fan in the middle of the story and watched what happened next. The result struck a chord with audiences, who at the time were so keen to escape the reality of the unfolding financial crisis that they were more than happy to suspend their disbelief. It would be a curmudgeonly Austen fan indeed who could not admire the adapter's intention of celebrating the authentic material, not traducing it.

Shooting this mini-series made me think about the "knowability" of an author. Does or should our knowledge of an author's life affect our appreciation of the literature they produce? A question to be posed about any artist. If we were to discover that Leonardo da Vinci was in fact an axe-wielding serial killer, how would it affect our appreciation of the *Mona Lisa*? And should it? A knowledge of authorship enhances our understanding in some ways, but also sways our appreciation of the art itself. We know so little of Jane Austen's true biography that her books have been left to speak for themselves. If we go to an art gallery, do we need information about the author to appreciate the work? Or if the only way we *can* understand a work is by knowing about its creator's background, or thanks to a written intention on the wall by its side, does it diminish its aesthetic quality? Conversely, are some books or plays brought before the world simply because their author is who they are, rather than because the work is any good? Eight hundred words, on my desk by the end of morning break tomorrow, please.

*

During the filming of *Mansfield Park,* while I would never say I found Harold Pinter to be a pussycat, he did morph from a lion who could rip your head off into, perhaps, a dozing tiger, exotic and purring in repose but still not to be messed with.

One afternoon between set-ups, Harold, Sheila Gish (who played Mrs. Norris) and I were sitting in canvas set chairs next to the sound trolley on the lawn at Kirby Hall. The lighting team were assembling a huge silk screen to shade the lawn from direct sunlight. It was going to be a while. I was leafing through a copy of *Private Eye.*

"Oh go on, Hugh, read out a funny story," said Sheila.

Suddenly the tiger stirred and, leaning forward round Sheila, pointed at me with a forefinger of warning.

"No. Don't," snarled Harold.

"Why on earth not?" asked Sheila.

His eyes were hooded, his voice dark, sentences coming out in staccato bursts.

"I'll tell you why, Sheila.

Years ago, when Antonia and I first got together,

a journalist – from that, that rag – wrote a piece about us.

Snide. Nasty piece.

Some time afterwards we were invited to one of these dinner party things.

Notting Hill.

We walked in.

Noticed this journalist,

among the guests

in the drawing room.

I tensed up.

Antonia clocked who I was looking at, grabbed my arm and said, 'Don't, Harold. Just don't.'

So.

I let it go.

Went in for dinner.

Everything passed off fine.

Ate and so on.

Then afterwards we go back into the drawing room for coffee.

They have coffee at these things, y'see.

And I'm standing by the mantelpiece chatting to someone.

And this journalist

comes over.

Glances out the window and he says,

'Excuse me, Mr. Pinter. Is that your rather lovely red Merc I noticed parked outside?'

And I said, 'Fuck off, you CUNT.'

Which I thought was pretty good!"

Harold broke into a grin of satisfaction, which developed into a huge guffaw.

It was the first time I had seen him laugh.

30

Below the Title

Some actors are brilliant at being an orange on demand, in front of a complete stranger. I admit I am not one of them. Advert auditions are just not my forte. For a while I gave them my best shot, turning up to cattle calls with a bunch of other blokes of roughly the same age and shape, most of us looking like we were hovering at an STD clinic. The nadir came when I traipsed to a venue in Westbourne Park one afternoon for a 2:30 audition. It was in the offices of a converted factory – utilitarian, a nod to art deco, whitewashed brick walls, exposed pipes, wire mesh windows on the doors, long stone corridors. Utterly soulless and therefore bang on message for the purpose in hand.

The assistant didn't look up as I forced open the massively heavy spring door. Three other patients on chairs around the perimeter of the windowless ante-room. The parquet floor looked good and solid. They knew how to build, back in the day.

"Take a form. Fill it in." She was sitting at a table in the middle of the room, studying a magazine. The closed door to the audition room behind her.

"Thanks," I said. "Can I borrow a pen?"

The look she gave me. Impossibly long, decorated finger nails that curled back on themselves. Definitely not a typist. "But I need my pen."

"I haven't got one on me."

The suck of the teeth. The handover of the biro. "I want it back, though."

"Well, yes. And thank you."

I sat down on one of the grey plastic stacking chairs, nodding a smile at Chlamydia, Gonorrhoea and Crabs. It was 2:10 p.m. I started to fill in the form. Name, age, height, weight, the usual. Then another standard question, about whether or not I had done any commercials in the last twelve months and, in particular, any that might conflict with the product under consideration today. I racked my brains. Let me think . . . lemmy think, lemmy think. No, no, to the best of my knowledge in the last year I had not taken part in any commercials, no, and definitely not a single one involving toilet paper. "None" I wrote confidently, dotting the full stop with a flourish before handing back the pen. The Claw took it without looking up and continued her Word Search.

I resumed my seat, studying first the ceiling and then my colleagues. Chlamydia was in whispered conversation with Crabs, so I nodded hello again to Gonorrhoea, a roly-poly man with a beard in a shell suit.

"What time you in?" he asked, nodding towards the door, the other side of which lay a hideous examination and our futures.

"Two thirty."

"Ha! Good luck with that. I'm two twenty."

"Well that's still" – watch check – "that's still eight minutes, so . . ."

"Yeah, but he's ten past," he continued, indicating Crabs, bodybuilding days on the wane, bursting out of his Nirvana T-shirt and not in a good way.

"And I'm two o'clock," chipped in Chlamydia. Big chunky chap, denim dungarees.

Mum and Dad – JP and Pat – newly engaged, 1951.

Dad, Nigel, Mum, Clare and a wannabe astronaut, Christmas 1969.

My outfit was made out of something that smelled awful and made me retch. The helmet had a green visor which broke off on Christmas night. By Boxing Day I'd decided not to sign up for the space programme.

Sunday lunch in Chetnole, Dorset, 1971.

Nigel let me have the beard he'd worn the night before as the Doctor in *King Lear* in the Sherborne school play. I kept it in a box for months.

Ernie's Incredible Illucinations by Alan Ayckbourn. Dulwich Prep, 1972.

L-R: Richard Sparkes, HB, Dominic Christie-Brown, Peter Cookson, Andrew Langford.

Water-damaged snap of my first job – understudying Ralph Fiennes as Lysander at the Open Air Theatre, Regent's Park, 1986.

Dear Michael
Use your eyes.
Keep your neck back
Don't make little gestures
Keep a sense of legato
He's a young Count with
an O in it remember

Feel it
Mark the changes of thought
Listen
Be clear –
Be confident
If you remember any of
these you'll be a good boy Love LO

First night note from Laurence Olivier to Michael Byrne when he played Claudio in *Much Ado* at the Old Vic in 1965.

Dick Whittington – Colchester Mercury, 1988.

In front of the Chorus: L-R Sian Howard, Susannah Jupp, HB, Derek Wright, Gary Sharkey.

"My name's Sarah the Cook … but you can call me anytime!"

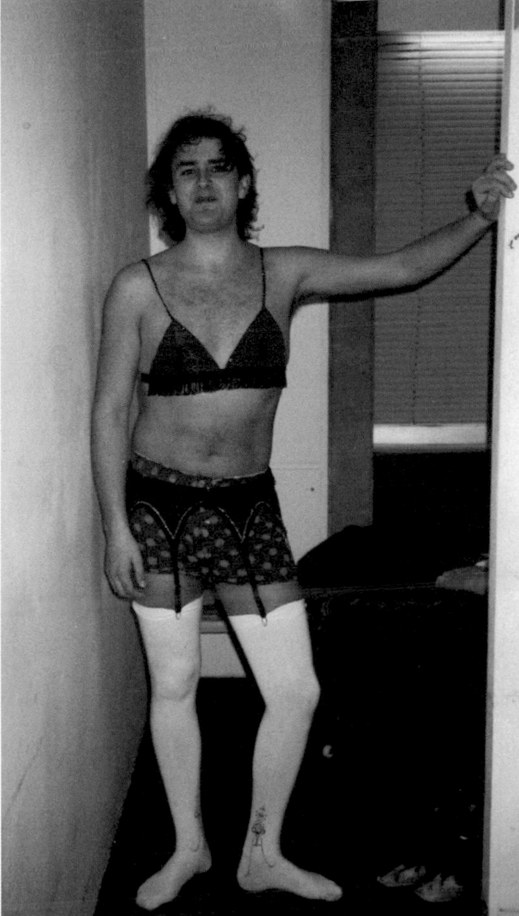

Charles Surface in *School for Scandal* at Olivier Theatre, National Theatre, 1990.

My stockings kept falling down and the elastic garters employed to hold them up cut off the blood supply to my thighs, so I asked the Wardrobe department to make me some simple suspenders. They opted for the full set.

New boy at the Royal Shakespeare Company, Stratford, 1991.

Anthony Ward's costume design for Sir Samuel Hearty in *The Virtuoso*, RSC Swan Theatre, Stratford, 1991.

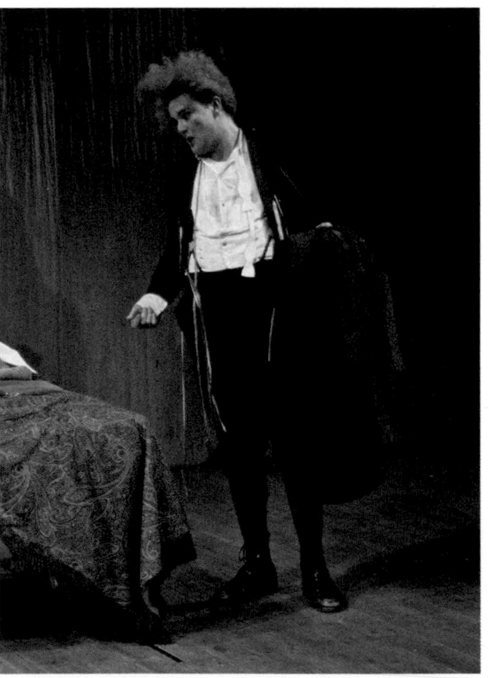

. . . and the end result.

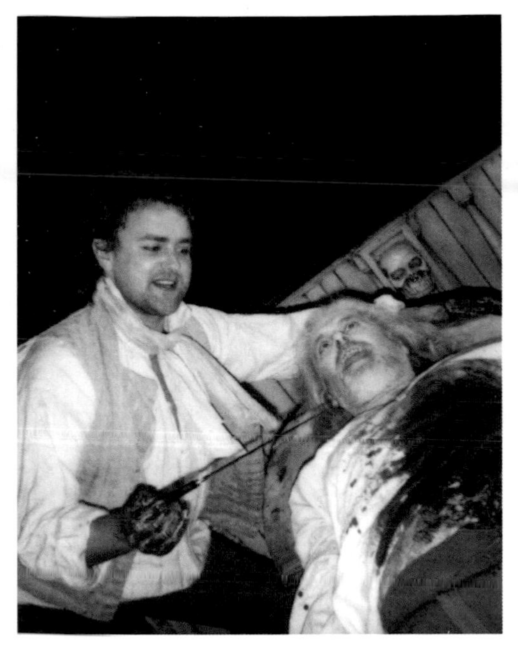

With John Cleese in my first film, *Frankenstein*, directed by Kenneth Branagh.

Bloody wasp.

Playing Dick Dudgeon, with Helen McCrory as Judith Anderson, in *The Devil's Disciple*, Olivier Theatre, 1994.

The cast of *Habeas Corpus* by Alan Bennett, directed by Sam Mendes. Donmar Warehouse, 1996.

Front row L-R: Sarah Woodward, Natalie Walter, John Padden, Nicholas Woodeson. Second row L-R: Imelda Staunton, Brenda Blethyn, Stewart Permutt. Third row: Jason Watkins, Celia Imrie. Back row L-R: Michael Haslam, HB, Jim Broadbent.

Lulu and me on the bridge in Stedham, West Sussex – newly engaged – 1998.

Notting Hill, 1998.

L-R: HB, Emma Chambers, Julia Roberts, Hugh Grant, Tim McInnerny, Gina McKee.

Clive Coote

█ Highbury New Park
London N5 2HG
█

Thursday

Dear Hugh

Many thanks for your letter, it was very kind of you. We probably are fucking barking mad not to cast you, and when we end up casting some talentless useless charmless fucker who screws up all the jokes, and the programme is consequently a stinking piece of garbage that ITV are too embarassed to broadcast, except maybe at four in the morning and it's only watched by four insomniacs and some pissed-up night watchmen, none of whom bother watching it to the end, and even my *family* don't bother watching it and my girlfriend is so embarrassed that she finishes with me, and I never get another writing job and have my pens and word-processor confiscated, and get drummed-out of the Writer's Guild, and end up drunk and alone and dying in some gutter, and my feeble dying words are 'H-u-g-h', then it will be our fault and our fault alone, and you can say I told you so and laugh quietly to yourself and pour another glass of fine wine.

Before that happens, however, I'd just like to say that you are an extremely fine and funny actor, and that I'm extremely flattered that you were so kind and passionate about the script. I hope that we do get a chance to work on something in the future, providing of course I ever *do* work again after this almighty casting fuck-up. In the meantime, you are perfectly entitled to smack me in the face if we ever meet, and that goes for Tom and Christine too. Though watch out for Christine, as she spits and kicks.

Best wishes

David Nicholls.

Having been turned down for a role in his mini-series *I Saw You* in 2001, I wrote to the screenwriter David Nicholls to tell him he'd made a catastrophic mistake. I still can't believe I did that. This was his reply. Thank God he has a sense of humour.

Make-up test for *Iris*. The only shot of Jim Broadbent and me together – we played Younger and Older versions of Iris Murdoch's husband, John Bayley. Pinewood Studios, 2001.

With Felix, reading scripts. West Sussex, 2002.

On my knees, signing away seven years of my life to CBS. 2005.

On the back lot at Warner Bros with my long-suffering agent Donna French, while shooting David E Kelly's pilot, *Legally Mad*, 2009.

"So what's the hold-up?" I asked.

"They're still at lunch," said Gonorrhoea, raising an eyebrow with meaning.

Well, lunch for a bunch of advertising executives at the expense of a toilet paper manufacturer – what's not to like? I began to fume inwardly. My fellow sufferers and I sat there for at least another fifteen minutes before footsteps, voices and laughter could be heard swaggering slowly along the corridor. The heavy door swung open.

"Fuck this door's heavy!" laughed STD Doctor #1 as he held it open for STD Doctor #2, who in turn stood aside out of deference to a third man, presumably the visiting proctologist who had paid for lunch, who stumbled in and headed through the door into the examination room.

"All right, lovely?" said Doctor #1, smiling boozily at Nurse Ratched With Talons. As he followed after Doctor #2 he let the door go and it thudded shut. The door opposite closed too, laughter echoing from inside the clinic.

Chlamydia stood up.

"Wait till you're called," said Nurse Ratched.

"But it's two thirty. They're here. I was due in at two."

She tapped a talon on her table. Chlamydia was about to sit down when the door to the examination room opened and Doctor #2 poked his head out.

"Less be having you then!" he slurred, and retreated. More laughter from within.

Clutching his form, Chlamydia entered.

I sat there reflecting on life and its meaning. About the confluence of events that had led to this moment. The childhood, the schooldays, innocent dreams and pleasures of being on stage, the moments of good fortune and the setbacks, navigating the path into adulthood, into a profession in which Rejection and the word No are, statistically speaking, more likely to feature than Acceptance and Yes! And just then, into this vortex of metaphysical contemplation, came a sound. At first it was a distant rumble, gradually growing in volume and proximity into a huge roar. It was coming, I realised, from the adjacent audition room, as chunky Chlamydia man in the blue dungarees began acting out what was being asked of him by the drunk advertising people. I can only imagine what the instruction had been but when you bear in mind that the four of us lined up to audition were all on the large side and the product was toilet paper, you only have to add the word "woods" and you're pretty much there.

Suddenly, an epiphany. Saul on the road to Damascus. The swirling cottonwool clouds in my brain parted, revealing a benign figure in a white beard and robes, solemnly intoning the words, "Hugh, Hugh. You too have the power to say No."

My breathing calmed in an instant. As if lifted by unseen hands I got up, floated over to the table and, borrowing a line from Peter Cook, said to the assistant, "I'm so sorry, I've just remembered I'm meant to be watching television this afternoon."

And with a thumbs up to my fellow actors, I pulled open the door to the corridor. It was as light as a feather.

It was while wearing this new armour of The Power of No that I answered the front door to the postman and signed for a large manila envelope. It was a script for a film called *Iris*, to be directed by Richard Eyre. The role, said the covering note, was Young John. I immediately sat down at the kitchen table and started to read . . .

Young John cycling down a hill with Young Iris. A carefree couple feeling the wind in their hair. I got to the end of the first scene, turned the page and read "CUT TO: John and Iris, many years later."

One bloody scene? I knew exactly the correct response to this. Puffing out my chest until it touched the breastplate of my armour, I picked up the phone.

"What do you mean, no?" said my agent a minute later.

"One scene? I mean, come *on*," I replied.

"Hugh, have you actually read the whole script?"

As she continued to talk – "You haven't, have you?" – I flicked on a few pages and then on some more, soon discovering that the story cut back and forth between the two timelines.

"Ever since that audition for bog roll, Hugh" – she was now coming to the end of a quite long and exasperated speech – "you've been an absolute arse."

A few days later I was in Richard Eyre's study at his house in Brook Green. He showed me a photograph of John Bayley as a young don at Oxford. A tall man in glasses with a slender face, wearing a tweed cap.

"I can absolutely see the likeness!" said Richard. "Can't you?"

I absolutely couldn't. "Yes. Absolutely. It's uncanny."

Well, I wanted the job. More than any other I had ever been up for, in fact. By now I had of course been through the script several times and knew it to be one of the best I had ever read. Intelligent, funny, heart-breaking, the story charting the relationship between the novelist Iris Murdoch and the academic John Bayley. The 1950s timeline explored the early days of their partnership, her sexual wisdom and his naivety; the latter years focused on Iris's decline into dementia. It was a love story set against the backdrop of Alzheimer's, the bitterest irony of all being the diminution of everyday language in a person for whom words meant everything.

Jim Broadbent and Judi Dench had already been cast as the senior versions of John and Iris. Richard said it would be a couple of weeks before I heard anything while he and his producers zeroed in on their Young Iris. The following week I learned that Kate Winslet was now on board and, true to his word, Richard rang me a week later. But it was not the phone call I was expecting.

"I can see no one else playing Young John in this film but you. However, our American friends feel they don't know you."

"They mean I'm not famous like the other three."

"Well . . ."

"They're right, I'm not famous. I can't even get a table at McDonald's."

"I've never asked this of an actor before," he continued, "but if you're prepared to do it, I know things will turn out fine."

He explained that on the following Thursday morning the key cast were gathering at his house to go through the script. Some of the producers would be there too. In short, he was asking me to audition at the readthrough. I had by now melted down my Power of No armour into a sensible paperweight, to prevent opportunities from blowing away.

"OK, but can I have a session with Jim to talk about how he's approaching the character of John Bayley? His stutter and so on."

"Unfortunately, he's in Italy shooting *Gangs of New York* with Leonardo DiCaprio." Of course, *now* those history books Mop Head had under his arm made sense. "Jim's flying in Thursday morning and coming straight from the airport."

Make it easy for me, why don't you.

"How about Kate, can't I get an hour with her?"

"Kate has childcare things this week. She can only join us on the day."

I could count my options on the fingers of no hands.

Thursday came, I arrived early. Richard led me downstairs to the empty kitchen where a long table groaned with croissants and fruit. No sooner had we exchanged pleasantries than he disappeared to answer the doorbell. Jim's legs appeared, descending the staircase. At least in him I knew I had an ally. We had appeared together in *Habeas Corpus* at the Donmar.

"Hullow, Hugh!" he said.

"Quick! Quick! How are you doing the stutter?"

"Haven't you heard der tape?"

"Tape?"

Turns out he had a recording of John Bayley from a BBC radio programme. I gritted my teeth. Great. Coulda been useful.

Doorbell. It was Judi.

"Hello!" she said, putting her bag down on the table. "This is going to be fun, isn't it?"

Not for me it wasn't, but I made all the right noises.

Doorbell. Producer Robert Fox. Doorbell. Kate Winslet.

"Hello, Kate, I'm Hu—"

Doorbell. Producer Scott Rudin. Burly New Yorker, unshaven, glasses, gravelly voice booming into his mobile, seemingly even when the lack of signal in the basement cut him off.

We settled at the table and the readthrough began. As I spoke before Jim it wasn't as if I could copy his tone, so I played the lines of the first scene in a vague flurry of nervous energy as the young couple bicycled down the hill, adrenalin pumping. Once Jim and Judi's scenes kicked in I gradually shifted my voice to match Jim's pitch and timbre, accentuating the stammer a little more than he did – a pointer towards the younger John not yet having learned how to control it.

Jim and Judi gave astonishing performances, even here at a kitchen table in W14, as the curtains closed on Iris's life. As the rest of us were drying our eyes, Judi chirped, "Oooh goody, lunch!" Richard offered wine and the company relaxed into conversation. But I was far from relaxed and couldn't get out of there fast enough.

However long it takes to get from Hammersmith to where the A3 crosses over the M25 is how long it took for the phone call to come, putting me out of my misery. I pulled off at the next junction, found an off licence and bought three bottles of champagne.

The next obstacle was rehearsals, or rather the lack of them, at least for me and Jim. By now I had read the trilogy of books on which the script was based and had listened to the tape of John Bayley's voice as an older man but that wasn't going to be enough. If you are trying to give credibility to the idea that you and another actor are playing the same person, albeit at different stages of their lives, you want a nod in the direction towards, not impersonation, but at least a shared DNA. But because of Jim's schedule there simply wasn't time for us to get together before he started shooting his scenes with Judi, which preceded my scenes with Kate. So, I asked Richard if I could watch some rushes of Jim in character. The message came back that the executives financing the whole shebang were adamant that no one was allowed to see any rushes, outside the top tier of production. It sounded bonkers to me that anyone on the team would want to prevent one of its key actors from developing his performance to the best of his creative ability. Richard thought the same.

One day we were at Pinewood Studios to test out the water tank for the swimming scenes. "Don't tell anyone," Richard murmured, surreptitiously palming me a plastic bag wrapped round an object the size of a book, as if it was a kilo of Class A drugs. Later that night, I drew the sitting room curtains in my flat, turned the lights down low and, checking the cat wasn't looking, inserted the VHS tape into the machine. Squiggles and numbers and scratches popped on to the TV screen as the previous day's rushes flickered into view. Finally, this was my chance to watch Jim at work. Except, as it turned out, of the six minutes of footage the first five were close-ups of Judi. However, Jim did feature in one shot. A wide angle as he walked across a supermarket car park with a trolley. And that was it. That was the sole visual reference on which, if I was to have any chance at verisimilitude, I was to base my performance.

About six weeks after we'd finished filming Richard rang me from the cutting room.

"We've just started to intercut the two storylines, from the younger generation to the older and back again. I was so nervous. What if we took one look and thought, 'This isn't credible, the audience isn't going to buy this in a million years'?"

"And?" I asked.

There was a pause and a sigh. "It works."

*

There is one scene in the film which was a masterclass in screen acting. I could have chosen several examples from Jim and Judi's scenes but obviously I wasn't involved in those. Towards the end of the film, after Young John has come to terms with Young Iris's liberated attitude to sex, she decides to tell him about her past, in full. John asks if he should take notes, only half in jest. He is unschooled in the ways of the world and vulnerable. Carefully but deliberately Iris proceeds to list the men she has slept with. One in particular, a soldier, whose proposal of marriage she turned down, went off to fight in the Second World War and never came back.

There were two cameras on Kate, side by side, one a medium shot, the other a close-up. On the first take, as she came to the passage about the soldier, Kate welled up with the emotion of the memory. Tears flowed freely as she revealed Iris's regret for having let him go to his death without her love in his heart. Off camera, I found it deeply affecting to watch. As the speech came to a close and just as Richard was about to call "Cut," Kate suddenly said, "Keep it running, keep it running, let's go again. Can I just get make-up in quickly?"

With the atmosphere delicately poised, her make-up artist nipped in with a tissue, dabbed away the tear stains, added a bit of powder, and away. Kate went back to the top of the speech and did it again. But this time through, she buried the emotion entirely. It was there in the words and in her eyes but there were no tears. Instead, the memory was something Iris had learned to deal with. If anything, the experience had helped strengthen her character's resolve to embrace life. Again, it was superb and powerful to watch. But again . . .

"Keep it running, keep it running, re-set," she said.

And with the crew still in absolute silence, back Kate went to the beginning of the speech. This third time through she found yet another tone, seemingly calm and matter of fact as she talked of her lovers, of Harry and Roger, of Oscar and Tom, but then suddenly the memory of the lost soldier caught her by surprise, pricking her eyes, an emotion Iris immediately pushed back down, determined to overcome.

"Cut!" called Richard.

On set that day was David Thompson, head of BBC Films. "If I could only take that footage," he said, "and show it to every drama student in the country . . ."

Each take was different, each totally believable. But as Richard said as we wrapped that evening, he now had a problem.

"How on earth do I choose which take to use?"

One surreal footnote to the whole experience came in a sequence when John calls on Iris at her digs. From the street he sees through the window that she already has male company. Against his better judgement he tiptoes inside, inches open her bedroom door and there spies Iris now astride someone on the bed, clearly the young man. John retreats awkwardly.

When it came to shooting the scene, something had happened to the Young Man – can't remember what. Anyway, there now was no Young Man on the Bed so Kate, ever practical and unfussy, called the 1st AD over and asked him if he would be so good as to lie down and let her clamber on top of him so they could complete the scene and we could all go home. Nothing to worry about, after all, his face wouldn't be seen anyway. Martin Harrison went bright red and mumbled something about having to call the shots. The 3rd AD was equally abashed. Eventually the tiny scene was completed and without too much further fuss. But I have to admit that the first time I watched the finished film, it was a slightly odd sensation to see myself as Young John peek through the crack in the door, knowing that the Young Man on the Bed . . . was also me.

Iris was my first experience of the significance of billing. The opening titles of *Monty Python and the Holy Grail* include a riff on the subject, via the means of Scandinavian subtitles initially involving a moose and eventually some llamas. This was a film I watched on a loop as a kid, so I have always looked out for Ands, Withs, Also Withs and And Introducings in movies and chuckled at the oddness of them all.

As negotiations for the *Iris* contract were nearing completion, my agent rang to say there was a problem over billing. I immediately fell into quoting Python. "Wik, alsø wik, alsø alsø wik?" I joked.

"What?"

"A møøse once bit my sister."

She was as baffled as you probably are. (Just look it up on YouTube. Trust me, it's funny.)

To this day I am not sure of the ins and outs of it all but the gist of the issue was that it had already been contractually agreed that only Jim Broadbent and Judi Dench would be above the title. Kate Winslet had come late to the party and frankly no one knew who I was anyway. Understandably, with Kate's standing in the industry, not to mention her prominence in the film, her agent was having none of this. My agent then argued that if Kate was to be above the title, then it made no sense to airbrush me – in a role of equal prominence – from the poster. So there was something of an impasse: between the powers-that-be saying they weren't budging, Kate's agent saying well in that case she's not doing it, and my agent being told if I wanted to withdraw that would be fine and perhaps Scott Rudin's rumoured preferred choice of Jonny Lee Miller might be available, take it or leave it, ducky. So, in the traditional showbiz spirit of beggars not being able to choose, we signed and left the grown-ups to bicker about the poster. In the end the marketing and publicity boasted three leading actors, or rather two *and* Kate Winslet. I wasn't even alsø alsø wik.

There was an interesting upshot to this. A few film journalists got confused. Let's not forget, they are busy people. Their job is to watch umpteen movies each week, scribble notes in the dark, read the press pack, interview the actors and listen to them droning on about how much they loved working with their co-stars (because they're contractually obliged not to say anything derogatory about anyone on the film in perpetuity), then write an article to a deadline, rinse and repeat. Inevitably they take short-cuts and sometimes don't absorb every last detail. Like who's actually in the film. The journalist from the *Baltimore Sun* wrote:

> All the performances in *Iris* are so persuasive that I rushed from a Manhattan screening room to a cafe interview with Broadbent under the impression that Broadbent played Bayley as a youthful man, too. Even though I knew that Kate Winslet and not Dench played the younger Murdoch, there was such a continuity of expression between the young and old Bayley that I couldn't wait to ask Broadbent how he pulled it off.
>
> "There are two actors," he said, setting me straight immediately, and kindly adding, "Don't worry; you're not the first." (Hugh Bonneville plays the young Bayley.)

In fact, it worked both ways. Years later, Richard Eyre told me about the film's composer, the late James Horner. "The whole time we were working on the music he thought that the actor playing young and old John was the same person. And he thought the name of the actor was Hugh Bonneville."

The film got a positive reception and significant praise for the actors (I have always been surprised that it wasn't more widely lauded for Richard and Charles Wood's wise, deeply humane screenplay). In fact, all three actors "above the title" were nominated for Oscars and all four of us for BAFTAs, Judi and Jim as Leading Actors, Kate and I as Supporting. It was my first nomination for anything, so it was of course an exciting evening. Black tie, free plastic bottle of water, the works. The envelope moment came.

"And the BAFTA for Best Supporting Actor goes to . . ."

It's true, at moments like this you really can hear your heart thump – *ba-dum, ba-dum, ba-dum.*

"Jim Broadbent for *Moulin Rouge!*"

Yes, Jim was being greedy that year, up for Leading Actor in *Iris,* too. Was I surprised that he won? No. Nor was I surprised when he went on to win the Oscar for *Iris* – albeit as Best Supporting Actor, strangely.

Was I happy about my BAFTA nomination? Do bears shit in the woods?

31

Impact

I've come to believe that in your early twenties you know everything and by the time you reach forty you haven't got a clue. It was certainly true in my case. Having auditioned for Bristol Old Vic Drama School and failed (idiots), I was offered a place at Webber Douglas and took it before I had the chance to fail my second audition at RADA. I may have just left Cambridge with a "Desmond" – a 2:2, as in Archbishop Desmond Tutu – but at this point I was pretty confident about life, its meaning and everything there was to know about theatre. I had read Simon Callow's book *On Acting* and hoovered up Stanislavski and Brecht, tried to read about Laban, polished off any number of biographies and was pretty much an aficionado. I deigned to visit theatres from time to time that summer of 1985 but honestly the lack of diaphragmatic breathing in some of these so-called professionals, and that production of *The Seagull* was passable but, really, the actioning, or evident lack of it, from Konstantin was unforgiveable.

I was a right know-it-all.

So it was in this spirit that I grudgingly accepted a friend's last-minute spare ticket to the Barbican to see Yet Another RSC

Production. I had been to a fair few in the last couple of years and, yes, many of them were fine to good, but I wasn't sure I needed another one, thank you, Tim. You can only eat so much ice cream, y'know. He then said he'd buy the ice creams, so I said I'd go. I didn't even ask what the show was, I just turned up. I knew the play, of course, but for some reason – probably because I had at least done *some* work for my finals – I had not tracked or even heard about this particular production. The lights went down and out of the darkness a black spider scuttled on to the stage.

"Now is the winter of our discontent . . ." began the six-legged creature, which I now realised was a man on crutches, his draping Tudor sleeves completing the optical illusion, "made glorious summer by this sun of York."

Within twenty seconds my thumb had, as it were, crept into my mouth. It was as if I was back at Greenwich Theatre, as a kid, watching the Firebird, or some other fantastical creation, sweeping me away into a story, making me forget about anything and everything else. All thoughts of breathing techniques and stagecraft vanished. This weird, twisted, funny, horrible man was telling me how wicked he was and how dastardly he was going to be. It was one of the most electric stage performances I had ever witnessed.

I've written only a handful of fan letters in my life, and one was to Antony Sher for that performance as Richard III. I didn't just congratulate him; as well as asking him about the genesis of his thrilling book about creating the character, *Year of the King*, I thanked him for reminding me what theatre can be.

Another fan letter was to the actor Iain Glen. He and I were first cast together in *Impact*, a real page-turner of a drama produced by Company Pictures for ITV. The story centred around Iain's character, Marcus Hodge, heading up a trio of air accident investigators, the other two being Sarah Parish and me. I played Phil Gorman, metallurgy expert, or something butch and intelligent like that. In the story, Iain's estranged daughter is due to fly over from Louisville, Kentucky, to visit him in the UK. The airliner explodes over a field in England and, yes, you guessed it, Marcus and his team end up investigating the debris, uncertain whether or not the girl was actually on the plane. High stakes, high drama.

The costume designer went to town making us look like action heroes. T-shirts and leather jackets, each of us with a natty hold-all known as a Go Bag, pre-packed and ready to grab and run with whenever the call came. We were gonna be as cool and slick as an SAS unit. Iain, Sarah and I were sent off to Farnborough, to spend a day with real-life air accident investigators. The first thing that struck me about Pete and his colleagues was that they wore quite a lot of grey. He himself had on a grey suit, white socks and grey slip-on shoes. He spoke in a very measured flat voice, the tone in which I imagine air traffic controllers are trained to talk: calm, unflappable, there's nothing to see here, and if there is, I've seen it all before anyway. What you might call grey. Brilliantly efficient in a crisis, catastrophically dull at parties. The bottom line was there was absolutely nothing SAS about Pete or his team.

Real life can be such a let-down.

Pete showed us into a huge aircraft hangar where bits of buckled planes were laid out across the floor of the vast space, taped off into separate areas, marking each tragic incident. Mangled engines, propellers bent out of shape, smashed cockpit windscreens. He talked us through the painstaking methods used to piece together the events leading up to an accident, the black box recorders being the most valuable starting point to explain a plane's final moments. He wasn't allowed to play us any recordings, he said, with the solemn tone of a man who has heard too many last moments, but he did share that the most frequent final utterance before the silence of eternity was the word "shit."

I had noticed a small plane to one side, its single propeller bent out of shape, its tiny cockpit charred and caved in. One wing was missing, the other was intact but skewed upwards at a right angle halfway along its length.

"Yeah, well, she was a burner."

"A burner?"

"These small planes, see, have wings in two parts that fold upwards, so you can store them easily in the hangar. You come along of a morning, push them out the hangar, fold the wings down, put a locking pin in each wing and off you go. Thing is, see, she only put one of the locking pins in. So, she gets up speed, takes off, and of course the wing without the pin flips up, plane does a somersault and nose-dives on to the runway. Boom. Burned to a crisp. Silly cow. Never forget the pin."

But Pete's tone of black humour faded away as we approached another incident they had been investigating. It needed no introduction. Hanging on a giant frame of scaffolding, a jigsaw of pieces painstakingly reconstructed fragment by twisted fragment, was the nose and part of the fuselage of Pan Am flight 103. The Lockerbie plane. Pete pointed to a puncture hole about the size of a football, several shards splaying outwards like the petals of an ugly metal flower.

"That's where the bomb went off."

It was August 2001 and we were to film first on the Isle of Man, that dollop of inhabited weather-beaten grass and drystone walling plonked in the sea between England and Ireland. Back in the noughties there were big tax incentives to film there. Any number of productions repurposed shitty freezing cow sheds as shitty freezing studios, and mediocre pubs suddenly became the best accommodation on offer.

The Mount Murray Hotel may now be a paragon of five-star service but back in 2001 it was pretty ropey, the staff seeming to change on a daily basis. Our film crew were the only clientele, and the manager didn't like us much. One night he chased Micky the grip round and round the ground floor of the hotel because he had dared to pull his own pint of beer from behind the bar, there being no barman on duty. Micky having fled, the manager declared the bar closed and that we'd all have to vacate. Chrissy our producer had a quiet word, pointing out that the sixty of us staying there were presently the hotel's only source of income and banning us from spending money might be just a little short-sighted.

Iain is a natural leading man. I would follow him into battle at any rate. Calm, authoritative, softly spoken with an Edinburgh lilt, a devilish smile and, with guitar in hand, a singing voice of honeyed milk. At the time Lulu was pregnant with our son Felix. One night, in the (now reopened) bar, Iain played us a song he had written years before about his own baby, Finlay, who by now was all but grown up. It was a moment when fatherhood was still on the horizon for me, but the lyric "son, put your hand in the palm of mine" has stayed with me down the years, as the sense of impending responsibility grew on me. That same night one of our co-stars talked about how once the job was over, in September, he was to take his own boy to university for the first time. There were tears in the man's eyes. I remember rolling mine: what sentimental bollocks; get over it, mate. Now, as I remember installing my own son at university, a school lifetime later, the whirligig of time brings in its revenges. No, that speck of dust is in *your* eye.

Apart from a fight one night in Douglas's premier nightclub, Paramount City, the Isle of Man portion of filming passed off without incident. We then returned to the mainland to film the main event, the aircraft wreckage. Company Pictures had purchased a disused Boeing 707 and were in the process of breaking it up, the art department creating a crash site across a couple of fields in Hertfordshire. And then came my generation's version of "Where were you when you heard that JFK had been shot?" I was in the car park at Tesco in Haslemere. It was around lunchtime, I was picking up a sandwich. I rang my agent about something and her assistant answered the phone, sounding distracted.

"Yes I'll put you thr— Sorry, but we've got the telly on in the office and something really weird's going on in New York. A plane's crashed into one of the twin towers."

Our producers did the right thing, postponing filming at the crash site and removing the fuselage from the field for several weeks. But it was too late: the design team had been papped preparing the site and so a couple of newspapers foghorned along the lines of "Insensitive ITV Commissions Air Crash Drama on Back of New York Tragedy," as if scripts are written and go into production within twenty-four hours.

I'm often surprised when I read how people think TV shows are made. In the case of *Downton Abbey*, one newspaper delighted in taking fantastically ill-informed potshots at the programme – tall poppy syndrome, of course. It alleged that two hours were cut from the US version of the first season because the producers felt Americans were too stupid to understand the plot. The fact was that ITV in the UK has advert breaks, whereas PBS in America does not. There may have been some tweaks for clarity but not two hours' worth. Once it's in print, though, it must be true. Another smear was that the actors were being forced to wear costumes that had been worn by other actors before them, implying that not only were the producers misers but also that we all stank to high heaven. While some costumes are indeed made specifically, the vast majority of clothes I have worn in productions down the years have been hired from one of the internationally renowned costume houses, such as Angels or Cosprop.

Ahead of the first season of *Downton Abbey* the press weren't particularly interested in the show. In fact, the publicity team struggled to get coverage. Period drama is old hat, nobody watches it, was the general mood. Only when the ratings went up in the second week, a rare phenomenon on television, did the tables turn. Suddenly, the ITV breakfast show wanted any of us, even the dog, next morning. Please!

Just as I was about to go on air, Peter Fincham, head of

programming at ITV, who had championed *Downton Abbey* from the outset, appeared on the studio floor to share his delight in the show's unprecedented impact. And from then on it snowballed. We gradually realised that the audience was far broader than the "normal" Sunday night audience. Teenage girls were falling in love with the sisters' characters. Going to pick up Felix from school one day, a nine-year-old lad came up to me in the playground and said, "I don't like that Thomas the footman." You're nine, for heaven's sake, I thought. What are you doing up at that time on a school night, and anyway, why aren't you playing *Minecraft*?

By the time it came to filming season two the location manager had to change the unit signs – the luminous markers that point vehicles towards the set – from "DA" to something less obvious. The scripts no longer had "Downton Abbey" written on the title page and watermarking them became standard. Security became an issue, burly blokes in hi-viz vests having to pull paparazzi out of trees when we filmed on private property, or perform vigorous interpretative dances to block their lenses when on public land. John Gundill, the manager at Highclere Castle, told me that in the first year we filmed there they had about sixty coachloads of visitors. With the first season having aired, by the time we came back to film season two, they had had six hundred coaches scheduled to visit. As the show became more of a goldfish bowl we became increasingly protective of each other as a cast and mindful of what was said in public, too. When Jessica Brown Findlay left the show in season three, her farewell party was held at a pub near Ealing Studios. There were balloons and decorations but to avoid spoilers and loose lips from nearby customers the bunting declared "Happy Birthday!"

We eventually completed the filming of *Impact* in October 2001, the sombre reality of the tragedy in New York never far from our minds. ITV never broadcast the show.

I had heard that Dominic Cooke's RSC production of *The Crucible* at the Gielgud was worth a look. Worth a look or not, my easy-going, guitar-playing pal Iain was playing John Proctor, so of course I was going to saunter along. The house was full, the production excellent, but then something happened in Act Four for which I wasn't prepared. Suddenly, I was no longer watching my friend being superb. I was watching the disintegration of a man in a prison cell, clad only in a soiled loincloth, as a cruel society clamped on to his spirit and began to squeeze tighter and tighter. Sweat began to pool in my palms as, before my eyes, John Proctor's dignity was eroded until only a husk of humanity remained, clinging on to the one thing he had left: his name.

It was shattering to watch. There will be those who remained entirely unmoved by the performance. Of course. What moves one person won't necessarily touch another. That's why theatre is unique and always personal and why reviews are so often pointless. But on that particular night, for me, something happened, that can only happen in a theatre, actor and role combined, transporting this member of the audience to a different, visceral level of experience.

"Dear Iain . . ." I wrote.

32

Head Girl

If a ninety-minute fireside chat can raise over a quarter of a million pounds, then maybe some good can come out of lockdowns. Mind you, if there hadn't been the need for a lockdown the need to raise funds for the Combined Theatrical Charities wouldn't have been quite so pressing, although it will never, alas, be absent.

In 2020 there was an online event on Zoom featuring five greats of the British theatre. Ken Branagh was a brilliant chat show host, steering the conversation and handling audience questions, typed into a Q&A box and sifted live, as if to the manner born. His guests were Dame Judi Dench, Dame Maggie Smith, Sir Derek Jacobi and Sir Ian McKellen.

They were natural and affectionate towards each other and characteristically self-effacing and faux forgetful but sometimes perhaps genuinely so. Old age. What struck me most was that the likelihood of getting five such people together in this format in "real life" was virtually nil. As we all know, Covid spawned new forms of entertainment, borne out of millions of people being housebound. And here were five of my country's greatest living actors in one virtual living room, as if with their legs curled up on the sofa, watched by thousands of people worldwide. And it really was worldwide. Ken read out some of the names and countries that waved hello on the screen as the event kicked off: South Africa, America, Ukraine, Australia, Russia. These, our beloved British best – global stars. While I wouldn't claim any of them to be bosom buddies, I have worked with them all over the years and each has left an indelible impression on me as an actor, along with some striking memories.

Immediately after the event I emailed Ian McKellen to say that for an hour and a half lockdown had seemed almost fun. He wrote back . . .

> We've just had a post-mortem when Maggie complained she couldn't get a word in becos we all talked too much – half seriously, as is her way. Yes, Ken was brilliantly in control. Jude drank some cough medicine just before we started, diluted in 3 pints of water. So throughout, she was dying to pee – that's acting for you
>
> It raised over £300,000.
>
> Wouldn't it be good if we managed to work together again? Our film with Natasha – fun in her trailer after-hours and lying out after a pub lunch in a field full of cows who sniffed us.
>
> much love Ian x

This is the moment when, in the movie, the image spirals, the music goes weird and we're transported back in time . . . to the autumn of 2003, when Natasha Richardson is producing and starring in *Asylum*, a film based on the novel by Patrick McGrath about Stella Raphael, a psychiatrist's wife who has an affair with an inmate (Marton Csokas) at the mental hospital at which her husband (Max, me) is a consultant. Ian McKellen played Dr. Cleave, Max's boss.

It had been a passion project of Natasha's for years, a role that played to her strengths as an actress: an almost skittish lightness of touch, coupled with a deep intelligence and an unpredictable vulnerability. She and her husband Liam Neeson had originally bought the rights with the idea that they might play opposite each other but the project had been so long in development that by the time it came to the boil Liam was (arguably) too old – and, to be honest, too famous – to play Edgar, the dangerous object of Stella's affections.

We were to film part of the story in a derelict hospital in Yorkshire and then on to a studio shoot in Dublin. However, the movie's finances were precarious. There was wobbly funding from the US. I heard a rumour that I was going to be paid via a basketball player in New Orleans. Towards the end of the UK shoot we sensed the wheels were in danger of coming off completely, the Irish producer saying he wouldn't allow us even to travel to Dublin until certain monies were in escrow. The insurers started getting twitchy and came to visit the set on the day we were shooting a staff party sequence at High Royds Hospital outside Leeds. My dance partner for the scene was Wanda Ventham, who seemed a little agitated.

"Don't worry," I said, "the insurers are just here to check up on their asset, not to fire anyone."

"Oh no, I'm not bothered about that," she said. "My boy's only recently started out as an actor, you see, and has just got a job at the Almeida Theatre, with Iain Glen. I'm a bit overexcited."

"That's wonderful news! What's his name?"

"Benedict Cumberbatch."

"Well, I'll certainly keep an eye out for him, Wanda," I said.

Oh God, I winced, another misguided young fool.

Over at the monitors, the producer Laurie Borg was looking a bit sweaty. Two men from the completion guarantee insurance company had just sat down in canvas chairs next to director David Mackenzie, who had headphones on, ready to watch the next take.

Looking smart in my dinner jacket and black tie, I muttered into my lapel mic, "The name's Bond. Completion Bond."

David smiled.

"Action!"

Natasha and I had appeared in the film *Blow Dry* together in 2000 but rarely in the same scene and so had only met fleetingly on that project. On *Asylum* we became friends. I called her the Head Girl because she was a great organiser and natural team leader, a role she relished. She'd also been head girl at St. Paul's Girls School. At the end of each day's filming she would suggest to Ian, Marton and me, or whichever combination of us were filming that day, that we meet for a cocktail in her trailer. Except "suggest" isn't quite the right word. It was more than a suggestion, yet it wasn't quite an order. She enjoyed and needed company, loved a cocktail but certainly wouldn't relish it as much on her own. So, the vodka and cranberry on wrap became a ritual each evening, as did the discussion of where to have dinner. In truth, she would already have decided where exactly we were going to dine, depending on her mood, but we happily went through the charade of discussing options nevertheless.

"Well, yes, we could of course go to the Indian but how about that Thai place?" she might say through a plume of smoke from a long, thin menthol cigarette. "Actually, I've booked a table."

The Thai it was, then.

My wife and I later visited Natasha's family home in the South of France. She was an impressive hostess, of course. Within minutes she had Lulu writing out labels in English and French for the shelves in the crockery cupboard, and when she "suggested" an itinerary for the following day, starting with a ten o'clock departure to go into town, we all knew that meant ten o'clock on the dot. Alan Rickman, another of the house guests, said, "Tashy, you are without doubt the second most controlling person I have ever met."

"Only second?" she giggled. "Who's the most controlling, then?"

"Emma Thompson," said Alan.

Natasha died after a skiing accident in 2009. I can hear her smoky laugh still. And I can see her and Ian, Marton and me, lying in a field near a village pub, a taxi ride outside Leeds, on a kind autumn Sunday afternoon with white clouds dancing up above. Into frame walk three or four cows, their gentle munching and sniffing providing the soundtrack for a perfect day off work, among friends.

33

A Brit in Hollywood

In his book *Adventures in the Screen Trade,* the screenwriter William Goldman writes of Hollywood, "Nobody Knows Anything." A phrase that covers everything from the startling incompetence of some of those in charge to the impossibility of predicting which scripts might become a hit and which won't. In 2005 I found out the truth of the expression for myself.

In February of that year I had been in Los Angeles for a "table read" – that's the We're Possibly Thinking This Might Become a Pilot stage of the development process, a method that production companies often employ as a way of sorting the wheat from the chaff before too much money is actually spent.

I had been to LA a couple of times now and found it a peculiar place. I don't think I'd ever been to a city that had no centre to it. European cities have grown organically over millennia. In California, in little more than a century – *boph,* there y'go, Beverly Hills – *boomph,* Downtown – *plomp,* West Hollywood. They quickly spread and merged into an amorphous urban mass, perched precariously on the edge of the San Andreas Fault.

With my table read commitments completed, my agent tacked on a couple of meetings before I headed home. It was pilot season, the time of year when potential new shows were lined up for casting. From hundreds of commissioned scripts across the networks, several dozen would be made into pilots, a handful would make it to air and one or two, if the studios were lucky, would become hits, run for a million years and bring in enough revenue to cover the losses of all the shows that didn't make it.

One script I really liked – it made me laugh, which let's face it is a good start for a sitcom – was *Everything I Know About Men*, written and produced by Fred Barron, whose credits included *Seinfeld, The Larry Sanders Show* and the British series *My Family*. He was to be what they call the show runner, leading a team of writers. Meeting Fred was my last appointment before heading back to the UK. I instinctively liked him. Fifties, a neat dark beard flecked with grey, big voice, bags of energy. I read OK. I was halfway to LAX when my American agent rang.

"What time's your flight tomorrow?"

"Er, it's tonight, Jeremy. I'm on my way to the airport now."

"OK. Turn around. Here's the thing. They want you to go back and read with Jenna Elfman in the morning."

Before I knew it, I was kneeling, literally kneeling, on the floor of CBS's Business Affairs office, with a pen in my hand and a contract on the coffee table. I was signing my life away, or potentially seven years of it anyway. For up to twenty-three episodes per year my soul would belong to CBS, if the pilot got picked up to be made into a series that is, and if the show lasted past the first season that is, and if, and if, and if. If it made it to season three, apparently, the contract would get tossed in the bin, agents would roll up their sleeves and everything would be renegotiated because you were now in a hit.

"Oh it will get picked up," Jenna assured me when we gathered six weeks later to make the pilot. "CBS want me on air." Jenna Elfman had had enormous success with a show called *Dharma & Greg*, which had run for more than a hundred episodes on ABC between 1997 and 2002. Tall, blonde, naturally funny, Jenna was smart. She had a great instinct for what worked and what didn't and was very hands on during the rehearsing and shooting of the pilot. This was to be her first major project for a while, her comeback show, and with her name on the credits as an executive producer she was determined to get it right.

The pilot was directed by James Burrows, a veteran of shows like *Cheers, Friends, Frasier* and, I believe, every episode of *Will & Grace*. There was nothing he didn't know about shooting a multi-camera sitcom. It's why he was so much in demand come pilot season. He was quiet, methodical, brilliant at creating the shape of the show, hearing its musicality and conducting it accordingly. On the recording night, for instance, he rarely looked at the action. Instead, he paced up and down in front of the audience seating, just behind the cameras, listening to the rhythm of the show and how the jokes were landing. If an actor's line crashed through a laugh, he'd say firmly, "Back up." He'd expect the actor to repeat the line, once the audience had settled, so that the next beat of the scene wasn't wasted. To a master technician like Jimmy it was quite simple: if the audience haven't heard the set-up of a joke, they won't laugh at the punchline. By the time we recorded the pilot we were well versed in his way of working. He delivered.

The show was indeed picked up, and production was scheduled to begin later in the summer.

Frazzled after our flight from England, it was nine o'clock on a Wednesday evening in early August when the taxi dropped us at the house we were to rent, south of Hancock Park in Los Angeles. As I had been shooting in Majorca earlier that summer, renting a house had taken place via sticking pins in a map and a very slow internet connection. Lulu and I had been crystal clear about the sort of place we wanted but perhaps the Mediterranean heat had got to us, because far from finding a three-bedroom house with minimal furnishing, aircon and a pool, for some ridiculous reason we had opted for what looked like a tiny English country cottage; it even had roses round the door. It had two bedrooms, no garden, no aircon and was fully furnished. But that would be manageable, we figured, because we'd told the agent that all breakables would need to be removed before we arrived with our inquisitive toddler in tow.

Things went wrong from the moment we opened the front door. All the knick-knacks and dinky ornaments were exactly where they had been in the photographs. There was leftover food in the fridge, pubey soap in the shower. It was as if someone had just popped down the shops and would be back in five minutes. It was like the *Mary Celeste*. To make matters worse, in the living room there was a huge portrait of a nineteenth-century cavalry officer on horseback, rearing up, sabre drawn and full of military ire. Little Felix took one look at it and burst into tears. It was hot and we were tired. But jet lag doesn't give a damn. With Felix fully awake at 2 a.m. and still going on about The Man! The Man! we were completely done in. By 9 a.m. we had decided to move out.

At 10 a.m., just as I was picking up the keys to our rental car, I got a phone call from an executive producer that heralded one of the most bonkers chapters of my career.

"Kew?"

She always found my name impossible to pronounce. There was something uneasy behind the smiley voice. I could tell.

"Well, yes. Hugh."

Pleasantries about the weather and the Californian sunshine. Then . . .

"Just to let you know we're going on hiatus."

Up to this point in my life my understanding of the word hiatus had been limited to hernias.

"Going where?"

"We're not starting work on Friday. We're going on hiatus. We may start up in two weeks. We may not."

"What? Why on earth did you let me get on the plane?"

"Because it only happened at eight o'clock last night."

We had landed at seven.

"What only happened?"

"Fred Barron was let go."

It took a moment for the news to sink in.

"Hang on – you fired Fred Barron?"

"I didn't. He was let go."

"You fired the creator of the bloody show?"

"As I say, Fred Barron was let go."

From then on, the American dream turned rapidly into a nightmare. We spent the following four nights in various hotels while trying to find another house. We saw an unfurnished house near Larchmont Village on the Sunday and – God Bless America – by Tuesday we were in and fully furnished. Now I was suddenly renting two houses, as the agent for the absurd country cottage with the scary fucking portrait and stuffed to the rafters with rinkydink ornaments was up for a fight.

And then the waiting began.

Our intention had been not to bother putting Felix into preschool, as we were only going to be in Los Angeles for four months that first season. However, the goalposts had moved. We now had no idea how long we were going to be stuck there and so we started to look for a school. Frankly, we'd have had better luck breaking into Fort Knox. It's a seller's market in LA. One head teacher told us, smugly, "Not even the Douglases could get a place here." We finally found one, run by a substantial woman in Roy Orbison dark glasses who wanted six months' fees up front. When I said I'd mail a cheque first thing she said, "I never trust the mail." I had to take the cheque round personally and put it into Jabba the Hutt's upturned palm, like I was paying off the Godfather.

Two days later we were sitting sullenly in a diner in West Hollywood when I got a call from the executive producer.

"Kew? I wish I didn't have to tell you this but—"

"But what?" I asked.

"The show's on hold again."

"Christ. Until when?"

"Possibly October. Or possibly November."

"Possibly?"

"Probably. Probably November."

"But possibly October?"

"Pretty definitely not October."

"So why did you say possibly?"

Things would have been different if we had decided to leave the UK and set up in LA full time. But that wasn't the case. I was there to do a job and then come home. Originally the only uncertainty was whether the visit was to be for a few months . . . or several years, should the show become a hit. While that would have been a nice problem to have, the present reality was horribly different. My only occupation right now was to sit around and wait. Unpaid, because I was only paid "per episode produced" and we weren't producing any episodes at all. I was living in Hollywood, paying rent with zero income.

"Let's go home," said Lulu. "They can call you when they're ready."

Hindsight is a gift we all possess but sadly very few of us are blessed with foresight. My eminently sensible wife, however, was. And I didn't listen to her when I should have done. As she said, problems are easier to face when on home turf. But I was blinkered, haemorrhaging cash, and saw only the logistical nightmare of skipping town now and having to commute for the rest of the contract, if indeed it ever got under way. According to my warped thinking, this was my LA agent's chance to put me up for an episode of a mini-series, or an arc in a serial to try and claw some income. Except one look at my visa and I realised I was restricted to working only for Touchstone TV and I wasn't entirely sure *Desperate Housewives* were particularly desperate for me. I engaged a lawyer to try and broaden the terms of my work permit. Another cash meter started ticking.

We met some kind locals, who held a welcome-to-the-neighbourhood party for us. We all wore name tags, which made everyone feel they were at a sales convention, but at least Felix got set up with playdates and I got set up with an entertainment lawyer to try and get me out of my contract so we could all go home. He failed.

The uncertainty and gloom of living in a city for no reason and with no visible means of support began to weigh heavily. The days passed with numbing repetition. We went to the beach a few times. Did Santa Monica, which in our dour mood held the same attraction as Brighton pier on a wet Thursday in February. Since having Felix, Lulu had conveniently developed vertigo, so Daddy had to butch up and go on the big wheel. Felix loved it and peered gaily over the side of the swaying bucket in which we were suspended while my life flashed before me, and I clung to the suspiciously rusty centre pole. On the beach that afternoon Lulu was told by a lifeguard (a proper *Baywatch* one with a pulled-in tummy, clutching a bright red lozenge) to remove Felix's armbands because they're illegal in Los Angeles county. The reason being they give the child a false sense of security. You could say the same about seatbelts if you think about it. Anyway, "Take care of your child, ma'am," he said, and squeaked off across the sand.

We went to Disneyland, gratis. I should sodding well think so since the company who brought about the hideous hiatus I found myself in was owned by Disney. Yes, it was great, but our hearts weren't in it and I came away never wanting to hear "It's a Small World After All" ever again.

Felix and I invented characters to chat to at bath times. There was Dexter, an LA hairdresser who advised Felix on colonic irrigation, and Ber-nard, Dexter's housemate, who ran the salon with him. Ber-nard sounded like a New Joisey thug and unless he took regular medication was prone to eating furniture. The finer points went sailing over Felix's head but we had fun, the three-year-old not registering that his parents were increasingly miserable.

By early October even the bath times had begun to lose their lustre as my enthusiasm for Tinseltown spiralled down the plughole. Meetings with lawyers, agents and Senior VPs of Whatever within the vast structure of Disney covered a few costs but ultimately got nowhere.

"Anyway, Kew, what's the problem? It's California and the sun's shining!"

Lulu suggested we write a black comedy about a Brit who goes to LA to do a sitcom that never starts. Trouble was I had virtually no sense of humour left. And she only mentioned the idea while thumbing through the directory for a divorce lawyer. A while later, when we heard about a show called *Episodes* doing pretty much the same thing, we dropped the idea.

The wearing, lapping waves of living in limbo had eroded our spirits like nothing I had ever experienced. One night I noticed that a peanut had got squashed into the hall carpet. Every time I passed it I thought to myself, "You should sweep that up." But I didn't. Over the next few days I must have passed it, zombie-like, thirty, forty times. On each occasion I'd think "Ought to sweep that up" but would simply walk on. I Just Didn't Care. On about day four of this flirtation with nihilism I somehow managed to reach for a dustpan and brush and dispose of the crumbs. That night, as together we nursed medicinal glasses of wine and smoked another twenty cigarettes, Lulu murmured, "I see you got rid of the peanut."

"Mmm," I grunted.

"Spotted it a few days ago," she mumbled, "but I couldn't be bothered. This isn't my house. This isn't my life. What's the point?"

(Cue jaunty music:) "Hoo-ray for Holleeee-wooood!"

Several weeks later the wheels of the project, static for so long, finally started to grind into action, when the all-new, brighter-than-white version of *Everything I Know About Men* came through cyberspace and off the printer. It was now called *Courting Alex*. Aside from Jenna, Dabney Coleman and myself, the rest of the cast from the original pilot had been replaced. My character was no longer her boss but her neighbour and the writers had decided that "Reginald" was a typical English name for me. I soon got that changed.

The night we recorded the new pilot I wrote to Fred Barron, who had given me the job in the first place back in the spring.

> This has been one big hairy bastard of a rollercoaster ... when the new script came off my printer two weeks ago, I thought AT LAST! I read it ... and was so stunned that I couldn't return anyone's calls for two days. The only way I can describe my feelings about the project is in terms of *One Flew Over the Cuckoo's Nest*: what was once the vigorous, surprising, unpredictable McMurphy had been lobotomised – safe, placid, functional. I in no way mean to criticise Rob and the writers for this – it's what CBS want, and I guess it's at the root of why you and they parted company. And what they've achieved in the days since that draft has been terrific. But the taping tonight had none of the atmosphere that our pilot had. I remember the roof coming off in some scenes. Tonight you needed a cattle prod to keep the audience involved. To make matters worse, 90% of them left at 10 o'clock because they were on a package tour from Universal City. By the time we did our half-hearted curtain call there were EIGHTEEN people left in the audience. I've felt like an automaton recently: turn up, try and do funny, go away. It's going to take a while to get over the hurt of sitting on my fat arse for three months, unable to work.

While the execs picked over the new pilot episode, like so many medical students over a patient – "ah, there's the funny bone" – we went on hiatus again for another fortnight.

A week later the new show runner, Rob Hanning, called to tell me the Suits were delighted with the way the first episode had cut together and that it had "tested" well (heaven forbid that any production team should be allowed to trust their own creative instincts) and that they'd used hardly any of the hasty rewrites that had been thrown at us on the night of the taping as a result of the comatose audience not laughing. I put the phone down feeling completely numb. I no longer knew what constituted quality. But hey, it was on the supermarket shelf in a bright, attractive packet, so I guessed I'd plop it into my basket and move on down the aisle.

Despite the mini road trip we took up the coast during the hiatus there was little that could lift Lulu's mood. The doctor diagnosed a whacking great episode of stress and asked if there was any chance of her going back to England and taking control of her life again. She and Felix flew home to the UK; I would follow for the Christmas break.

The network announced it was going to give the show a prime-time slot at the end of January 2006. With this in mind I really did have to put the misery of the last few months behind me and turn up to work with a smile on my face. Which, given time, wasn't difficult. The cast were talented and my character did at least have some vim. But what I had first tasted as a crunchy baguette packed with salami was now thin white bread with a sliver of processed cheese on top.

In the run-through for the next episode, one of the tall willowy execs (all the execs seemed to be tall and willowy) yawned all the way through. It was funny to watch this quasi-scientific appraisal of our work as an outsider. As the run-through moved from set to set, tall canvas-backed chairs were laid out in front of each performance space. And, like a school photo, the same people sat in the front seats. No one dared sit where the teachers sat. I regularly counted forty people watching these run-throughs. Each week three of them would say hello. I knew their names and what they did. Each week the other thirty-seven would walk past, studiously avoiding eye contact. I don't know who was more wary of whom. But it certainly made for an atmosphere of Us and Them.

After we had run the twenty-one-minute show, all the execs would go off into their boarded-off corners, the Studio (Paramount/Touchstone) in one area, the Network (CBS) in another, to discuss the patient they'd just examined and would then formulate their prognosis and issue their prescription for the writers. Meanwhile, we actors would be banished to our dressing rooms – literally banished, not allowed even to get a cup of tea from "craft service," at the back of the set, while the executives were in committee.

Twenty minutes later we would be called back downstairs. More often than not the upshot would be that the writers would need to go off for another afternoon and evening in the writing room, with pizzas and phone calls to say Darling, I'm Sorry But I Won't Be Home For Dinner. For all my misgivings about the white-breadness of the show's new format (and whatever they themselves may have thought about what they were being instructed to write) they were a talented team. After any rehearsal, whenever I felt inclined to mention a "bump" in the writing, it had been spotted by all of them long before I brought it up.

Tuesday 13 December

Did the Network Run-through. Suits and Tall & Willowies in abundance. In this week's episode I had a romantic storyline with a woman who runs an art gallery. They cast a brilliantly sassy hispanic actor, Yvonne. She was great to work with. Director happy, Producers happy. Everyone happy. So we do the Network Run-through, are corralled into our dressing rooms, and then half an hour later are lassoed for notes with Rob and the team. Discuss the first scene, tweak some lines, at which point Rob blurts out "Oh I forgot to say, we'll be having a new Rita tomorrow." I look round the group, aghast. Everyone has a similar reaction: a look skyward, an awkward glance down to their script, whatever. Only Jenna remains unmoved. Straight-backed. Doesn't flinch. Rob adds that the Network just didn't like her. "Well, if the Network says no, there's no shifting 'em," says Jenna. Inscrutable.

Apparently the T&Ws, unanimously, were astonished that she'd been cast in the first place. They thought she was "coarse." Granted she turned up for today's rehearsal in a leopardskin poncho thing, hair all over the shop, looking more Bois du Boulogne than Gallery Owner. But still, we were all in civvies and none of us look The Part at Run-throughs. Point is, that was it. Decision made. Ditch her.

"Next!"

God it's so fucking cut-throat here.

I got Yvonne's phone number from Production and called her to say I was sorry. I didn't want her to think I'd had anything to do with her being fired, which she could easily have done since I was the one she was acting with primarily and because everyone passes the buck in this town. She appreciated the call but obviously felt like shit. Another nasty taste to leave in my LA mouth.

After a brief Christmas break – Lulu already feeling much better now that she was back in her home environment, Felix thrilled that no one had stolen his toys in his absence – I flew back to Los Angeles to work on the remaining episodes. On my way in from the airport I saw a huge billboard of Jenna on the corner of Fairfax and Beverly. It was one of those where a cut-out image extends above the top of the rectangular hoarding. In this case it was her head. Unfortunately, the extra bit had slipped so it looked like she'd dislocated her shoulder.

One evening an obscenely long stretch limo arrived to take me – just me – to the Wind Tunnel gallery in Pasadena, where CBS was holding its mid-season press launch. I poured myself a vodka from the crystalled in-car bar and jokily shouted a question to my only companion, the driver, twenty feet away about how the weather was down there (I was later driven home in a saloon).

Once at the party, I bumped into the head of publicity and asked what figures CBS would "need" from the premiere of the show the following week. Answer: between 13 and 15 million viewers. Below 10 million would be catastrophic, apparently. He'd been doing his job seven years, so I asked him whether he'd worked on shows that all the way through production were dead certs, only to go on air and flop, and vice versa. "All the time," he cackled. And it really was a cackle. High-pitched, manic, revealing a man for whom instincts about taste on the one hand and the market on the other had clearly parted company some time ago. "*All* the time," he repeated, with feeling. "You *never* know." William Goldman again – Nobody Knows Anything. I had recently seen billboards all over town, and I mean *all* over, advertising *Emily's Reasons Why Not*. ABC must have spent millions promoting this show. It got pulled off the air after one episode. "Millions" ... "One." Two small words. And such a difference between them.

The morning after the first episode of *Courting Alex* went out, a manager acquaintance rang to tell me it was a hit and he could fix me up with a realtor to help me buy the house I would definitely be needing to buy for season two and beyond. "And if at *any* time you feel you need a manager, buddy . . ." he added.

I wasn't convinced on either count.

Tuesday 7 February 2006 – email to a friend in the UK:

> *Courting Alex* has been on the air for three weeks; pretty bad reviews. CBS have given it the best possible slot on a Monday night, sandwiched between the Charlie Sheen show *Two and a Half Men* and *CSI: Miami*. Both these get boffo audiences (15m and 18m respectively). We got about 14m on our debut and have now slipped to 12m, which is still in the Top 20 for the week. I find the whole thing baffling and am amazed that we've retained as many viewers as we have. Maybe America can't reach for the remote control because it's died in its armchair and the emergency services have yet to notice the smell.

At the Monday table read for the next episode, one of the Suits who hitherto had never said hello came over and shook my hand, full of congratulations. I felt a bit nonplussed, and when a second one came over and did the same I mentioned it to one of our producers.

"It's simple. The ratings are holding up," she said. "Have you noticed how there have been more executives at the table reads recently? Same thing. They went away when the show wasn't testing well, but now the ratings are OK, they're coming back."

I was soon to be released back into the wild (England). For how long remained to be seen: perhaps our show would be recommissioned for a second season, or maybe it would be plopped in a dumpster. Either way, in a week or so I was to be on a plane home, twelve episodes in the can (thirteen including the original pilot that was never aired). I had already begun packing up my stuff, unsure whether to put it in storage until season two or ship it home for good.

I was at rehearsals when I got a message from my landlord that he needed to show the house to a realtor on behalf of a prospective tenant that afternoon. The house was tidyish but there were papers and files spread out all over the den, pans and stuff strewn across the kitchen, not to mention packing boxes by the back door. So as soon as there was a break in rehearsals I whizzed back home and tidied manically.

The landlord pulled up in his Porsche. He usually pitched up in the Bentley – maybe it was dress-down Friday. We shook hands. I had always got on with him and his partner, both of whom were as buff as Colonel Buff from Bufftown, as each finger-shattering handshake reminded me.

A moment later another car arrived. I clocked the number plate: MG ♥ AB. Out got an exceedingly slim woman, lips pouting, high heels. The landlord introduced me but I missed the name because at that very moment a passing car honked its horn (just like my Leonardo DiCaprio experience). Perhaps the passing car driver knew her; to me she just looked familiar. Maybe I'd met her at a local do. She struck me as quite eccentric, the way she appraised the rooms, and squinted up at the skylight, a faraway look in her eyes.

"I just *love* your house," she said.

I muttered something about it not being mine exactly and she went off on to the front porch to make a phone call. I was wrapping stuff in the kitchen when the landlord sweated in, asking for matches – "Now she wants a goddam smoke. Hasn't brought her own goddam lighter, of course. Disgusting habit." The woman teetered around the garden, fag in hand, drawling into the phone. "It's kinda yellow and white clapboard. No seriously, I think you'd like it." Eventually she and the landlord shook hands and off she went. He shut the front door, leaning against it with a sigh.

"Jeez! *Hollywood* people!" he exclaimed, rolling his eyes.

"That's realtors for you, eh?" I chuckled.

"You think she was the realtor?" he asked, his expression faltering.

"Yeah, I guess they can be as tricky as their clients," I said.

"The realtor cancelled. That *was* the client."

Once again my celebrity antennae had failed, apparently. I had mistaken Melanie Griffith for a local estate agent.

A week later I was back in soggy West Sussex. Chill, damp. Welly boots slathered in mud. I looked on them now with renewed affection. The mud you can't help bringing into the house because you've been for a yomp across a Green English Field; the losing your sock in them when you try and shake them off. It felt wonderful.

The next day my US agent phoned to say *Courting Alex* was being pulled off the air. The ratings had gone from 13 million on a Monday to 4 million in its new slot on a Wednesday, proving either that people only laugh at the beginning of the week, or that our show had only survived in its initial slot on the Monday because it was the drooping head between two hit shoulders (*Two and a Half Men* and *CSI*).

The production had had FAILURE stamped on it since Fred Barron had been fired and the execs had tried to reverse-engineer a sitcom based on their leading lady and two of her supporting actors. I met Fred for coffee in London. Afterwards I dropped him a line.

> It was great to see you. It felt like we were two survivors of a ghastly shipwreck being brought together for the first time since being hauled from the sea; very therapeutic. Honestly, this last year has been the most bizarre of my career: from getting the job by accident (I didn't even know

> what "pilot season" meant), in a town in which I had no desire to live, to seeing the show I adored disintegrate before my eyes, only for it to re-emerge as Frankenstein's monster.
>
> Hope the root canal isn't too dreadful. I've had so many my jaw resembles a map of Venice. Keep in touch.

To this day I have never been told officially that my contract has been terminated; Hollywood execs are way too nervous to take on such responsibility. But in the middle of May that year I read online in *USA Today* that *Courting Alex* had been cancelled. Almost a year to the day from the show being picked up, it was finally over.

A few days later I stopped to fill up the car at our local ramshackle petrol station, not much more than a junkyard of bits of old vehicles with a pump that was probably made out of some of them. I was greeted by Jason, in his oily blue overalls.

"Well, if it isn't our local minor celebrity. The other night we was talking about famous people in the area and I forgot all about you. Best I could come up with was June Whitfield."

It was good to be home.

34

Diary of a Nobody

There's a question that usually arises two drinks in. You're at a friend's house and you've been in the corner with a stranger for half an hour now but there's no easy means of escape. We've run through the standard checklist: how do you know Mark and Sarah; do you live round here; did you see the match; what about that thing on the news; what field do you work in – oh right – so do you know – small world. Then there's a pause, and then here it comes . . . "One thing I've always wanted to ask you actorrrr types: how *do* you learn all those lines?"

Trouble is, if you try to answer their eyes glaze over; the thrill for them was asking the question in the first place, like confronting a lawyer with "So! How do you defend the bloke if you know he's guilty – answer me *that*!" I usually reply to the learning lines question that being paid helps, then try to steer the conversation on to something of mutual interest, like Mark and Sarah's famously gifted children.

But since you and I aren't stuck in a corner at a party, I'll share, briefly. Memory is like a muscle. Exercise it and it strengthens. At junior school we had to learn a poem a week and recite it to the class. It helped that I liked poems and also enjoyed reciting, so learning by rote came relatively easily. But I've never found learning by rote in theatre constructive, as it constricts your approach to what's happening around you. If you turn up with the lines pre-learned, pre-baked if you will, then your brain is in danger of being inflexible and less open to whatever is thrown at you by your fellow actors during rehearsals. In theatre, lines sink in best, for me, in three dimensions, once you start blocking the show, when one line, spoken in the space, leads to another, prompting, or being prompted by, interaction with others, or by a move. If the dialogue involves pouring a cup of tea and giving it to someone, the lines will tend to bed in along with the physical action. Then, going over the lines at night, recalling the day's actions in the rehearsal room, helps the lines sink in further. The repetition of scenes in the next rehearsal further solidifies the layers. Gradually, the lines you've learned and rehearsed become a learned scene, then an act, then, God willing, the whole play.

Learning lines for film is different, to the extent that sometimes you don't ever really learn them, not properly, not in the way that they remain layered in, engrained and embedded, there to be recalled the next day and the next, maybe even a decade later. You nearly always shoot out of sequence and rarely cover more than ten pages of dialogue per day – more on a soap, way more, fewer on a drama filmed on location, even fewer if several hours in the day are taken up with costume and hair changes in a period show. With the dialogue never to be repeated, inevitably the memory trace is shallower as you learn it, to the extent that often it's a case of "learn, shoot and forget." This means that if you have to re-shoot a sequence even just a week later, you'll probably have to re-learn the lines because they won't have stayed with you. At least, that's true in my case. But give me the script of a play I did ten years ago, and after an hour of study most of it will have come back.

One hybrid experience I had was a two-hour monologue for television. No allowing the lines to sink in by rehearsing with co-stars, through the process of repetition. With time for rehearsals on a TV schedule a limited luxury, I had to learn it up front, by rote.

Originally an illustrated serial in *Punch* magazine in the 1880s, *Diary of a Nobody,* expressing the views and values of Mr. Pooter, a lowly office clerk from North London, was then published as a book and it's never been out of print. It's very funny and touching, too. With Andrew Davies having smartly adapted the book into a monologue, I set aside three weeks to learn it and set off daily for walks near my house, script in hand.

One afternoon, having parked my car and headed into the woods, I got so absorbed in my lines, going over and over them until I was confident they were cemented, that by sunset and time to go home I suddenly realised I had no idea where I was. I spent the next thirty minutes plunging through the forest in various directions, completely disoriented and increasingly anxious; there was no mobile signal and this was in the days before phones had maps. Just as dusk fell and it was all getting a bit *Blair Witch Project,* a woman appeared, walking her dog. Desperate, I pleaded with her to tell me if she knew where on earth I was and if I was even in the same county as the car park.

"Yes, it's thirty feet that way," she said, pointing.

"Oh."

But the interesting thing was that when it came to filming on the set – in Mr. Pooter's front room, or in his office – whenever I turned to address the camera, with each line I uttered, at the very same moment as the words left my lips I could see in my mind's eye the exact tree I had passed as that particular line had lodged itself in my memory. Full disclosure: there was an autocue, too, as a safety net. But you can usually tell when someone is using one – the eyes flicker – which is why I learned the whole thing, but it was good to have it there in my peripheral vision.

The next question the bloke in the corner asks, of course, is "Are you 'resting'?" He's delighted to quote what he knows to be an insider's technical term, although it's a word which I have rarely heard an actor use. I just answer, "No, I'm unemployed. Another drink?"

35

Hidden on the Hard Drive

There is a scene in the 2010 film *Burke & Hare* in which my character, Lord Harrington, addresses a group of learned colleagues. In the background of one angle on me is a supporting actor with a face not unlike my own. It's the only time my brother Nigel and I ever appeared together, either on stage or screen. He used to do a fair amount of work as a supporting artist. He'd told me he was doing a day on the film. I introduced him to John Landis, the director, who made sure we got to be in the same frame.

Nigel was without doubt one of the main reasons I became hooked on acting, because he was into it too. When I was growing up he was, to little me, off in the distance, already a grown-up. During term time he was away at boarding school and a somewhat brooding presence during the holidays. When he seemed most alive was when he was on stage. As a kid of seven, eight, nine, watching him in production after production in the school hall gave me a taste for it. I was captivated. He was exotic. He was very funny in company with others, popular, lots of friends, a string of girlfriends – rarely serious ones though, and mostly short-lived – loved being the centre of attention. He was also irascible, unkind to my sister when they were both in their teens, and utterly foul at times to my parents. He was never physically violent but his words were. I can see a young me locking myself in the bathroom, sobbing, as he laid into Mum and Dad about something. They took it on the chin, never raising their voices, ever. It must have been infuriating for him, the eldest, desperately trying to leave the nest but not yet able to fly. Sometimes I wish we'd been a family of plate throwers and shouters, letting it all out, soon to blow over. But you live by example, and Mum and Dad just weren't built that way.

Nigel's anger during his later teenage years can be partially attributed to pain. He had Perthes' disease, causing problems in the hip and pelvis, but it went undiagnosed until he was nearly twenty; sometimes he must have been in agony without knowing why. Subsequently he had two hip replacements, one of them twice, and had associated health issues for many years. Another cause of frustration was not knowing what he wanted to do with his life. He fared moderately in his A Levels, not to the Oxbridge standard to which he had aspired; he didn't get in. Like my father and sister, he was a good linguist. He went off to be a welder's mate in Hamburg for a bit and then to Montpellier University in France but he didn't complete his degree. He came back to England without much of a clue as to what was going to happen next. What happened next was he got a job in an insurance firm called Brown Shipley. It would do as a stop-gap until he worked out what he really wanted to do. As it turned out, marine insurance was to be his life for the next forty years.

Well, perhaps not his life. It's what he did to earn a living. What he really wanted was to be involved in theatre. But as the first born, with two more kids to support, and with little or no knowledge of the industry themselves, Mum and Dad were in no position to point him in the direction of the stage. So, he worked in Lloyd's during the day and did amateur dramatics by night. The Lloyd's Players, I think they were called, put on dramas, comedies and a big musical once a year. He then moved on to the British Rail Players, who had the lease on two extremely damp arches underneath Waterloo station. After privatisation they became the Network Players; trouble with rent and the evil landlord, he told me, began almost immediately and never abated during the twenty years he was involved with the group, as performer, director, treasurer, secretary, chairman and frequently barman. For several years, until Eurostar moved to its permanent home at St. Pancras, the trains' smelly rubbish bins were located right opposite the theatre entrance. Audiences weren't actually advised to bring a lavender bag to mask the smell but it would have been helpful. On a hot summer night, watching Network's take on some forgotten classic, the aroma was something else.

One day, about five years after I had become a professional actor, Nigel invited me over for a beer.

"What do you think about me turning professional?"

My heart sank. I had been asked that question a few times by people and always found it impossible to answer. I still do. You could be completely confident in someone's ability but they might never get a break – witness half my class from drama school. On the other hand, you may not personally rate someone but who are you to shatter their dream? There are plenty of actors of dubious quality with magnificent careers. But this was my big brother, asking his little brother for advice.

"It needn't be just acting. It could be presenting," he went on. "I mean, Clive Anderson went from being a barrister to a presenter, didn't he. Nothing to stop me making a similar move from insurance."

I told him how much I enjoyed watching him in his shows and that I knew how much pleasure he derived from performing. However, I added, there was one significant difference between his current world and mine: a salary.

"At the end of every month a cheque goes into your account,"

I said. "Actors never have that guarantee. But if you think you could cope with going for a year, maybe more, without the phone ringing with a job offer ... if you reckon you could handle that level of insecurity and do other jobs to make ends meet, then fine, go for it. But if you need routine in your life and a sense of security, then don't give it a second thought. It's not for you."

Another thing I, to this day, say to aspiring actors is: if you are having a "bit of a think" about "possibly acting" alongside a couple of other options in life, for heaven's sake explore the other two. Because except in very rare cases – and as precious as this may sound – acting isn't an option, it's a compulsion. You need to do it and you will put up with all manner of crap in order to pursue it. But it owes you nothing and it's often feast or famine.

"I quite like the idea of TV production, too," he said, more eager by the minute. It sounded to me like he was clutching at straws rather than answering The Call. Nevertheless, I phoned a friend of mine who had irons in many fires on the production side of the industry. He agreed to meet Nigel for lunch.

A few days later I rang my friend to thank him for having given up his time.

"But didn't Nigel tell you?" he said. "He cancelled."

"What?"

"He was offered a promotion at work and decided to take it."

Nigel hadn't told me, and we didn't speak of it again. I was relieved he'd recognised that, for him, job security mattered more than an insecure, precarious career on stage and in the freelance world. But it didn't mean he enjoyed the world of theatre any less, as one day I was to discover.

I was at lunch, on 5 April 2017 to be precise, with my first employer, David Conville, now retired from the Open Air Theatre. We would meet once a year, the rendezvous being made via a lot of barking down the telephone from Dorset about why my proposed dates were completely untenable, in his uniquely bombastic, baffled tone, mystified as to why on earth I had suggested them in the first place. He'd take me through his diary, ruling out suggestion after suggestion.

"No, I mean, look, of course I can't do the twenty-eighth because I have to see Malcolm – dreadful old bore but there we are – in Andover." The name of the town being pronounced as if it was situated within the ring road of Hell. The sound of a page turning in the little Letts diary. "And, no, the third isn't going to work, is it."

"Isn't it?"

"Well no, obviously it's not, because I've got the dentist."

"Right. I didn't know."

"It's in the diary. Nice fellow. Terrible teeth."

Eventually we'd find a date and we'd meet up, his eyes a little rheumier, his untrained eyebrows even more adventurous than last year.

That particular lunchtime we'd reminisced happily, as ever, about characters from "The Park" and my baptism into the profession. As coffee arrived, I excused myself. En route to the loo I looked at my phone, which had been on silent. Two missed calls from a number I didn't recognise, one voicemail. I dialled in. It was a colleague of my brother's.

"Nigel hasn't turned up for work today. I wonder if you might have any idea . . . ?"

In the four decades of his working life Nigel had never not shown up for work. He was a man of routine, even down to the number of times he dunked his tea bag at breakfast. A bachelor, he lived alone in Camberwell, South London, a ten-minute cycle ride from his beloved Network Theatre underneath Waterloo station. The voicemail had been left an hour earlier. I called back. The man answered.

"He's dead." But that was my unspoken thought, not the man's words. I just knew it.

"Since I called you, Hugh, two of the team from our office went round to his house. There was no reply. The police came.

They broke down the door. I'm so sorry. It looks like Nigel died in his sleep."

Following a visit to the UK, my sister Clare had just landed in Hong Kong, where she worked. I phoned her. She immediately booked a flight back again. We would break the news to Dad together. As he was living with dementia, we agreed that delaying telling him by a couple of days was not going to make much difference.

As any bereaved adult knows, the administration that comes with death is so involving and confusing that grief can go and bloody well wait in line for a bit, sometimes for months. When Mum had died three years previously, I had cast myself as the office manager of death, getting all the paperwork together, trying to sift the stuff of a life. I now did the same with Nigel. Keeping busy makes you think you are contributing in some way. You are in the short term, yes, but you are also masking things. Shock, in my case.

The front door frame was split where the police had broken in, although the locksmith had done a good job of a temporary repair. Upstairs, the duvet on his bed was a bit ruffled but the place had been left tidy, with respect. There were his spectacles on duty at the bedside.

I sat down at the computer in Nigel's study. I pressed the space bar and it sprang into life, and by some miracle the password wasn't required. I was then able to access the file where most of his passwords were stored. Having gathered the key bits of financial and insurance information I needed, I started to get nervous. What else was I going to find on the hard drive? You read about secret lives being uncovered after death: three families turning up at the bigamist's funeral; long-lost illegitimate children laying claim to their inheritance. Maybe I was going to discover a deep well of perversion, hideous horrors involving the dark web.

In fact, there were no such revelations. What I discovered was surprising in a different way. As I sifted through folder after folder, both on the computer and on the shelves above his desk – the concertina files, the box files, A4, A5, foolscap, plastic wallets, thick manila envelopes stuffed with papers, the external hard drives, particularly the one I found ominously half hidden on the top shelf – what they revealed was something simple and therefore all the more poignant. My brother lived, breathed, was 100 per cent totally committed to and in love with The Theatre. Every aspect of it. There were reams of production notes from Network Theatre, photographs, scripts, theatre programmes, committee minutes, audition lists, lighting plots, front-of-house rotas, costume budgets, bar takings spreadsheets, scene dock To Do lists. His passion and devotion to the watching and the putting on of plays, in his case for the sheer pleasure of doing so, far outstripped my own.

A couple of days later my sister and I visited Dad, then still living in his own home. I went into the sitting room ahead of Clare, to introduce the idea that his daughter was home unexpectedly. He was at the piano, in a jolly, animated mood.

"Ah, my dear fellow!" He got up from the piano stool and approached me excitedly. "I'm so glad you're here! Now listen, I have to make a will. Because I haven't got one, you see. And I think this flat must be worth a bit and so I need to sort it out."

"It's OK, Dad. It's all been taken care of."

"But it's important, you see," he continued empathically but without anxiety. He was in a good place today.

My sister came in and he gave her a kiss hello, not remotely surprised to see her.

"Why not sit down, Daddy?" said Clare.

"Right you are."

We pulled two chairs close to his and sat, gently taking his hands in ours.

"Dad," I began, "we have to tell you that a couple of days ago Nigel died in his sleep."

With barely a flicker to register the thought he said perkily, "Did *he* make a will? Because I bet his place is worth a bit. Poor chap. He hadn't been ill, had he?"

His darling, funny, sometimes grumpy son, the one who did plays under the soggy arches at Waterloo, was now, to Dad in the misty lowlands of dementia, not much more than a passing acquaintance.

Nigel was sixty-one. He'd been talking about retirement, planning yet another production at Network; reunions with "The Rhinos," his cricket team of "creaky old men"; catching up with his five adored godchildren. My big brother had gone, just like that, overnight. He'd had a stroke.

All the questions I'd never asked him. Why didn't you propose to Pippa? Why did you never want children? You loved children. What held you back? What caused you the most pain in life? And, as I looked down one last time into his open grave, adjacent to Mum's so they could chat, "Were you content, Nig?" I'd never asked him that. But I did now know something for sure: for the countless hours after work and the many, many weekends he devoted to it, Theatre gave him a sense of purpose. It fulfilled him, giving his life meaning. Above all, it made him happy.

36

Mr. President

Twitter can be a nasty place, but occasionally it leads to something quirky and fun. A couple of years into the run of *Downton Abbey* someone pointed out to me that Ronnie Wood of the Rolling Stones had become a fan of the show and had recently joined Twitter. He posted a picture of himself holding a *Downton Abbey* DVD in one hand, a cup of tea in the other, with his pinkie finger poking out. I commented that Alastair Bruce, our historical adviser on the show, would have had a fit. The notion of sticking out your little finger when drinking anything is Just Not On. Our correspondence continued on- and offline for a bit and within a few days we had come up with the idea of a charity fundraiser in the form of afternoon tea at The Savoy for a pair of *Downton*/Stones fans. That's quite a crossover. We raised good money, and in the end the two winners were on their way. One man flew in from Germany, the other from Milton Keynes. Although I suspect the latter came by train. It turned out they were both massive Stones fans; Ronnie even recognised one of them. I might as well have been the waiter. While Ronnie signed the plethora of memorabilia they had brought with them, I ate a cucumber sandwich in the corner and thought about a similar moment that had occurred some months before.

An invitation had come via the *Downton Abbey* office for Elizabeth McGovern and me to visit Washington DC as part of Prime Minister David Cameron's first official visit to the USA. There was to be a day of events in mid-March 2012 to celebrate the Special Relationship. Actors such as Idris Elba and Damian Lewis were also being invited, along with a number of British entrepreneurs and business people, all doing their bit for soft diplomacy. With a convenient break in filming and our spouses in tow, Elizabeth and I set off to America.

At Washington Dulles airport, Elizabeth and her husband Simon Curtis sailed through customs. Of course they did, she's American. Once at the immigration desk I stated the purpose of my visit . . .

"Well, it's rather exciting, actually. There's a thing on the White House lawn tomorrow morning, then lunch at the State Department, then dinner at the White House!"

The immigration officer was having none of it. Even when I pulled out the official invitation and displayed the full itinerary he really wasn't going to a happy place anytime soon. Lulu and I were escorted to a holding room where we joined forty or so other suspicious characters like us who were clearly trying to pull a fast one. Half an hour later we were called forward and quizzed. The interrogator held the thick embossed invitation up to the light. Not quite sure what he was expecting to see shining through, but eventually he sighed, stamped something or other and let us through. We'd ruined his day.

Next morning we gathered on the South Lawn at the White House for the Arrival Ceremony, a traditional Washington spectacle to welcome visiting dignitaries. Pink blossom on the trees. There were marching bands, a nineteen-gun salute, speeches by the President and the Prime Minister, national anthems, a review of troops, all the pomp and circumstance of a state occasion.

We McGonnevilles were among the hundreds of well-wishers, waving our little Union Jacks and Stars and Stripes.

The nickname McGonneville, incidentally, had come about during a limo drive to the Golden Globe Awards a year earlier when, during the slow crawl through LA traffic to the ceremony at the Beverly Hilton, the driver had to name-check his passengers at numerous checkpoints.

"McGowvin and Bone-a-vile?" he said at the first. He was already tired and looking forward to an early night.

"MacVin? And Barningvil?" at the second, vaguely.

At the fourth time of winding down his window for another bored clipboarder, he just said "McGonneville," and it stuck.

The pageantry on the South Lawn drew to a close and the crowds dispersed. Our partners were up ahead when a young woman rushed up to Elizabeth and me.

"I can't believe you're here! I so love your show! Could I get a picture?"

"Sure!" said Elizabeth.

The woman whipped out her camera . . .

"Here, you take the photo."

. . . and handed it to Elizabeth, who was all of a sudden cast as an extra in someone else's movie.

A bit like me, taking afternoon tea at The Savoy with the two auction prize winners, neither of whom cared two hoots about *Downton Abbey*, even if they had just about heard of it. As Ronnie Wood listened to Mr. Germany describing exactly which seats he had sat in at not only Hanover 1982 and 1990 but also Hamburg 2003 and, lest we forget, 2007, my tea plate slipped off my knee and the contents fell on to the floor. I was dying to make a joke about the rolling scones but, reading the room, I thought better of it.

The Truman Building, which dominates the romantically named C Street in Foggy Bottom, Washington DC, is the home of the

US State Department. While most of the building is a homage to functionalism, several floors up you come out of the elevator, through a door and enter a movie set from a bygone era. The Diplomatic Reception Rooms represent a gilded age and boast items of Americana from across the nation – porcelain, silverware, furniture. The décor and upkeep, the person escorting us was quick to point out, being paid for from legacies and donations and not from the public purse.

In the principal dining room Hillary Clinton, then Secretary of State, hosted a lunch for us visitors from over the seas. I sat next to a wonderfully gossipy woman who pointed out who in the room was on their way up, down, out, and who had the worst halitosis. On my other side was a lady whose husband worked in the White House on Joe Biden's vice presidential staff. So, over a three-course lunch I got a rapid education in American political life. It was riveting.

Towards the end of the meal, as guests were beginning to disperse, a tall, fit-looking man came over to say hello. I recognised John Kerry at once and started to stand up, just as he began to crouch down. A rather odd dance ensued with the pair of us bobbing up and down, like two men on one of those railway handcars that moves along the tracks on the see-saw principle. Eventually we found a middle ground, me half standing, Mr. Kerry stooping, hands on knees. He told me how he'd had a bad back recently, a detail of personal medical history I had not anticipated from my first encounter with the former presidential candidate. All I could think was the bobbing wouldn't have helped.

"Haven't been able to sleep because of it," he continued. "So, the other day I'm wide awake at four in the morning and I put on the DVD of your show. My wife had been going on about it, you see, and I figured it would get me all drowsy and help me go back to sleep. Well, sir, I have to tell you, I was still there at noon. Completely hooked."

He patted my shoulder and moved off.

The White House in real life, a bit like Tom Cruise, isn't as big as it looks on screen. Substantial, yes, but not massive. It's not Versailles, or Blenheim. You're not going to get lost in it. Or if you do, a bloke with a worm hanging out of his ear will unlose you in about four seconds. The reception rooms on the first floor are impressive, with high ceilings and portraits of political figures observing from history.

That evening we joined a line to shake hands with the President and the First Lady and the Prime Minister and Mrs. Cameron.

Just before we had left for the trip, Felix, then aged ten, had thrust a letter into my hands.

"Will you give this to Mr. Obama?"

It asked two specific questions, about the President's views on the police being armed and also what he felt about the potential harmful effects of violent video games on children. "If you could get back to me," Felix's letter concluded, "that would be hugely appreciated. It's OK if you don't reply – I'm only 10."

"Right, well. Um . . ." I said.

"Just make sure you give it to the President."

I didn't tell him this was about as likely as him getting the raise in pocket money he had recently been campaigning for but I said I would do my best. So, during lunch at the State Department I asked my new best friend, whose husband worked at the White House, what the protocol was on such things. If I were to reach for something in my inside pocket at the point of being introduced to the President of the United States, for example, would I immediately sense four red dots on my forehead? She assured me it would be fine and the President wouldn't mind in the least. Moreover, said my lunch companion, she would make sure Felix got a reply. I knew that wouldn't happen but it was nice of her to say.

It was my turn next, as the line of guests in black tie moved from the East Room through the Green Room into the Blue Room, the one with the bay window that you can see through the pillars of the famous South Portico. "Oooh look, he's taller than on the telly," I thought, turning my Tom Cruise theory on its head. The President was my height. I used to say with confidence that I was 6ft 2in but I've definitely shrunk. His handshake was firm, his smile efficient. I asked if he watched *Downton Abbey* with the First Lady, as we had heard she liked the show. He replied that he was currently glued to *Homeland* but maybe some time he'd get to a *Downton Abbey* box set on Air Force One. It was my cue to move on. Carpe diem, I told myself.

"Mr. President, my son would never forgive me if I didn't at least give you this."

I pulled the envelope from my inside pocket. No red dots on my forehead. His smile was broad now.

"Tell you what, let's get a photograph, so you can prove you did."

A turn to the photographer. The handover of the envelope. *Click*.

The dinner was memorable. John Legend and Mumford & Sons played. The President remarked in his speech that the last time there were this many Brits in the White House, they burned it down, in 1814.

Next day we boarded the plane home. As we found our seats, Lulu spotted George Osborne, then Chancellor of the Exchequer. She collared him, getting straight into policy matters, specifically our son's complaint about pocket money. The Chancellor recommended an increase well above inflation, amounting, I think, to a 20p rise. A display of reckless fiscal abandon, what with Osborne's austerity policy already kicking the nation when it was down.

Some weeks later a letter arrived in a cream envelope.

"Dear Felix, thank you for your thoughtful letter," it began. "It was a pleasure to meet your Dad this spring, and I appreciate hearing from you . . ."

The letter went on to commend Felix for addressing the challenges of the age as his generation had an important role to play in shaping the future. It finished by urging him to endeavour to improve the lives of others. And below the text, the unmistakable signature of Barack Obama.

I sat there for a moment, stunned and moved by this epilogue to our trip to the White House, effected, I had no doubt, by my lunch companion that day at the State Department.

"Felix," I said, choking up, "*that* is from the President of the United States of America."

"I know," said the ten-year-old, "but he hasn't answered my questions."*

Later that same year, having been to Los Angeles and New York, a group of ten of us were back in Washington for a pre-Christmas visit, promoting season three of *Downton Abbey*. The British Ambassador, Sir Peter Westmacott, hosted a reception for us in the Residence, a magnificent Lutyens building in Embassy Row. In the splendour of its main reception room – brown marble pillars and glittering chandeliers – he spoke of the "*Downton* effect" and the growing affection with which the show was held in the United States. We then mingled with guests, the movers and shakers of Washington. I can say with confidence that of all the *Downton Abbey* events I have attended over the years, and there have been many of them – Meet and Greets, Q&As, In Conversation Withs, impromptu fan encounters – by far the most bustling and pushy crowd, barging each other out of the way to get a handshake and a photo with one of us, were the great and the good of Washington DC. And the pushiest of them all? Alan Greenspan, fighting his way to the front like an actor spotting the last chicken wing at the buffet.

---

* A couple of years later Felix asked me to give a letter to David Cameron, who was going to be at a lunch I was attending. The Prime Minister kindly accepted it. Felix's missive was about global warming. A few months later he got a reply from a stroppy intern saying that the government had a far better record on climate change than the opposition. One way to charm a twelve-year-old.

Following the reception we hopped into cars and were driven to an appointment that I don't think any of us will ever forget. Thanks again to one of my lunch partners at the State Department, who had the ear of the First Lady, we were given a night-time tour of the White House. I had seen the reception rooms on my previous visit but there was something special about touring the building "after hours," with the lights down low and the rest of the house apparently asleep. The seasonal decorations were beautiful and I lost count of the number of Christmas trees, with their twinkly lights, baubles and tinsel. There were cookies laid out for us, with best wishes from Mrs. Obama. Elizabeth McGovern, feet sore from standing at the reception for hours on end, took off her high heels and plonked them on one of the dining tables as we wandered from room to room, our late-night guide pointing out the significance of the paintings and the furniture. Then to the West Wing. In a room lined with TV screens monitoring broadcasts from around the world, the two Marines on duty stood bolt upright on recognising us. One of them said BBC News was the only channel they had on 24/7 because they trusted the quality of its reporting.

As we were about to be shown in to the inner sanctum we then had to put our cameras and mobile phones in pigeonholes, before passing through a secure door. Noticing a hi-tech boxed device on the wall next to it, Una Maguire, one of our publicity team, asked the Marine, "So is that some sort of palm-print scanner, then?"

"No, ma'am," he replied. "That's hand sanitiser."

We were shown into the John F. Kennedy Conference Room, better known as the Situation Room, from where eighteen months before the President and his advisers had watched the operation to capture Osama bin Laden. A moment of history played out on a screen in a small, windowless room in Washington. And yes, I did sit in The Chair. Finally, with our cameras and phones restored to us, we visited the Briefing Room, taking it in turns to stand at the podium pretending to be Jay Carney, the current Press Secretary, taking questions from journalists, with our host, Bobby Schmuck, joking along with us. However, the laughter freeze-frames in the memory. The very next afternoon, 14 December 2012, the President stood at that same podium, promising the people of Sandy Hook all the help they required. The shootings in a school in Connecticut that morning had turned the White House in to a place of sombre reflection as yet again America's relationship with guns was brought starkly into focus, my young son's letter to the President suddenly painfully appropriate.

Has anything changed?

37

Table for Waltz

As I was under contract to *Downton Abbey*, there was no way I could do *The Monuments Men*, George Clooney's film about a band of art historians and museum curators trying to rescue and account for cultural treasures in Europe during the Second World War.

When I read the script, filming was still several months over the horizon and by that time we would be in the thick of shooting season four. However, as fate would have it my American agent, Jeremy Barber, also represented Julian Fellowes. Words were exchanged. Having been an actor himself, Julian recognised the value of opportunities like the one that now presented itself for me and he took up the cause with Gareth Neame, his co-exec. Julian offered, effectively, to write me out of two episodes so that I could shoot the American film. We had lost Dan Stevens and Jessica Brown Findlay as Matthew and Sybil, and Siobhan Finneran as Miss O'Brien at the end of season three, with no hard feelings; they had come to the end of their three-year option and hadn't wanted to renew. So, attempting to let me scoot off for a few weeks to do a movie in the middle of *Downton Abbey* was a kind gesture, not without a hint of reward for having stayed with the show. There was also a sense of karma being in play, as well. Bob Balaban was in the cast of *The Monuments Men*. It was he who had brought Julian on board to write *Gosford Park*, for which he won the Oscar. Without that film, *Downton Abbey* probably would never have come into being. With all that in mind, Julian championed for me to be released to do the movie, Gareth kindly agreed, and Jeremy Barber worked miracles getting both filming schedules to fit.

The film was based at Babelsburg Studios and was shot in a number of locations in Germany and the UK. George Clooney leads from the front and clearly has the best time, developing projects he cares about, with people he likes to be around. The atmosphere on set, even in the big set pieces, was relaxed and fun.

"Do you know Bill Murray?" he asked when we first met in Berlin for rehearsals. I hadn't had the pleasure. "Put it this way, I'll be at my place in Italy. He'll call and say, 'George, I'm at the airport.' And he'll just arrive at the house, and after a week I'll explain that I have to head back to the States for work or whatever and he'll shrug and say, 'OK, have fun.' And he'll wave me off and he'll just . . . stay. In my house. You'll like him."

Lulu and twelve-year-old Felix were in Berlin for some of the shoot, as were two of Bill's sons. Bill invited Felix to hang out with them one night, while Lulu and I went out for dinner.

"Don't hurry back," said Bill as we dropped Felix off at his room, "we're playing Monopoly."

Having collected him at the end of the night, I asked Felix how his evening had been.

"It was very nice and they were all very friendly but I can't quite work Bill out," said Felix. "At one point, he started talking to me about integrity."

"Integrity?"

"About how in life it's important to be truthful and not to cheat. And how in Monopoly it's especially important to be really honest, otherwise the whole game falls apart."

"Well, that's fair enough, isn't it?" I said.

"Yes, but two minutes later, when the boys weren't looking, he grabbed some cash from the bank, passed it to me under the table and said, 'I'll give you two hundred for Pennsylvania Railroad.'"

Some of the UK filming was at Camber Sands in Kent. My agent said she might pop down and say hello on the last day, which was due to be a Thursday. However, as often happened with George at the helm, he had got so far ahead on the schedule that he decided the final day was superfluous. I mentioned this in passing to my agent when I phoned her on the Wednesday morning.

"Yeah, likelihood is we're going to finish today, in fact. Around lunchtime."

There was an ominous pause.

"What do you mean, today? But, but, I'm coming tomorrow. I'm coming to meet George Clooney tomorrow."

"Well, I'm very sorry, but he won't be here tomorrow," I said. "None of us will."

"You're NOT SERIOUS," said Donna.

She slammed the phone down, and within ninety minutes had arrived on the set. That's quite a feat from central London. We did indeed wrap at lunchtime, and many of the cast and crew spent the rest of the day in the courtyard of The George Hotel in Rye drinking rosé, my agent thrilled to have met her hero, and Jean Dujardin doing impressions of various members of the animal kingdom.

Eight months later we were back in Berlin for the Film Festival to launch the film. In an Italian restaurant one evening, packed with our cast and production team, I was sitting at the head of one of the long tables when the maître d' suddenly appeared at my side.

"You will move, please. Herr Waltz."

I wasn't sure which charm school the maître d' had trained at but it needed to have its accreditation removed. I followed the direction in which he was gesturing. The actor Christoph Waltz had entered the buzzing restaurant and was currently a few tables away shaking hands with John Goodman.

"Oh, I see."

The prospect of the two-time Oscar winner coming to sit with us was quite exciting.

"Sure," I said. "No problem."

The maître d' nodded at two waiters who deftly glided in like a pair of cygnets from *Swan Lake*, whisked my place setting away from the head of the table and moved it to one of the long sides. I made everyone else scooch along so we could accommodate the Austrian star. Fresh cutlery and table linen were laid with a flourish at the head and we carried on our conversations, looking forward to being joined by our new best friend.

Two minutes later the maître d' materialised again, clapped his hands, and with a flick of his head instructed the two swans to remove the place setting as Herr Waltz was evidently *not* going to be gracing us with his presence – he was over by the front door now, on his way out, chatting to our producer. Another nod of the head from the maître d' indicated that I should resume my place at the head of the table and not disturb his evening any further. Fine. I moved back again. One of the swans, now more of a grumpy duck, dumped the napkin across my lap.

Five minutes later I was just tucking into my spaghetti alle vongole when the fucking maître d' and the two geese appeared once again.

"Look, mate . . ." I began.

"But is Herr Waltz."

Suddenly the Inglourious Basterd was at the very next table, leaning over a publicist, talking to Bill Murray. One of the buzzards pulled the napkin off my lap, the other yanked my chair from under me, and the maître d' pirouetted the place settings in readiness for our esteemed gatecrasher. Then, as I finished the last clam, I looked up only to see Herr vanker Waltz disappearing through the front door. The maître d' bowed unctuously at the departing Bond villain then nodded to the two vultures, who immediately turned their gaze towards me.

"Don't," I said. "Just don't."

Bill Murray wasn't meant to do *The Graham Norton Show*. Originally it was going to be Matt Damon, Jean Dujardin and me. But it became clear that Jean wasn't entirely comfortable about holding his own on a British chat show speaking in a second language. Jean's English is good – better than my French anyway – but I could sense his unease. Backstage at a press event in Berlin I asked Bill if he had heard of Graham Norton.

"Have I heard of Gray-ham Norr-ton?" he mused.

"He's a chat show host in the UK. Would you be up for it?"

"Sure. How does this fit?"

He had undressed the little Paddington Bear that was travelling with me and was trying to put the coat back on.

A week later we were in London for the UK premiere of *The Monuments Men*. The cast met at Claridge's for a glass of champagne before setting off to the Odeon Leicester Square.

"Hey, this is Janine and her boyfriend Karl," said Bill, introducing a young couple who were with him at the bar. "Janine works here at the hotel. But it's her evening off, so I said she and her boyfriend should come to the movie." I had also heard he'd given a pair of tickets to a random guy in the street who had asked for directions. I don't know if that was true but I could easily believe it.

Once we were at Leicester Square there were photographs in the foyer with the cast and some veterans and relatives of the Monuments Men themselves. There was one elderly lady in a wheelchair. Bill immediately went and perched on her lap and gave her a kiss on the cheek.

"Bill, you could have broken her legs," I said.

"Some people see an old lady in a wheelchair. I see ... Party Girl!"

He had made her night.

Towards the end of the *Graham Norton* recording that evening, Matt declared it the best fun he'd ever had on a talk show and, having sung the closing number, Paloma Faith dived across our laps. We drank champagne from her shoe, Bill threw plastic fruit at the audience, and the episode won a BAFTA.

38

Going Back for More

These days everyone is a film maker. We have smart phones that turn us into one-person production companies. We can spend hours watching couples in their kitchens dancing annoyingly well in synch, beautifully produced. At least that's what I do, the watching bit anyway. In recent years actors have had to learn about ring lights and have one on standby in case the agent calls. I bought a green screen during the first lockdown of the pandemic and spent many happy hours sending films to my family trying to convince them I was in a variety of exotic locations and not in fact in the next room. However, the wonder of all this accessible equipment has brought with it the rise of the self-tape as a form of auditioning. While useful and inevitable during a global health crisis, in most other circumstances it's reductive and a travesty of what auditioning should be about.

In the good old days – and I'm only talking ten years ago – you would go to a casting director's office somewhere in Soho, up the rickety stairs, and sit cheek by jowl with four other Yous in a waiting room that was in fact a kitchenette and office combined, chairs jammed against a dripping radiator. And since there were only four chairs, one of you Yous had to stand, or crouch, depending on how confident you felt, pretending not to study the pages of script. A cupboard door would open – turns out it's not a cupboard, it's the audition room – and out would come another You. Eye contact, recognition, a gesture of spread thumb and little finger, followed by a quick tremble of the hand clutching an invisible glass, indicating that once this whole bloody thing is over let's phone each other and meet for a pint, that single mime class at drama school finally being put to good use. Off the You goes, clumping down the narrow stairs, and the next You goes into the cupboard, shuts the door, and you finally get a seat by the radiator. One of the other Yous is chatting merrily to the casting director's assistant. Of course he is – wanker. Known her for years. They were probably at college together, so he's further up the food chain already.

Eventually it would be your turn to go into the cupboard, or the abattoir as it might as well be known, what with the blood and tears and carcasses of careers and dreams swilling all over the floor. There'd be a video camera on a tripod, pointing at you like a stun gun, and a technophobic casting director grappling with changing the tape while trying to hold a bit of paper with your name on it in front of the lens. And, God willing, there would also be another human being, seated, present to authenticate the slaughter. A human being otherwise known as the director, opposite another human being, you, the living breathing lamb about to be put into its misery. The point is, it was a live encounter, in which the director actually got to see the whites of your eyes and quite probably smell your fear. In fact, *definitely* smell your fear because the window was always shut due to the compulsory drilling noise from the building site next door.

The more astute reader will detect that I have never been very comfortable at these sorts of auditions, the ones with the camera lasering into your brain even though you're trying to pretend it's not there. One to one with the director, or producer or casting director, fine. In fact, all of them together in a room with you naked under a spotlight, fine, because it's you they are seeing, the three-dimensional you. The taped you, grabbed takes in between drilling, is two-dimensional, tinny, and not the real you. The decision-making Suits who cursorily flick through the tapes in their office or hot tub have not an inkling of your pulse, of your personality, nor of your potential. And they're probably going to fire the director anyway.

Having someone competent behind the camera is a plus. I auditioned for the title role in the US mini-series *John Adams* three times. It was meant to be twice. The first time, I met with a human, Gary Goetzmann, one of the executive producers, at the Playtone offices in Los Angeles. We chatted, the meeting went well, it was great. But, I said, surely I'm too tall. John Adams was short, it was part of his punch. Gary waved it away and said they'd be in touch.

They did get in touch. I was back in the UK and got a call to go and meet Frank Doelger, another human being, who was co-exec on the show. I had met Frank on *The Gathering Storm*, a TV film about Churchill starring Albert Finney, and I knew Frank to be an excellent producer. So when I found him in charge of the video camera I felt as relaxed as I was ever going to be. I read the scenes with him and they went fine.

"But surely I'm too tall," I said, getting up to leave. "I'm six foot two. John Adams was five seven. It was a thing, wasn't it, part of his punch."

Frank waved the issue away. "Look, if everyone believes in you for the role, it'll be fine," he said, shaking my hand. "Anyway, we can always dig a trench."

I suddenly pictured a network of trenches snaking round the fields of Virginia, with me in a powdered wig toddling around up to my calves.

A few days later my agent called asking me to go back in to meet Frank again. It was all rather urgent because he was flying back to the States that afternoon.

"Again? Why? I'm too tall for it anyway."

"Frank said you were great. He said just please go in and do it all again, exactly what you did before."

"But why? He's got 'exactly what I did' on tape."

"Hugh." I recognised the tone in Donna's voice. It meant stop whining like a wuss and just do as requested.

Frank opened the door to the casting suite, welcoming but looking strangely sheepish. I did the audition all over again. Only once I had finished did he finally fess up.

"I, er . . . Hugh, the audition . . ."

"Auditions, plural, Frank."

"Both terrific, seriously. But somehow I – ha-ha – somehow I mislaid your first tape."

What's the right thing to do when someone holds up their hands in sincere apology? You smile and pretend it's fine like a good boy because you want the bloody job. Although I suspect my smile was rather clenched and unconvincing. I didn't get the job. Apparently, the bosses at HBO took one look at the (second) tape and said aside from anything else I was way too tall.

"John Adams was five seven," Donna explained, debriefing me over the phone. "Apparently it was a thing, gave him his drive, you see."

"You mean his punch."

"His what?"

Sometimes, though, technology works to your advantage in unexpected ways. Before the rise of the machines, when the journey up the rickety stairs was the usual way of auditioning for an overseas production, Donna sent me a script for a US pilot. It was to play the lead in a sitcom, a Chicago lawyer who could sing, dance and play the ukulele. I checked through my CV and, no, thought not, none of the above were listed under my Additional Skills. Although I had intended to read law once upon a time, did that count? I phoned Donna and told her that living nearly two hours from London there was absolutely no point in me flogging up to town simply to climb into an attic cupboard and go on tape between the crashes of next door's wrecking ball for a part I had absolutely zero chance of getting.

"And anyway, I swore I would never do another sitcom in LA," I said. And I meant it.

Donna sighed. A pause. An impasse. Then she said, "You've got a video camera, haven't you?"

After a lot of huffing and puffing I conceded that I had and that I would put myself on bloody tape, then somehow get it uploaded; I had at least heard of FTP, although I was less certain in which order the letters went and absolutely no idea what they meant. As usual it all had to be done by yesterday. I needed someone to read the off-lines but my son was at school and Lulu was out for the day. Then I heard the vacuum cleaner in the living room. Giselle may not have been gunning for a job in Hollywood but I explained that destiny was calling, so would she mind turning off the Hoover and joining me on the landing. I sat her down behind the camera, pressed record, and together we went through the scenes. She was way better at reading the off-lines than most casting directors and I think the surprise probably registered on my face. Something registered anyway because I got the part.

A week later Tom Hollander rang and said he was going on tape for a David E. Kelley pilot set in a Chicago lawyers' office. I told him to hold his horses and not go up the rickety stairs. "I'm on my way." I packed my camera kit, extension leads and tripod in the car and drove to his flat in Portobello, where together we rehearsed and recorded two or three dialogue scenes that the characters shared. Tom got the part and off we went to LA. We had a great time working on the pilot, which had a quirky energy and a fine script, David writing new scenes daily on his trademark yellow legal pad, left-handed. Working with talents like Kristen Chenoweth, Loretta Devine and Charity Wakefield was a blast, and once our three weeks were up I had forgiven Los

Angeles for its previous bad behaviour and was actually looking forward to working there again.

However, by the time I got back to the UK, the studio had started giving notes on what we had filmed and would I please go back to re-shoot a couple of scenes. When I landed back in LA ten days later the couple of scenes had turned into half the script, and by the end of the whole process the show had turned into something I don't think even David E. Kelley recognised any more. The studio certainly didn't, and *Legally Mad* didn't get picked up. Still, the whole experience showed me that self-taping, painful and impersonal though it is, sometimes pays off. And also, never underestimate your cleaner.

The most unusual self-tape I did was in a place called Ouarzazate in southern Morocco, where I was filming a two-part TV version of *Ben Hur*, playing Pontius Pilate. I had never heard of Ouarzazate until this job came along in 2009 but it's been the go-to desert location for any number of sword-and-sandal epics ever since David Lean shot part of *Lawrence of Arabia* there in the early sixties.

We were staying at the Berber Palace Hotel, which played one jazz tape on a loop at all times and in all public areas as, I assumed, a form of torture, like a hideous foreshadowing of *Squid Game*.

The email came through via the clunky dial-up internet connection: please would I put myself on tape for a new show HBO was developing. Our rabbit-hutch dressing room trailers were parked up with a spectacular view across the hot, barren landscape, the Atlas mountains in the distance. It was about the most unlikely backdrop for a self-tape in the history of the genre. And I told the lucky viewer that, too. With one of my co-stars, James Faulkner, behind the camera I showed off the wonders of the desert of southern Morocco, a hint of smugness in my voice, letting it be known that my career was truly international and whoever was watching this tape would be lucky to get me before I disappeared off on another exotic project. Uploading the tape took an age but it eventually whooshed over the internet horizon.

The very next day – literally the next day – twenty people from HBO arrived at the hotel on a recce for the very show for which I had just auditioned, *Game of Thrones*. Frank Doelger shook my hand and joked about his faux pas a few years before. "Taping for shows, huh? You never know what's going to happen, do you?" He winked. Well, I can tell you what happened. My services weren't required, and Iain Glen was brilliant as Ser Jorah. And like I said, never underestimate the person reading the off-lines: James Faulkner played Randyll Tarly in seasons six and seven.

It doesn't get any easier with age, nor with the progression of your career. Not so long ago I was sent a script and a selection of scenes to record myself on tape. The accompanying instructions from the casting director were threefold:

1) TAPE SCENES: Please include a few different options of each scene.
2) SLATE: A physical full-length slate.
3) General introduction/chat about recent work or any reference to this period of time/role.

I stood in front of my bedroom cupboards and recorded the scenes, then a full-length slate, meaning a wide shot showing me head to toe, and then I turned on the spot to confirm that I wasn't after all a cardboard cut-out. Finally, crossing my fingers that the casting director's assistant wasn't going to bin my tape in favour of the other You with whom she'd been to college, I introduced myself to the grown-ups who might eventually watch my tape, in this case the producers, George Clooney and Grant Heslov.

"Hello, I'm Hugh Bonneville. I've appeared in TV shows like *Downton Abbey* and *W1A* and in movies like *Notting Hill*,

Downton Abbey 1 & 2 and the two *Paddington* films. I also appeared in *The Monuments Men,* produced by George Clooney and Grant Heslov . . ."

I sent the video files to Donna, whose office assistant nowadays has to spend half their working day on the uploading and submission of self-tapes.

"It's all a bit awkward, Hugh, isn't it?" said Donna once she'd watched the material. "I mean, I don't *have* to send it. I could just say you'd be happy to consider an offer, but really, they already know your work and you shouldn't have to read."

I told her no actor worth his salt is above a bit of professional humiliation from time to time, it keeps us on our toes. "And besides," I said, "it'll make a good paragraph in the book." The last sentence of which concludes, by the way, with our protagonist learning that he "wasn't quite right" for the role in *The Boys in the Boat.*

39

A Dog's Life

It was the second year of filming *Downton Abbey* and the first day on which I was to be reunited with Pharaoh the dog, played by the lumpen Labrador Rowley, who had only ever shown the remotest bit of interest in life when a whiff of sausage passed his nostrils.

In fact, the very first shot of Lord Grantham, descending the grand staircase at a stately pace, faithful Labrador at his side, was only achieved because I had a wodge of chipolatas secreted in the palm of my hand.

I didn't grow up with dogs, apart from an ill-advised foray into the world of a beagle called Plush, so named because on the way back from the kennels he threw up on the back shelf of the car and the vomit smelled of braised pheasant, apparently. We used to go to a pub called the Brace of Pheasants in a village called Plush, hence the christening. I loved this dog but he bit everything, including me, when I was stupid enough to go coochy-coo once too often with my face way too close to his. He nearly ripped my cheek off.

I came home from school one Thursday afternoon. I was about eight. I dumped my cap and satchel in the hall as usual, went into the kitchen for a glass of squash as usual. Halfway through telling Mum about exactly why it wasn't fair that I had come last in swimming again, as usual, I noticed something unusual. Where was Plush, leaping all over me, tail wagging, dappled brown and white coat smelling warm and familiar?

Mum's eyes watered and she told me that after another complaint from a bitten neighbour she had had to "take him to the vet."

I cried that night like never before. I had an elder brother and sister and friends enough but Plush was my closest confidant. I had told him everything.

Rowley, in the first year of *Downton,* certainly didn't inspire love, nor the inclination to share my inner thoughts. He just sat there. Less a Pharaoh, more a fat Sphinx.

On my first day of season two I was in the hall, chatting to the show's creator Julian Fellowes, when a runner appeared holding Robert Crawley's best friend, Pharaoh. Except it wasn't Pharaoh. It was a completely different dog.

"They're ready for you on set, Hugh," said the runner.

I looked down at the dog. Its tail was wagging keenly, its eyes bright, its tongue popping in and out in time with its panting breath.

"Who's this?" I asked.

"It's Pharaoh."

"No it's not."

"Yes it is."

"I'm sorry, but this is not the dog we had last year."

This was a lively young thing and bore absolutely no relation whatsoever to its predecessor. And now Julian chipped in.

"No one will notice."

"Julian, it's a third of the size, has twice the energy of the last dog, and in case you hadn't noticed, she's a bitch."

The runner put his hand to his earpiece. "Er, sorry, but they really are ready for you."

Even the dog seemed to be dragging me towards the set.

"So what are we going to call her?" I asked the author.

"I don't know. Shall we keep it Egyptian? What's the female equivalent of a Pharaoh?"

The first assistant director's head now popped through the library doorway, politely glaring at the runner that Time is Money.

"Who was that Egyptian goddess?" I asked. "Osiris? There were two of them. Or was that the male one? What was the other one called – Isis?"

Julian shrugged. "Fine. Isis it is."

And so we went on set, both of us wagging our tails.

It turned out that "The Castle" – a catch-all phrase referring to Highclere's management – had decreed that male dogs were not acceptable on the premises because they upset Lord and Lady Carnarvon's own male dogs, and since the estate could do without a lather of canine competitiveness, from now on only bitches were permitted. I was grateful for the explanation. Even though Rowley was a personality-free zone I was glad he hadn't kicked the bucket. Although, that was a thought to hold on to.

We were shooting season five when I was made aware of a geeky chart on the internet that analysed in detail how old everyone in the show would be in real life, with the series having started in 1912. Julian had always intentionally blurred the passing of time, allowing the story to dictate the pace rather than having too literal a time structure. Nevertheless, each season was by this stage covering roughly a year and the world of geek was getting nervous about the credibility of Isis living to such a grand old age. As most British people of a certain type are more likely to express feelings about their animals than they are their own family, I thought it might be fun to kill off the dog. Julian took my suggestion and ran with it. We began shooting in the spring of 2014. News of Isis looking poorly escalated during the story, culminating in a scene in which Thomas Barrow carried the devoted but fading pet into the library to be with her master. However, there was absolutely nothing wrong with Millie (as I think this one was called). Tail wagging and tongue panting, she was one perky Labrador. Short of tying a label round her neck announcing Ill Dog, there wasn't much we could do. In the end I suggested we stick a rug over her to denote Not Much Time Left. It seemed to do the trick.

In June that year Islamic State's atrocities in the name of God became more prevalent when it launched an attack on Mosul. In August the US-led airstrikes began on Islamic State positions, and by the time our show was on the air in September, ISIS was front-page news most days. Some newspapers concluded that having witnessed the rise of ISIS in the autumn of 2014, *Downton*'s producers rushed to remove the dog. The scenes were in fact filmed five months previously and the storyline developed six months before that.

Following the death of Isis the dog, the TV series concluded with the arrival of Tia'a (pronounced "Teo"), a yellow Labrador puppy for Robert. She was adorable.

Cut to the first movie of *Downton Abbey*, filmed in the autumn of 2018. We first see Robert, Earl of Grantham, coming down stairs, a more mature Tia'a at his side. The inseparable duo then head into the dining room for breakfast.

The bitch playing Tia'a was about two years old and very friendly, a real light in her eyes and a penchant for bacon treats in her tummy. After a few takes she was persuaded to do roughly as she was told and accompany me down the stairs and into the hall. We got the shot and the cameras moved on, setting up now in the dining room.

Then, in a sequence of déjà vu, Tia'a was presented to me for the next part of the scene. Except it wasn't the enchanting bitch that had accompanied me an hour earlier. This was a larger animal altogether and, in fact, the proud owner of a penis. I looked quizzically at the hapless runner . . .

To this day I haven't been able to get a straight answer about why the female Tia'a got the sack. I doubt for a second that "The Castle's" policy on female versus male dogs being present had done a complete one eighty. Another version has it that Julian Fellowes, who by chance was on set that day, was appalled by the degree of fluff in her tail. Apparently, no self-respecting member of the aristocracy would have a Labrador with even a hint of wool about its body – an indication of poor breeding, according to sources. Despite trying to lose the fluff by smoothing the tail with KY jelly, expertly applied by Mark from the make-up department, making it look like a slick saveloy, the bitch had to go. So, in the first *Downton* movie, it's one dog walking down the stairs with me and quite another who gets the bacon treat in the dining room.

40

So That's All Good

As a kid I used to get a Saturday morning bus to a flea market in East Greenwich to buy gemstones with my pocket money. Calling them gemstones is a bit fancy, they were little more than buffed-up pebbles, and the ones that weren't buffed up rattled around in a tiny tumble dryer contraption Adrian Thingy from round the corner had lent me until they at least looked clean. Amethysts and agates – dendritic blue, green moss, carnelian – garnets and jaspers. Asprey couldn't hold a candle to my collection. I kept them in a little wooden box divided into sections. Having cast myself as a Collector of Interesting Things I decided to offer out my services. I set about examining my brother's stamp collection and quickly realised, with him away at boarding school, that it would be eminently sensible for me to take it over. No need to involve him in the details of the transfer.

I bought a book from Stanley Gibbons in The Strand that revealed where the stamps had come from and their likely value. I got into swapping stamps with other collectors around the world, keenly checking the morning and afternoon post for envelopes from faraway places.

There were certainly one or two among Nigel's own stamps that were worth treasuring. I noticed he also had several commemorative sets still joined together. There was the group celebrating the centenary of Winston Churchill's birth, for example; a quartet of stamps of British polar explorers; fourpenny, sixpence and one and thruppence stamps fanfaring the football World Cup of 1966 and England's famous victory. All these and hundreds more were neatly arranged in date order in several albums. However, I felt that my brother really didn't have my eye for layout. Having so many bunched up together spoiled The Look when one turned the pages. It would be so much better if the stamps were laid out in a more regular fashion. At least, that was my expert opinion. So, I spent one rainy afternoon carefully tearing each of the stamps along their perforations, separating them from the strips on which they had arrived . . . and in doing so devalued my brother's collection by about 99 per cent.

Once Adrian Thingy from round the corner had pointed this out to me I immediately put the albums and any remaining loose stamps I could find in a large box and hid them in the attic. Fortunately, Nigel had already moved on to bigger boys' things like smoking and girls and university and never asked what had happened to his treasure trove from younger days. There were, it has to be said, still some quite valuable stamps inside the various ageing envelopes that had been used for swaps or thematically grouped: Pacific Islands; South America; Antipodes. The box travelled with me from house to house down the years, my intention being to sell the handful of valued items and buy Nigel a handsome present, like a big blow-out dinner. It would be a gift of congratulations with an implied apology bringing up the rear. There was a fourpenny Battle of Hastings, a blue tuppence ha'penny Royal Wedding of George VI, as well as a rose-pink penny stamp from the reign of George V, among a few others. Together worth not a fortune but a tidy enough sum.

My wife is a creative woman and is restless unless occupied.

One day, out walking the dogs, she came across an abandoned wooden cable drum, about three feet in diameter. That afternoon she went back in the car to pick it up. Over the following days she cleaned it up and painted it a vibrant red, deciding it was the perfect height, when on its side, to be a coffee table. It looked great, but I could sense she wasn't satisfied; it was lacking something. When I came home from filming a few days later, Lulu emerged from the sitting room, a pot of glue in her hand.

"Come and look!" she grinned, leading me to where the cable drum was now in pride of place.

You can do a bit of pi r squaring and calculate how many postage stamps it would take to cover the area of a coffee table that has a diameter of three feet. And boy had she achieved it. Spread across the surface of the cable drum were hundreds of my brother's stamps, depicting not only images of beautiful birds from faraway climes, European locomotives and bridges from the four corners of the British Isles, but also a number of stamps which, as soon as I recognised them, made me utter an involuntary high-pitched *hmm'num*. There they were: famous battles, royal jubilees and a couple of recent monarchs. All overlapping each other, glued in a collage and now trapped beneath the circular glass top Lulu had had made, sealing their fate for ever.

Over the years, though, I would say my favourite hobby has been studying jobsworths in their natural habitat. Give someone a clipboard, control over a door, or a bunch of keys, and personalities transform. The commissionaires at the BBC – security guards by another name – are legendary. Brilliant at their job of checking that only the right people go in and out of the various buildings, helping out with queries, and pointing people in the right direction. But they are also, traditionally, such sticklers for the rule book that a visit to Broadcasting House can be an experience of Kafkaesque frustration. I suspect that when the BBC first came into being these gatekeepers were drawn from the demobbed military, former sarn't majors and the like. Veering off course from the rules by one degree would be More Than My Job's Worth, and this has become part of the unwritten Commissionaire's Code. No one gets past them, and when they do, permission feels like it is being granted with the greatest reluctance.

We filmed chunks of *W1A* at Broadcasting House. It was an observational comedy about management, set within the walls of the BBC. While our production team did take over a corner of the fifth floor we were, in effect, interlopers. This meant that, at first, we didn't have passes to get into the building. So, a runner had to spend the first hour of each day going up and down between reception and the fifth floor escorting actors to work. This involved going through the internal revolving doors that could only be operated by a pass and so, without an official BBC employee by your side, you had to show your temporary pass to a commissionaire and ask them to swipe theirs to let you in. That was all perfectly understandable, but things got surreal once we started filming in reception.

The BBC lanyards we wore were of course props. Having finished a scene and with all the crew and runners busily helping our little unit move kit around, guerrilla film-maker style, I headed for the revolving doors and asked a commissionaire to let me through, so I could nip back up to the fifth floor to change for the next scene.

"You'll need to use your pass."

"I haven't got a pass."

"Well what's that round your neck, then?"

"That's a prop."

"A what?"

"Look. It doesn't work."

To prove the point I pulled the prop pass on its retractable cord and placed it against the sensor on the metal pillar by which we were standing. The revolving door remained unmoved by my attention.

"You'll have to get a new one then," said the commissionaire.

"No, you're missing the point. It's not real."

"It's got your photo on it."

"Yes, that's me in the photo."

"Says Ian Fletcher."

"But that's not me."

"You've got a pass with your photo but somebody else's name?"

He grew an inch as his suspicions twitched, sensing a possible invasion.

"I'm an actor," I sighed.

"Are you now?" He put his hands on his hips, subtly adjusting his belt.

"Yes. You know I am because you've been watching us filming here in reception for the last hour. I even saw you laughing."

"Yes, I found the lady you was talking to quite amusing."

"Yes, which was when that bloke in the puffa jacket over there, the one with the walkie-talkie, came over and asked you not to look at the camera."

But now the commissionaire was nodding at a man in a wheelchair. "Morning, Mr. Gardner, let me save you the bother," he said, popping his pass on a pad. The adjacent glass door swung open and the BBC's security correspondent passed through into the interior.

"You let him in all right," I muttered.

"Sorry, sir?"

"Please can you just let me through? I need to change my costume."

"I can't let you through without a pass."

"OK, look, my visitors pass is upstairs in the pocket of my jeans. I forgot to transfer it to my costume."

"Then you'll have to sign in over there please, sir," he said, pointing to the reception desk. "I mean, you could be anyone, Mr. Fletcher."

*

I had first heard the name Ian Fletcher in the autumn of 2009. In Parliament Square, to be precise. It's strange how sometimes you can remember inconsequential moments in detail and yet can forget whole weeks and months relating to more momentous events. I was shooting a scene for a short film when, between set-ups, Paul Schlesinger rang. He had produced writer/director John Morton's brilliant *People Like Us*, a spoof radio documentary. John's writing was sublime, full of brilliantly drawn characters and situations, nudged to the edge of credibility. Paul explained how John was now developing a new show about . . .

"Yes, I'm in."

. . . the administrative team that . . .

"You can stop there, Paul. I want to do it."

. . . was working to deliver the Olympics for London 2012. At their head would be the unflappable Ian Fletcher, surrounded by a group of well-meaning but largely incompetent colleagues. A lot of meetings, with all sorts of crap being hurled at the organisers and daft obstacles jeopardising what was to be the biggest national event in a decade. The great thing about the show from John Morton's point of view was that it had high stakes baked into it: the opening date of the Olympics themselves. The programme was for BBC Four, but as so often in the revolving-door world of television commissioning, the person who had welcomed the project had gone and the new head wasn't perhaps as committed. Apparently, there weren't enough jokes per page and the scripts were too long for a thirty-minute programme.

One of the reasons Jon Plowman has been so respected as an executive producer of comedy shows over recent decades is because he can brilliantly navigate commissioners and broadcasters while at the same time protecting the Talent, in this case his writer/director. John Morton simply doesn't write gags, at least not in the Gag Per Page sense. His comedy arises from gradually revealing characters' fallibilities and confusions against a backdrop of increasingly complicated situations. As for the page count, John's dialogue plays extremely fast, it's as simple as that. Jon Plowman saw the project safely through from commissioning to production, with producer Paul Schlesinger then juggling script, cast, crew and schedule, freeing John Morton, with his directing hat on, to do his job of bringing his scripts to life.

We filmed the office scenes for *Twenty Twelve* high up in One Canada Square, a skyscraper at the heart of Canary Wharf. There were amazing views across North and East London and with a long lens you could see the cranes and hard hats of the Olympic Park itself. But there wasn't a lot of time to gaze out of the window. The budget was minuscule and the filming unit tiny, and it had to be nimble, what with the high page count to achieve each day and a style of delivery that meant everyone had to be on the ball, all the time. As a cast, while the cameras were being set up we would sit round the table in conference room scenes running the lines over and over. When there was a tea break, we ran the lines. During lunch, we ran the lines. In scripts like John's, where every dot and dash is significant, where there can be four different meanings behind the word Right or Yes or No, subtext is everything. So, the pressure was always on to deliver his dialogue with the fluidity of natural speech but with an unrelenting forward momentum, barely acknowledging the interjections and tics that pepper everyday conversation. There is musicality in writing like John's, a rhythm that you tinker with at your peril. If one player in the orchestra suddenly struck out at their own pace, or hit a bum note, the whole thing fell apart and sounded wrong. Switching metaphors now, if any of us fluffed a line it felt like a member of the relay team had dropped the baton. There would be a collective sigh of sympathy and we'd go back to the start. Sometimes it felt incredibly tense – not tense in the sense of fractured relations but in the sense of anticipation, like at the start of a race, or the first baton raise at a concert (batons central to both metaphors: discuss). I frequently had key lines scribbled on the notepad in front of me for fear of being the one to let the side down. Luckily my character had every cause to refer to briefing notes from time to time and with judicious editing it rarely looked as though I was cheating.

As the Olympics approached, the Great British national sport of Cynicism limbered up in the pubs and in the press, ready to express its flabby, sneering, lazy self in action. The Games were going to be a disaster, Britain couldn't organise a piss-up in a brewery, or if it could it would be a brewery like the Millennium Dome that had promised to blow our minds and in the event was Quite Interesting. Our show danced around the fringes of all sorts of potential Olympic disasters and the phrase about life imitating art sprang to mind on more than one occasion.

The first episode was broadcast in March 2011. The main storyline was about the launch of the countdown clock going wrong. That same week the real Olympic countdown clock was unveiled in Trafalgar Square and promptly broke down. Thanks to a kink in the metaverse I was asked by a journalist to comment on the predicament as Ian Fletcher, who always put a positive spin on things, however dire the situation. "The clock hasn't so much stopped," said Ian, "as paused to reflect on the exciting journey that lies ahead. So that's all good."

A later episode featured a Brazilian Olympic delegation visiting London ahead of Rio 2016. Unfortunately, the coach driver taking them to the Olympic Park to meet the chairman of the London Organising Committee Sebastian Coe put the wrong postcode in the satnav. The result was the delegation ended up in a traffic jam on the North Circular and never got to shake hands with the great man. When it came to the Olympics proper, a number of American and Australian athletes took more than four hours to reach the Olympic Village from Heathrow, because the coach driver "wasn't familiar with London." We were fortunate that Lord Coe gamely agreed to appear in the show, which headed off at the pass those who thought we were out to sneer at the Games. If John Morton was out to satirise anything, it was management-speak and office culture, the meaningless twaddle that comes out of people's mouths at certain types of meetings, which others present fail to call out for whatever reason. On top of that there's the sinking feeling that anyone who has been in any meeting, or sat on any committee, be it a parish council, a charity fundraiser or a FTSE 100 board, will recognise: you just know she isn't going to do what she's been asked to do and he certainly won't because he didn't understand the task in the first place.

The show started small, on BBC Four. When shows get nominated for awards inevitably it draws attention to them, so understandably Jon Plowman and Paul Schlesinger nudged the powers-that-be to put *Twenty Twelve* forward for some. The word came back that it wasn't feasible to do so, because the competition was so hot. But when some of us were nominated for British Comedy Awards and the show won Best Comedy, the people upstairs yawned into action and took the show on to the bigger sister channel, BBC Two. It didn't make any difference to the budget. Comedy has historically always been the poor relation of Drama when it comes to putting money on the screen but *Twenty Twelve* grew an audience, some of the catchphrases passed into the vernacular for a while, and the show went on to win RTS, Broadcasting Press Guild awards and the BAFTA for Best Comedy.

With the majority of my *Downton Abbey* scenes being shot at Highclere Castle and the world of Ian Fletcher being in central London, I spent several weeks hopping between a jet ski and a stately galleon and I am forever grateful to the production teams of both shows for enabling me to scuttle up and down the M4.

Twenty Twelve came to its natural end, with the final episode being broadcast just as the real Olympics hove into view. We were filming season three of *Downton Abbey* at the time and a dozen of us were fortunate enough to be invited to the opening ceremony as guests of NBC, the American broadcaster of the Games. On my way into the Olympic Stadium that night I must have been stopped six or seven times by officials, each of whom said how eerily close to the truth *Twenty Twelve* had got.

As anyone who was there in the stadium for the opening ceremony will attest, it was a spectacular evening. I have watched it again since on television and it looked amazing even on a small screen. But being there . . . the drumming tingled me from the outset, the drizzle early on, then the scale, the spectacle, the vision, the invention, the swirling thrill of imagination and celebration. Overseen by director Danny Boyle, the commitment, focus and sheer talent of those thousands of performers and technicians was astonishing. Arts and sports combining in celebration.

I was back in the stadium just over a week later. Having applied for tickets for a number of events, Lulu, Felix and I got lucky in the ballot for what came to be known in Britain as Super Saturday. Our seats were on the final bend of the running track, in the north-west corner, the finishing line off to our right and the long jump pit a way off on the opposite side. There was a huge electronic scoreboard about twenty rows up behind us and to our left, so occasionally one of us would turn round to check on distances jumped and times run, then report back to the other two. After several goes at this, Lulu told me there was a bloke sitting just below the scoreboard who must be an avid fan because every time she turned to look at the board, he seemed to be waving at her. And since she didn't recognise him, she said, it must be me whose attention he was keen to attract. So, on the count of three we turned round together.

"Where?" I asked.

"There," said Lulu through the side of her mouth like a trainee ventriloquist, as if he was going to hear us in a crowd of eighty thousand. "Four rows down from the board, seggen in from the gangway."

I upped scope, followed the co-ordinates with my eyes, and

zeroed in. There indeed was a man, four down, seven across, about our age, cheerily waving in our direction. I recognised him.

"Ah yes," I said to my wife. "That's your ex-husband."

With Jessica Ennis-Hill's and Greg Rutherford's gold medals already in the bag, by the time Mo Farah came round the final bend on his way to 10,000m glory the stadium was at fever pitch and the noise was deafening. Like the rest of the nation, I was on my feet, shouting myself hoarse. In fact, when I went to work the following Monday to film *Downton Abbey*, I could still barely speak. The script supervisor wrote a note to the post-production team that I would need to re-record all my dialogue for that particular day.

For those two remarkable weeks in August, when London shone and the nation bathed in its glow, I think Britain felt truly Great and the Kingdom properly United, in a way I hadn't felt in my adult lifetime. It certainly felt a less torn nation than it did just a few short years later, when the vote on being part of the European Union divided public opinion and even families, my own included, albeit unwittingly.

"Which way are you going to vote on Thursday, Dad?"

"Where am I going on Thursday?"

"I'm taking you to the polling station, Dad. The referendum about Europe."

"Europe? I helped found a medical society that brought lots of us together, urologists from across Europe. Lectures and wotnot."

"Yes, but the vote on Thursday . . ."

"The what?"

I adjusted his hearing aid, and while I topped up his tea explained once again the binary decision on offer.

"But I like being part of Europe. Who's making us do this, old boy?"

"So you're going to vote Remain, Dad, are you?"

A few days later, as he got back into the car at the village hall after voting, I strapped his seatbelt across him.

"All OK, Dad?"

"Oh yes. I put a cross against Leave."

"Right. OK. Why exactly?"

"A cross means no. And no, I don't want to leave Europe. Leave us in Europe. I think Europe is good."

As anyone who has accompanied a loved one on the dementia journey knows, there are often streaks of sunshine between the clouds.

As the 2012 Games were such a triumph, thanks largely to Ian Fletcher, what next for the man "who had delivered the Olympics not only on time and on budget but also very much in London?" I had wondered aloud if the Armed Forces or the NHS, both bureaucracies under public scrutiny and with more tentacles than an octopus, might present opportunities to tie themselves in knots. But as ever, John Morton – quiet, introspective, with antennae extraordinarily alert for someone who by his own admission "doesn't get out much" (apart from floodlit five-a-side football on Tuesday evenings in north London when, by all accounts, he is the most aggressive, demonic player on the pitch) – came up with something that was unexpected, odd, but at the same time right under his nose.

It was a time when the BBC was being systematically got at by media entities (when isn't it?) for being publicly funded and either pinky lefty or a puppet of the right, depending on which paper you opened, which radio station you listened to or which channel you watched – their own levers, of course, being pulled by a mere handful of proprietors. And with the ticking clock of charter renewal also on the horizon – the terms under which the BBC operates and is funded – why not bring in the go-to Man of the Moment, Ian Fletcher, as Head of Values?

When the BBC opted to give up its television studios and offices in White City it retained a couple of buildings just north of the iconic Television Centre. One or two were chrome new and contained a lot of people with BBC lanyards, but the one in which we initially filmed the majority of office scenes for *W1A* was derelict. The meeting rooms for the show were constructed in cold, abandoned work spaces. A huge photograph of Morecambe and Wise hung along the back wall, which was then replicated on a wall on the fourth floor of the real Broadcasting House, at least on the days we filmed there. So, "walk and talk" scenes would start in the White City set and, with the two iconic entertainers as a visual cutting point, would then be picked up in the building at the top of Regent's Street. This allowed for the labour-intensive scenes – the meetings – to be shot on a set over which the team had total control, while the tops and tails of scenes were shot at Broadcasting House itself, while hopefully not getting in everyone's way too much.

Our dressing room, such as it was, was in the Director General's office, or at least where it used to be. The building had been completely decommissioned, even down to disconnecting all the utilities. The nearest loo was therefore miles away, in one of the chrome-new lanyardy buildings, and being lanyardy this meant more revolving doors and more commissionaires. In turn, this meant that any time a member of the cast or crew needed a pee, the entire production shut down for fifteen minutes while we formed a crocodile of the needy and a runner with a working pass would escort us along the empty corridors, down in the one lift that worked, past the security guard and his Sudoku, and across the deserted goods-in yard towards shiny building lanyard land and a functioning toilet.

When we weren't filming in the clapped-out building in W12 we were either out on location or at the BBC's principal home in London W1. The front door of Broadcasting House shouldn't be confused with the front door of Broadcasting House. There are two of them, you see. Of course there are. There's an Old one and a New one. Blue lanyards meant you had clearance for one entrance, red for the other, or possibly both – I never got sufficiently far up the vetting ladder to find out. This is all you really need to know to get a sense of the show itself, all a bit odd but worryingly plausible.

There were no dressing rooms in New Broadcasting House because in this new building the BBC no longer made television programmes, or at least not the sort that involved people hanging around during the day, or getting into funny clothes and putting on make-up. Unless you include news and weather presenters. But presumably, went the thinking, Huw Edwards and his colleagues could whack on a bit of lippy using a phone torch.

The design of New Broadcasting House was also clearly intended to maximise eavesdropping and hinder creativity. All open plan and hot desks, it wasn't unusual to come across executives crouching in stairwells trying to secure sensitive deals on the phone, or see meeting rooms like "Dr. Who," "Basil Fawlty" and "Mr. Darcy" occupied by solitary figures, deep in thought with their eyes closed.

You would have thought BBC employees would be unfazed by having a film crew dotting in and out of their workplace. In fact they were probably the most selfie-hungry group of people we ever came across. When filming in the streets we might get a couple of people coming up to express disinterest but here at the home of smart, too-cool-for-school media types, per square inch there was more "It's not for me it's for my wife/son/uncle – loves the show – you have no idea how true to my work life it actually is" than we had ever encountered. We were filming back in the days when behind-the-scenes photos were frowned upon but BBC employees were sensitive to the fact that pictures should not be put in the public domain. Well, most of them were.

One afternoon we were filming by the glass wall overlooking the newsroom. A few of us were grouped for a reaction shot to a scene that was unfolding down below when Frank Gardner came past on his way out of the building, presumably having filed his latest report on Islamic State. He asked for a photo. Of course we agreed. After all, we were trampling all over his office, it was the least we could do. The only thing we asked in return was that he didn't post the photo online as we didn't want to leak any spoilers about the show. Plus, we could all get fired. How we laughed. I mean, this was Frank Gardner OBE, for heaven's sake, the BBC's celebrated security correspondent. If anyone knew about discretion, he did!

A week later the photograph appeared in the *Guardian*.

41

There Is Nothing Like a Dame

It was like Stanley meeting Livingstone. Only this time the adventurers were two dames, one of the British Empire, the other of Hollywood. It was two minutes to eight on a freezing cold morning in winter at Highclere Castle. The *thrwump thrwump* of Lady Carnarvon's hooves – or those of her horse, I should say – had just passed by the library windows, her ladyship off on her daily ride through the February frost. The unit cars were processing like a funeral cortege up the drive from base – all of four hundred metres away on the hard-standing by the castle's ticket kiosk, but a welcome luxury on a cold day like today.

I was already on set, chatting to one of the riggers halfway up the main staircase as below the crew bustled about their work. Mine turned out to be the perfect vantage point. Dame Maggie was standing in the middle of the hall in a warm duvet coat, a variety of which had become standard issue for the wintry months of filming; come the summer – when, ironically, we filmed the Christmas specials – it was all hand-held electric fans and ice lollies.

"Arrival on Shirley," crackled a walkie-talkie somewhere.

Shirley MacLaine, Broadway and Hollywood star. She'd

worked with Alfred Hitchcock and David Niven, Billy Wilder and Jack Lemmon, Bob Fosse and Peter Sellers; she'd won an Oscar for *Terms of Endearment*; Golden Globes, BAFTAs and Emmys dripped off her CV. She was also the sister of legendary Hollywood actor and ladies' man (back in the day) Warren Beatty.

A commotion around the double doors in the entrance hall and in she came. This wasn't her first day on set, so we'd got over being starstruck. But it was her first encounter with Dame Maggie and we were of course intrigued to see how it would play out.

Similarly clad in a duvet coat over her make-up robe, drowning her small frame, Shirley strode into the main hall. Maggie turned and smiled. Shirley, in full sail now, flung her arms wide and pulled her into an embrace. From my place on the stairs I got the perfect two-shot, in profile, as these two legends came together in front of the fireplace. There were smiles and laughs and a palpable sense, at least for me, of a magic moment as two great careers collided.

Maggie didn't think they'd met before.

"Oh yes we have, I remember distinctly," chimed Shirley. "Backstage at the Oscars. Must've been forty years ago."

"Really? Backstage? Were we presenting?"

"I guess. And not winning. Right?"

"I was probably face down in a cake," said Maggie.

When she had first arrived to work with us, Shirley's acclimatisation had required a degree of diplomacy from our producer, Liz Trubridge. Not satisfied with the hotel room she had been offered, Shirley requested a tour of other available suites. As the manageress walked ahead of them, showing them various rooms, none of them the right configuration, Shirley observed rather loudly, "You can tell she's wearing Spanx."

In the end, Shirley approved the layout of one room but preferred the shower facilities in its neighbour. So she took both.

Her glorious stories on set were matched by her interest in the younger generation, recreating Bob Fosse moves with Michelle Dockery and Tom Cullen, directing them how to thrust their hips just so, while across the room, Laura Carmichael showed Maggie another cat video on YouTube.

The dining room scenes were another opportunity to eavesdrop on two legends and once again I had the best seat in the house: slap bang between the two grandes dames, Maggie on my left and Shirley, as Mrs. Levinson, guest of honour, on my right.

"I was having an affair with Danny Kaye, you know." I didn't but I did now, and so did most of the table. "I guess he was kinda in love with me. I was shooting in Paris and he wanted to take me to dinner at his favourite Chinese restaurant in Manhattan."

"When was this?" I asked casually, trying to make an affair with one of the most beloved entertainers in cinema history sound as routine as a bus timetable.

"I dunno, fifty something, maybe nineteen sixty tw— I dunno. *Irma La Douce,* maybe. 'But I'm shooting in Paris, Danny,' I tell him on the phone, 'I can't just get on a plane to New York for dinner.'"

"Well, no," I concurred. I mean, obviously. Not on a school night.

"So he flies over in his jet. Comes to the set. The producers are begging me not to leave because what if something goes wrong, like there's fog and delays and next thing their schedule gets screwed? I say, you'll figure it out. Anyway, what the hell, I get on the plane and we fly to New York and he takes me to the restaurant and at the end of the meal, you know what he does?"

"I've no idea. Pays?"

"He calls over the waiter, who presents me with a fortune cookie. I open it up. I unfold the little paper inside. I hold it up and it says 'I love you, Shirley.'"

"Wow!" sighed Elizabeth McGovern from across the table.

"I get on the plane and next day I'm back on set."

"That's amazing," swooned Michelle Dockery.

"Yeah well, maybe. But five thousand miles for a fortune cookie?"

I was still trying to calculate the plausibility of Danny Kaye chartering a private jet to fly from Paris to New York and back for dinner in the days before Concorde. In fact, even *during* the days of Concorde. While I moved on to working out precise flight times, the difference in time zones and let's not forget jet lag, a thought occurred to Shirley and she leaned across me to Maggie.

"Do you think Danny and Larry ever had a thing?"

"Olivier? Oh don't ask me, I never have a clue who's doing what to anyone."

Shirley shrugged, leaning back into her seat. No big deal. By now I had given up trying to stress-test the veracity of the story. Who cares? It was a story. A good one, engaging and tall.

"Was there a Mrs. Kaye at the time?" I asked.

"I guess so. I dunno." Shirley took a swig of the coloured water from her wine glass. "I kinda used to lose track. I had lovers all over the world. Overseas was fun. This one time, three in a day."

"Oh darling, you have been busy," chipped in Maggie.

"I know," sighed Shirley. "I did all the work, my brother got all the credit."

42

Tummy Ache

"We'll never get either of them," I said.

"It's worth a try, though," replied Jonathan Church.

It was the spring of 2015 and we were sitting in his office at the Chichester Festival Theatre, where he was the artistic director, discussing who we might approach to direct Ibsen's *Enemy of the People* the following year. I had mentioned two names. Roger Michell wasn't available and Howard Davies said yes straight away. We couldn't believe our luck.

I had worked with Howard once before, on television, in an adaptation of William Boyd's *Armadillo*. The odious Torquil Helvoir Jayne is probably my favourite ever character. I even persuaded William to toy with giving Torquil his own spin-off show, but sadly it never gained momentum. I don't think Howard enjoyed working in the world of television that much. He kept forgetting to say "Cut"; he much preferred watching the actors doing their thing. But he was a master of theatre.

Over lunch we discussed the play and the role of Thomas Stockmann, the moralist who turns whistleblower when he discovers the town's water supply is poisoned. He is at first lauded for his discovery but then the town, led by his own brother, the mayor, turns against him and his world begins to fall apart. But, to the last, Dr. Stockmann never compromises. Characteristically dressed in a denim shirt, with captivating blue eyes and once ginger hair now grey, Howard spoke with infectious enthusiasm about the play. We agreed that Christopher Hampton's adaptation, while impressively fluent, was especially faithful to Ibsen's original in that it was long. Too long. We cut it substantially before we began rehearsals, batting versions back and forth before arriving at a shape (and length) that suited us. Howard's genius as a director was his practicality. If a line didn't feel like it was working in what is a hefty, repetitive play, we cut it, trimming and trimming again throughout rehearsals. Howard badgered away at what made the best, clearest sense to the audience. But the greatest lesson he taught me – and it is both self-evident and second nature to some actors – was about playing the moment.

Following an early run of the play, when we first began to get a proper feel for its architecture, I had worried that William Gaminara and I were having way too much fun in one particular scene when we pushed the idea of two squabbling siblings to its comic maximum. Far from being adults arguing the rights and wrongs of shutting down the town's water supply, risking economic ruin on the one hand and public health on the other, they were suddenly aged ten and eight once again, involved in a slanging match as if over a broken toy. It was fun to play because it was just as brothers do behave, but, I said to Howard, surely the tone contradicts the characters' behaviour in other parts of the story. In the final moments of the play, for instance, we're watching a man on the edge of a nervous breakdown. Tonally the two don't match.

"Life doesn't match," he said. "We behave differently when we argue with a sibling than we would do in a public debate. Even our voices change depending on who we're talking to." I immediately thought of my mum's telephone voice. "Two brothers having a verbal pillow fight one minute," Howard continued, "are still the same people who might be addressing the town council the next, or seducing a lover the next."

As actors, story tellers, we often get bogged down in wanting the narrative arc to smooth into a logical journey from A to B. Howard's point was that life isn't like that, and it's life we're telling stories about. It was the single most liberating acting note I have ever been given. Blindingly obvious, of course, but too often forgotten. It served me greatly when I next did a play, three years later in the same theatre, William Nicholson's *Shadowlands*. It's a painful, beautiful account of late-flowering love between the author C. S. Lewis and an American devotee of his work, Joy Gresham. Under Rachel Kavanaugh's direction, Liz White and I pushed the comedic tones of the unlikely couple's tentative courtship, confident that the shattering pain of the later stages of the play, when Lewis is losing the love of his life, would have all the greater impact. Playing each beat for the moment that it is, not knowing what is coming next.

It was precisely the same thought behind a comment Julian Fellowes made to Laura Carmichael, Lady Edith in *Downton Abbey*. In season three Edith fell in love with a publisher, Michael Gregson, played by Charles Edwards. Halfway through season four Michael went off to Germany (and Charlie to fulfil a theatre contract) with no sense of if or when he would return. With each new script revealing nothing about her destiny, it started to prey on Laura's mind. Eventually she asked Julian what was going to happen to Lady Edith as the uncertainty was affecting how she was playing the part – was Michael Gregson to return in, say, six months' time, or never? Julian's response was that no one knows what's going to happen after tea, let alone in six months' time. Play the moment. As we do in life.

We all learned lessons during the filming of *Downton Abbey*. For instance, Lily James, as Lady Rose, learned that it's OK to stop in the middle of filming a scene if something is going wrong.

It was a dining room sequence, and the camera was on her as she served herself some chicken that was being offered to her on a salver. Except the plate onto which she was placing it hadn't been re-set since the last take. Ever the professional and a subscriber to the principle that the Show Must Go On, Lily plonked a healthy portion on to the tablecloth in front of her, all the while carrying on conversation as if nothing was awry.

I learned about different colours of blood. In the final season, Robert Crawley looked a bit peaky during one particular dinner and then suddenly erupted from his chair, spouting blood across the table as his stomach ulcer burst.

A few weeks prior to shooting, a group of us had gathered at Ealing Studios to rehearse the sequence on a mocked-up set of the dining table, complete with white tablecloths. A medical adviser talked it through with me, director Michael Engler and our make-up designer, Nic Collins. When Robert vomited across the table, he would first be coughing up blood that had pooled in his stomach. This would be relatively dark in colour. The second spasm would be of freshly pumping blood and would therefore be brighter. We discussed at length how to get the liquid into my mouth with the minimum of fuss and get the shot in the fewest number of takes, because removing and re-setting the tablecloths and place settings could take up to twenty minutes, not to mention changing my clothes as well as those of anyone who came in my firing line. There was talk of an elaborate pipe system that would feed up through my costume and, if shot from the right angle, give the appearance of blood projecting from my mouth. In the end, I suggested I just take a mouthful of the fake dark blood and give it a go. I sat down at the rehearsal table and on the count of three I got up from my chair and retched dramatically. Unfortunately, the fake blood just blobbed out of my mouth on to my chin and plopped on to my T-shirt. Only a speck or two landed on the tablecloth. After a few more attempts I worked out how to get a decent spray going and via an advanced television technique known as getting a make-up artist to crouch under the table, we developed a method of supplying the blood while the cameras were rolling. Having splurted the first wave, Giorgio would hand me the next cup of blood from under the table and, thanks to the magic of the editing suite, I could continue to throw up where I'd left off.

The observant will have noticed that there were fewer flower arrangements than usual on the dining table for that dinner scene, strategically placed away from the landing strip, and also that they were all white, designed to heighten the contrast with any blood that might hit them. Everything was thought through. On the day, we had three cameras, the castle's table had additional layers of cloth to protect it, and the carpet too was covered with a prop one in case of spillage. Personally, I had only one objective and that was to spray my darling screen partner Elizabeth McGovern, sitting opposite me as she had done for six seasons, with as much blood as I possibly could. Thanks to a quick study on YouTube of the physics of the parabola just before I went on set, I successfully splattered her with gore on the first take. The shock on her face was unrehearsed, as was the costume designer's fury.

43

Darkest Peru

The reason I asked Richard E. Grant if I could take a photograph of him with Paddington Bear was because I wanted to win a bottle of champagne. Since completing shooting the first *Paddington* film at the end of 2013, Studio Canal had sent a memo round to the cast and crew asking for photos of Paddington in unlikely and far-flung places. It was just something to keep the bear present in everyone's minds during the long months of editing until the film reached the big screen. And there would be a bottle of champagne for the winner. So, I set to.

Richard joined us during *Downton Abbey* season five, so he was a prime target, at the dining table in black tie, Paddington poking out of his wine glass. I captured Paddington doing pre-flight checks as the co-pilot on a flight out of Heathrow. He featured on a rooftop in Berlin, sat on Bill Murray's knee, he was on *The Graham Norton Show* (but got cut), George Clooney and Matt Damon posed with him on the red carpet for *The Monuments Men*, he was on a sunlounger in Spain, he observed the BBC newsroom from the viewing gallery. Paddington travelled far and wide during the following spring and summer while director Paul King sweated away in the editing room and Framestore and its hundreds of genius computer artists gradually brought to life the little bear from darkest Peru for a whole new audience.

Like many Paddington devotees I had been dubious about the idea of introducing him to the big screen. Giving Michael Bond's beloved character the Hollywood treatment had disaster written all over it. But as soon as I read the opening sequence, with its intrepid British explorer weaving his way through the jungle explaining how he was "carrying only absolute essentials: map, rations, modest timepiece and travel piano" over images of "forty native porters carrying cases, furniture, a grandfather clock, billiard table and piano" – well, I was in.

Director and co writer Paul King and I sat like two patients in a dentist's waiting room outside producer David Heyman's office one January afternoon in 2013. That was our first encounter. I have often joked about Paul actually being Paddington Bear but I really do mean it. At least the big-screen version of him. Every director's tone and taste comes through in the finished product and with Paul it was there from the beginning and manifested itself in the very nature of the bear. There is a natural warmth in both and, if not a wide-eyed innocence, a certain way of looking at the world. Slightly off kilter, enquiring, optimistic but alive to the absurdity of everyday life, too. All those qualities are there in Michael Bond's writing and so it seemed to be a completely natural fit of director and leading character. Martin Scorsese found De Niro and then DiCaprio. Paul King found Paddington Bear.

But once we were out of the dentist's waiting room and into the chair with David Heyman it soon became clear that dates were going to be an issue. I was contracted to *Downton Abbey* until August and they were hoping to shoot earlier in the summer. I bit my lip and tried to look casual – you win some you lose some. Never mind, would have been fun. But I was lucky: Paul and David were prepared to wait until the autumn, and in fact it would give Paul more time to develop the script. He was like a terrier with it. While he was clear about the overall arc of the story, Paul was eager to develop each character with the actors.

Sally Hawkins and I spent several sessions together with Paul, improvising, batting ideas back and forth, gradually shaping the dynamic of the Browns' relationship and their attitudes to the stowaway bear who, thanks to a chance encounter on Paddington station, comes to live with Henry and Mary Brown and their children Judy and Jonathan at 32 Windsor Gardens.

Tone is always the essential and often elusive ingredient in a script. Paul had been circling around the idea of the Browns being in crisis at the beginning of the story and Paddington's arrival being the catalyst that brings about change for the better in all their lives. The word "crisis" had Sally and me heading off down what turned out to be a cul de sac. We would improvise a grumpy, silent partnership one day, a crockery-throwing volcanic marriage the next. Crisis? We can give you crisis! Paul would pace up and down the office, or latterly the rehearsal room at Elstree Studios, staring at an invisible point on the floor some feet ahead of him, his head to one side, one hand sweeping back his flop of dark hair as he worried away at whatever it was that wasn't working. He wrote out in meticulous detail the beats of the journey the Browns should go on as the story progressed. For a while during rehearsals we came across as a couple the audience would want to see get divorced, so spiky and miserable they seemed. The breakthrough came when Paul sent us Woody Allen's *Manhattan Murder Mystery* to watch, in which Allen and Diane Keaton play a couple who, while not at each other's throats, are lacking energy in their lives. Their suspicions about the mysterious death of a neighbour set them on a quest that ultimately rekindles their marriage. So, not a marriage in crisis, but a bit meh. They just didn't know they needed a stranger from Peru to fix things. So we started improvising again, this time Henry's stress levels about having a bear in the house being something that Mary can help him with, even during an argument.

"Are you doing the breathing?"

"I'm doing the breathing."

During rehearsals we had a stuffed bear in the room, not Paddington but a relative of his perhaps, just to have an ursine observer in our midst. When it came to the readthrough at Pinewood, Colin Firth donned a blue duffel coat and had a "motion capture" camera strapped to his head. A scaffolding gantry was erected, several feet high, on which the cast were arranged with their scripts, so Colin, down below, had to look up at whoever he was speaking to, as Paddington would. In this way Colin's facial expressions were stored in the computer ready to be used for reference when creating the bear.

The studio sets, built at Elstree and Leavesden Studios, were stunning. Having seen the Browns' house as a mere shell in late August, walking into the finished hallway a few weeks later was a revelation. It felt like home. I have lost count of the number of people who have said they really, really, *really* want to live at 32 Windsor Gardens, the tall narrow house with the beautiful tree design on the back wall and the amazing spiral staircase, perfect for baths to bump down. Gary Williamson's designs in both *Paddington* films were as immaculate as they were imaginative. Perhaps my favourite visual joke is that he placed a great big foot made of plaster just next to the bottom step in the hall – the foot of the stairs.

Lindy Hemming's costume designs, too, were brilliantly thought through. Mr. Brown starts the film in suits of grey, his colouring pale and conservative, reflecting the risk-averse risk analyst he is. Once he begins to be affected by Paddington, his colour palette becomes a little more relaxed, even adventurous, browns through to orange and glorious pink when he disguises himself as a cleaning lady. By the end, when Paddington is in mortal danger, and Mr. Brown has become a man of action, he's in a blood-red T-shirt. And that was just my character's arc.

Paul King was involved in every detail, his imagination

brimming with ideas, always wanting to improve what he was shooting. Mr. Brown opening the bathroom door and being hit by a wall of water, followed by Paddington bumping down the stairs into the kitchen, is a key moment in the first *Paddington* film. It obviously required a huge amount of water to have built up behind the door so that when it opened it would knock a man flying. The guys who created the water tank, inside what was effectively a small shipping container, spent weeks trying to perfect the effect. Every few days Paul would go off to watch a test during a lunch break. Every time he would return to set dissatisfied. The water either sprayed out too wide or, frankly, just looked like a dribble, and the Bathroom Door Day would be shunted down the schedule yet again. Eventually it worked perfectly. And trust me, it really was a wall of water.

Paddington, of course, has a marmalade habit and rarely came out of his trailer before lunchtime. Therefore a variety of methods were employed to give us mere mortals somewhere to look in his absence. Sometimes it was nothing more than a stick with a bit of pink sticky tape at 3ft 6in, which is where Paddington's eyes would be. Often, Lauren Barrand, an actor the same height as Paddington, would don his blue duffel coat and red hat and walk through shots with us. Colin wasn't on set but he had recorded his dialogue and so that was played back to us for reference. More often than not, however, rather than us reacting to the rigid rhythm of a pre-recorded tape, the actor Gus Brown would provide Paddington's lines from off camera, adjusting his pace and tone according to the action. For some of the sequences, Javier Marzan, a superb physical comedian, would step in, trying to look small. When we rehearsed the scene in the tea shop at Paddington station, for instance, it was Javier who created the bear's antics with the teapot and buns, and who initially sat opposite me when I learned his name in bear language, which of course is Grrrearawarrr. Not to be confused with Grraweearrr, which is extremely rude. It was Javier, too, who was part of the team that created the Sellotape mishap, working out the various steps and turns Paddington might take that would result in him winding himself up like a mummy, the sequence being filmed and then refined and filmed again, eventually providing the basis for the CGI team. Fortunately, Javier's invaluable contribution over several months wasn't confined to behind the scenes. In the finished film he can be seen as the soldier in the sentry box at Buckingham Palace who shares his tea with the bear from darkest Peru.

Paddington is of course a polite young bear, but in the finished film the British Board of Film Censors detected a mumbled "bloody" from a disgruntled Guardsman as he shoos Paddington from the sentry box. As a result, the film was slapped with a PG rating and not the U any person in their right mind would have given it. However, apparently my being dressed as a cleaner and flirting with a peculiar security guard also contributed to raising the health and safety alert to PG.

Paddington and Mr. Brown need to gain access to the archive at the Geographers Guild. They spot an abandoned cleaner's cart. Mr. Brown dons the cleaner's overalls, Paddington hides in the waste bin, and off they go into the depths of the building. Just as Paddington sits down at the archive, Barry the security guard beckons to the cleaning lady (I christened her Myfanwy after Myfanwy Price in *Under Milk Wood*) and engages her in conversation.

The audience never sees the photo on the security pass Myfanwy is wearing but evidently it is of a large woman with a prominent facial feature that has now gone ("I 'ad it lasered") and one arm. Costume designer Lindy Hemming had put a photo of herself on the pass, so when Simon Farnaby as Barry pulled various contorted expressions as he reacted to the photo on the pass, all I could picture was Lindy, who is anything but the gargoyle the audience presumes to be in the photo.

Barry comments on an apparent discrepancy in Myfanwy's features: "I see the arm's grown back."

"It's a false arm," says Myfanwy.

Barry then tests out the validity of this claim by sticking a pin in Myfanwy's arm.

"We can't do that!" I said to Paul and Simon during rehearsal. "We'll have to put one of those 'don't try this at home' disclaimers on the screen."

"Don't be so wet, Hugh," said Paul. "Every kid thinks sticking pins in grown-ups is funny. They'll love it."

"You love it, you mean."

I was turning into Mr. Brown.

"Lighten up," said Paul, ever in the mind of the ten-year-old, which is why he was so in tune with Paddington and the spirit of Michael Bond.

I am a stickler for credibility within a story. If I don't believe it could happen, even in a fantastical imaginary world, if the internal logic of the world isn't convincing, you've lost me. I did a thriller called *Knife Edge* that involved flashbacks to the time a murder was committed. I thought the script was OK but something kept nagging away at me about the story, what I call a speed bump. It sort of made sense but – *ba-dum* – there was a kink somewhere that kept distracting me from the narrative. I started to look more closely at the timelines in which the two story strands took place and by employing my (albeit limited) maths skills soon realised that my character (the baddie – oh, given it away now) would have been about six when he went on his killing spree, even though he was clearly meant to be an adult at the time. I put this to the director when we first met. He initially waved it away with "the audience won't notice." But never underestimate your audience, and if I can detect a speed bump on reading a script, they surely will when watching the finished version. In the end the issue was addressed to a degree but it was blurred and, to be honest, fudged. The film didn't trouble the box office anyway.

When it came to how Myfanwy the cleaner was going to look

in the sequence with Paddington at the Geographers Guild, Lindy Hemming came up with some brilliantly funny ideas, outfits that would transform Mr. Brown from uptight City worker into fag ash Lil. But I was adamant that the audience had to believe that every item had come from the cart itself. I had a particular image in my mind of a "thing" that goes over the top of a functional overall. Because my powers of description were so poor and my drawing even worse, Lindy didn't know what I meant. After three sessions of trial and error I said, "No, it's a thing, with a thing here and a thing up here and a thing. You know."

At last she asked, "Do you mean a tabard?"

"Yes! Like I said, a tabard!"

Graham Johnston had fun with the make-up and at first I looked like Danny La Rue on a night out up west. But again I said we needed to focus on the cleaner's trolley, which is why in the end Myfanwy's rouge and eyeshadow look like floor polish.

Halfway through the edit David Heyman called to say that Colin Firth was no longer going to be the voice of Paddington. I didn't query the ins and outs of the decision but the "conscious uncoupling" was perfectly amicable. The biggest risk was a commercial one, in that Colin's name had already been announced and any change in personnel during a film's journey to the screen can create uncertainty and titbits of carrion for the vulture press. There had already been a very funny but potentially damaging series of memes doing the rounds online of the bear looking like a figure from a horror film. A two-dimensional image of Paddington in duffel coat, hat and holding his suitcase. It was, literally, inanimate. It had a soulless look, lacking in spirit and, yes, potentially sinister. David Heyman and the team just remained focused on editing the movie. The proof of the pudding was going to be in the eating. The first time I knew the naysayers would have to eat their words was when I went to the cutting room and Paul showed me a clip of Paddington with his head down the loo. The animated bear was a revelation. The texture of the fur, for starters, blew me away – and hearing Ben Whishaw's voice for the first time, with its tremulous optimism mixed with vulnerability, gave Paddington an instant classic identity in the pantheon of ursine superstars.

Rosie Alison, one of our executive producers, had nurtured the project from the very early stages, making sure that Michael Bond and his wife Sue as well as Karen Jankel, Michael's daughter who looked after the Paddington franchise, were kept in the loop. While the project had cost tens of millions of pounds and Studio Canal needed it to work for audiences around the world, in a way the only person whose opinion really mattered to David, Rosie, Paul and the team was Michael Bond. He and Sue attended a screening in London. The quote he gave after the screening was, thank God, "I came, I saw, I was conquered."

Michael and Sue loved guinea pigs, as does my wife. One afternoon the Bonds invited us for tea at their house by the canal in Maida Vale. We took with us a flat-packed cardboard castle as a gift, an adventure playground for small furry creatures. While Lulu and Sue got down on the floor and set about the construction – side A refusing to co-operate with flange B – Michael and I oversaw things from the tea table, although tea had actually given way to a bottle of champagne, Michael's tipple. We talked about the history of Paddington, a subject which he must have been asked about a million times but of which he never seemed to tire, writing new stories for the bear every year since he first saw him in Selfridges department store on Christmas Eve in 1956, bought him and put him on his mantelpiece. His love of guinea pigs had taken on a new life in the Olga da Polga books and would certainly outlast the cardboard castle our spouses triumphantly erected that afternoon. Several storeys high, with turrets and battlements, the guinea pigs loved it. Thereafter, every few months Sue sent us a photograph of the castle and its inhabitants as they gradually nibbled away at their fortress. Eventually it was reduced to a modest one-roomed bungalow.

I got home that evening to find a bottle of champagne waiting for me from Studio Canal, thanking me for my efforts in the photo competition. The accompanying note didn't say whether or not I had actually won but who cares, a glass of champagne with Paddington's creator was prize enough for one day.

Michael Bond appeared in the first *Paddington* film, sitting outside a café, raising a glass of wine to his creation as the bear first took in the sights of London. He died on the last day of filming for *Paddington 2*, aged ninety-one.

44

Plan Z to Outer Space

None of us involved in *Downton Abbey* have ever taken its success for granted, but there is no doubt that as three seasons turned into six and then a movie, it became as familiar and comfortable as a favourite sweater. When it came to the second film, however, after everything all of us had been through during the pandemic – isolation, fear, loss – I looked on each day of the job with renewed appreciation. Coming up the drive and glimpsing the tower of Highclere Castle had always given me goosebumps, but the feeling seemed more potent this time round, knowing that the audience for the film we were making would be more than ready for a slice of big-hearted, escapist entertainment.

We were fortunate to make the film at all. The start date had been pushed back because of the lockdowns in 2020. We were finally scheduled to shoot in the spring of 2021, most of the cast being able to commit because there wasn't exactly a lot of work around. The idea had been to film the French scenes first, while Michelle Dockery finished a Netflix project. Also, the crickets would be less noisy earlier in the year. However, because of Covid it looked increasingly likely that filming on French soil was going to be impossible. One afternoon in February executive producer Gareth Neame phoned the production designer Donal Woods to say he was probably going to have to pull the plug on the film because France was simply too much of a gamble. Donal sought a few days' grace while he and location manager Sparky Ellis put their heads together in an attempt to find a solution. Working round the clock, they drew up a list of locations in the UK that could feasibly double for the scenes set in the South of France. A house at Longniddry outside Edinburgh had an interior that could pass for the entrance hall of the villa near Toulon. Manderston House in the Scottish Borders could be bleached white thanks to CGI and pretend to be the exterior. Its kitchens could get away with being called French. Trebah Gardens near Falmouth might work for Tom and Lucy's seaside dip. Chilly, though. There were tropical gardens in Bournemouth, or the Italian gardens at Hever Castle in Kent; Gunnersbury Park in Acton could provide a dining room, as could Twickenham Town Hall, would you believe. As for the streets of a charming French fishing village, well, they would have to be green screen. Talk about an amalgam. But it could work, just about. The ideas were presented to Focus Features, who agreed that if the worst came to the worst Plan Z would be put into operation. The film could go ahead.

Downton Abbey was always billed as an ensemble show, as a cast we won three Screen Actor Guild Awards for being so. But we all knew that Highclere Castle was really the lead character. And we all knew that Maggie Smith ran a pretty close second. When I was first offered the role of Robert Crawley I asked Gareth Neame who they had in mind to play Violet. Had I been drinking tea at the time I would have splurted it out when he answered, "Maggie Smith."

"Good luck with that," I laughed, "She'll never do it." She was in her late seventies when we started the television series and we shot the second film more than a decade later. So, do the math, as they say. A pretty remarkable age to be working in any profession. I was as intimidated and intrigued by her on my last day of shooting with her as I was on my first. Her reputation preceded her, of course. A living legend. Famously waspish, razor-sharp intelligence and utterly instinctive comic timing, with the ability to turn to pathos and even to deep emotion in a heartbeat. My first proper scene with her was in the drawing room at Highclere. Electric lights have been installed and the stage direction indicated that Violet shields her face for a moment against the glare. "It's like being on stage at The Gaiety." On the day, Maggie used her fan, flicking it up as a screen against the new-fangled illumination but she kept it there for what seemed like ages, ramming home the point of her character's authority, her distrust and distaste for electricity as well as sustaining a comedic beat long after anyone else would dare. In the theatre it would have received a laugh that rose and fell and then rose again with the sheer audacity of the actor's bravura. At least, that's how I read it. I was in awe. And I remained that way for more than ten years. She could be beady, sure, and laser-like in her put-downs. If the script supervisor approached after a fumbled take she might put her hands up as a shield of defence and waft her away, or mutter, "Oh gawd, 'ere she comes." She would test each new director, too. On their first day she might suddenly find a problem with the motivation for a line, or question why she should sit here and not there. If the director came back with a clear, confident answer then she would be, if not putty in their hands, then certainly agreeable. Show weakness or doubt and she would eat them for breakfast. There were good Maggie days and not so good ones. The production team learned not to call her first thing, filming her in the middle of the day and letting her loyal stand-in Ros Rosenberg read in dialogue for the shots when she was off camera at the end of a long afternoon. Gradually a balance was struck and the best Maggie was the one that was captured on screen.

She had three exits, really, from the world of Downton Abbey. To be honest, I thought Violet would die between films and that we would open the second movie with her funeral, because Maggie always said each outing was her last. In fact, she often seemed happiest on her last day of shooting each season. However, while her unflappable agent, Paul Lyon Maris, would reassure her that there was indeed no need to do it all over again, nevertheless somehow she was always there at the next readthrough.

I think it was Alastair Bruce, our stalwart historical adviser, who did some numbers on the back of an envelope and calculated that over the years we had spent the equivalent of something like three months, twenty-four hours a day, filming in the dining room at Highclere Castle. So Maggie's final day on that particular set was a significant one for all of us. To while away the time between set-ups, on the occasions when leaving the room to relax off-set was more trouble than it was worth, we would chat or sometimes play games. Wink murder was a favourite. If there were, say, eight of us at the table, eight small bits of paper would be folded and placed in one of the silver mustard pots. This would be passed round for each player to extract one of the pieces. However, one of them would be marked with a cross, denoting the murderer. With the game afoot the challenge was to carry on chatting and for the murderer to wink at their intended victim without the wink being spotted by anyone else. The victim would then choose their moment to die, either elaborately, perhaps by swooning off their chair and collapsing onto a grip who was trying to lay some track, or maybe by plunging face down into an imaginary bowl of trifle. One by one people would keel over, those left alive knowing their days were numbered but also having a better chance of deducing who the murderer was and pointing an accusing finger, thereby saving their skin. Look, I know it wasn't the most productive use of the endless chunks of ten-minute gaps we contended with but it passed the time.

After Maggie's final shot in the dining room, director Simon Curtis announced the fact that this had been her last meal and Elizabeth McGovern presented her with a silver mustard pot as a memento. Her final appearance as the Dowager Countess was a tiny moment in the hall, watching the film within the film. I wasn't there for that but her penultimate farewell was obviously the most significant, her death scene. Inevitably, it took all day and there were continuity issues to do with pillows being too high, too low but there wasn't the sense of irritation that often crept into such scenes when minor details became editing problems. Everyone sensed this was a different, special day. As we rehearsed, Maggie frail in bed, the rest of us gathered round respectfully, I couldn't help but whizz through my memory bank of moments I had witnessed, not just from our show but from her career. The film and television performances, like Desdemona to Olivier's *Othello, The Pride of Miss Jean Brodie, California Suite, Room with a View, Talking Heads, Gosford Park, Harry Potter;* stage performances like *Lettice and Lovage, Three Tall Women* and *The Lady in the Van.* I wished at that moment that I had seen her perform with her first husband Robert Stephens (he was an astonishing Falstaff in the main house at Stratford when I was performing next door in The Swan) in *Private Lives* or *The Recruiting Officer.* Above all I wished I had seen her in revue with Kenneth Williams. I could picture them gossiping in the dressing room before the show, sending people up, the air crackling with camp laughter and dagger-sharp derision. Early on in filming season one of *Downton Abbey,* knowing their affection for each other and in an attempt to break the ice, I asked her about her friendship with the comic actor and famously acid wit. She immediately turned her head to one side and looked down, putting her hand up defensively. "I can't," she said, "I miss him so much." I had evidently touched a nerve. I dropped the topic and never brought it up again. Some years later a friend of mine rang to say he was going to meet Maggie at a dinner party and asked if I had any tips. "Well, you both love Wimbledon," I said, "but don't mention Kenneth Williams." A few days later I called my pal and asked how the dinner had gone. "Oh, we got on famously. Great tip about Wimbledon, thank you. We talked tennis for ages. And there were brilliant stories about Kenneth Williams." Good days and bad days, I guess.

Having run the lines of her death scene we began to rehearse. The kaleidoscope of all these memories flickered across my mind as the Dowager Countess took in first cousin Maud, played by Imelda Staunton, then her grandchildren (Michelle Dockery and Laura Carmichael) and then, as she turned her head towards me, her screen son, she did something I don't think she had done in the entire series. For the first time in the decade and more that she had played my mother, Maggie Smith reached out, took my hand in hers and gave it a gentle squeeze. From then on, No Acting Required.

For the first six weeks of shooting it was touch and go as to whether we could travel to France, as Covid policies in the UK and Europe chopped and changed. Two elements of Plan Z in fact proved helpful. It was decided to shoot the French party scene on the terrace of Wrest Park in Bedfordshire, whatever happened. It gave the design and costume departments flexibility, dressing the dozens of supporting artists locally, rather than trying to design, supply and fit a whole array of extras, dancers and musicians in a country to which they couldn't commute and for which, post-Brexit, the carnet documentation would be a nightmare. Seeing the finished movie no one has questioned the fact that the orangery and the terrace party are in fact in a completely different country to the rest of the villa. The other survivor was the cross-Channel ferry. Originally there were plans to shoot on a French boat of the period that was due to be in Monte Carlo when we were to be in South of France but again the Covid restrictions and uncertainty of our schedule made this risky. It turned out that the only vessel in British waters that was of the right look and scale was the Royal Yacht *Britannia*. We were the first film crew ever to film on board. In the movie it heads off to France, leaving the white cliffs of Dover behind. In reality, we never left the quayside in Edinburgh, where it is moored.

There came a critical moment towards the end of May when a decision had to be made. With a deep breath and a roll of the dice, the producers decided to press Go for Plan A – France – still with no guarantee as to what the Covid rules would be in a month's time. The design team travelled ahead and began to prepare the villa at Le Pradet, while at Highclere we continued to shoot the film within the film and the ending. In the event, the movie gods smiled on us and we were, finally, able to head to the South of France where, at the end of June, the crickets were in full voice, necessitating a lot of audio re-recording in post-production.

On arrival cast and crew quarantined for a week in various hotels. Those of us staying at the Hotel Juana in Juan les Pins stared longingly towards the beach through the bars of our gilded cage, whining about having to hang about on poolside loungers in glorious sunshine, while Britain experienced one of its soggiest fortnights in years. The night before shooting recommenced we screened Truffaut's *Day for Night* on the hotel terrace. Made in 1973, it's about a film crew shooting a movie in the South of France. It was a special evening, popcorn under the stars, our close-knit crew watching a film made by and about their forebears. It starred a young actress called Nathalie Baye, in one of her first screen roles. Next morning we went on set to shoot the Crawley family's arrival at the French villa, and there was Nathalie, now our Madame de Montmirail.

With the world premiere of the second *Downton Abbey* film done and dusted in London, a month later we were set to fly to New

York for the press junket and US premiere. However, Penelope Wilton (Isobel Crawley) and Michael Fox (Andy the footman), both recently recovered from Covid, were still testing positive and had to stay at home. The rest of the cast who were available made it to the hotel on South Central Park, reuniting with some of our colleagues from production. From day one on the project Simon Curtis's enthusiasm for the film was infectious. I've never known a director take the time to come to each of the principals" homes to discuss their role, make notes and provide feedback to the writer. Simon did. Admittedly it was months before production and we were in a window between lockdowns and people were pretty much at home anyway, but it was telling nevertheless. Throughout the filming, too, he made sure everyone felt looked after, crew and cast alike. In fact, he probably spent more time organising quizzes for us all than he did on his shot lists. He was always looking for the fun amid the hard work. Sometimes the two combined. Part of the story involves a revelation that my character might have a long-lost half-brother. It turns out not to be the case but to sell the idea, Simon suggested that Jonathan Zaccaï and I find an unconscious gesture that could hint at some sort of genetic connection. So, when our characters meet for the first time, a split second before we walk into the villa we both scratch our ears. It's a tiny moment that no one has ever noticed but it tickled Simon and it took us several takes to perfect the timing.

The morning after arriving in New York I was paired with "our wife" Elizabeth and the interviews got under way. Press junkets are one of the dafter by-products of the entertainment industry. They're affectionately sent up in *Notting Hill,* when Hugh Grant's character casts himself as a journalist from *Horse & Hound* in order to gain access to his new movie-star friend while she's doing interviews. The reality is even more dotty. Of course, publicising a project is a necessary part of the process, don't get me wrong, but every journalist who enters the room for their allotted five- or six-minute slot with the "talent" invariably asks exactly the same questions as the journalist who has just left, clutching their notepads and dictaphones or, these days, their memory sticks. All parties involved in the interview know it, all parties slap on a smile and get on with it, complicit in a hideous conspiracy to bore the technicians who have to film and listen to our hamster wheel of chatter squeaking relentlessly for hours on end.

Covid introduced everyone to the notion of the Zoom junket, consisting of all of the above but now in two dimensions, making the experience as impersonal as the self-tape audition. Over that weekend in New York we recorded fifty, maybe sixty interviews this way. We kept trying to change our answers, at least a bit, just to prevent the poor recording guys from hurling themselves out of the window. But with many of the cast present, doing the same as Elizabeth and me in different parts of the building, the sense of the band being back together – and pulling together – prevailed. Then we heard that executive producer Gareth Neame had tested positive and couldn't travel to America. We were dropping like flies. But the show must go on and the following night the US premiere was held at the Metropolitan Opera House, the first time a film had had its opening there.

Highclere Castle's first appearance was met with a round of applause. There were huge laughs, audible sniffles, pin-drop silences throughout and a rapturous ovation at the end. Watching the fruits of our labours that night brought home to me once again the unique quality of cinema. The sensation of sharing a story with hundreds and hundreds of strangers in an auditorium, a giant screen magnifying every moment. As one, being moved to laughter and tears in a powerful shared experience. And up there, too, larger than life on the silver screen, some twenty people I regarded as friends ... my second family, almost. Judging by the online response the film received, it was a sentiment shared by many of our audience.

There was a second cause for celebration that night. I had met Bob "Farmer" Hines on a visit to NASA at Houston a few years previously. At the time he was being strapped into his space suit, prior to being lowered into the vast swimming pool in which a replica of the International Space Station lurked beneath the surface. We had kept in touch since and I congratulated him when I heard that he was to be part of Crew 4 that was heading up to the ISS in the spring of 2022. In reply he said he was sorry to miss the opening of *Downton Abbey* and perhaps they could have their own premiere in space. This got me thinking. Calls were made, strings were pulled and just as we were heading into the Met for our own premiere, I received a message that a link had just been sent up to the ISS and the crew would be able to enjoy the film when next they had some down time. My first thought was that when watching a film in zero gravity, popcorn might not be such a great idea.

45

Coming in to Land

Truth can be as funny peculiar as fiction. There is a scene in *To Olivia,* which we made in 2019, in which Roald Dahl and his film star wife Patricia Neal wait anxiously in a hospital corridor. Two vulnerable people desperate for news of their daughter, who has been rushed in by ambulance stricken with measles. There is a moment of silence, then, at the far end of the corridor, a figure in a white coat appears, a young doctor. He approaches tentatively. The Dahls look at him pleadingly, longing for some crumbs of comfort. The doctor hesitates.

"Miss Neal . . . ?" He pulls out a notepad and pen. "I'm such a fan. Can I have your autograph?"

During pre-production I had questioned the tone of this beat. It was clearly an authorial moment of light relief to temper the darkening mood of the film. But no, co-writer/director John Hay reminded me, it wasn't made up: Patricia had written about this darkly comic moment in her autobiography. So, the doctor stayed in the picture.

On the wall outside each bedroom at the dementia care home where Dad now lives is a laminated sheet with a photo of the resident and a few lines of biography. "JP is a retired surgeon. He has a daughter, Clare, and a son, Hugh." Next to it hangs a memory box, displaying a few items of memorabilia. The medal ribbons from his mess dress, from National Service days in the Royal Navy; photos of him and Mum as a handsome young couple and of Hillside Cottage in West Sussex, the house they loved for so many years. The sailing boat he shared with a cousin and a surgeon friend, in which we would cruise the Solent or head over to Normandy; an etching of Greenfields, the house in East Sheen in which he grew up; the Latin grace from Cambridge days that until recently he could recite to the nurses here, making them clap with delight. A pair of Spencer Wells, too, a scissor-like instrument to grip suture in place during an operation, and, of course, a stethoscope. More than ninety years of a vibrant life compressed into a Perspex box on a wall.

Inside the room, now, at his bedside, I turn the pages of the old red volume to Chapter 2 and continue reading aloud. Kipling is his favourite author, and although for me *The Jungle Book* will forever be a Disney movie, to him the words echo from his childhood, when he first read and fell in love with the stories. But I know he can't follow the narrative any more. I'm a form by his bedside, making sounds in a familiar tone. He has lived at Langham Court for just over a year now. The staff have been kind, the company understandably eccentric, the overall mood of the place positive, accepting of Fate as it unfolds, sometimes quickly, usually slowly, but with only one direction of travel.

I study him. Eyes half closed, his mouth agape, his breathing shallow . . . now slowing . . . now stopped . . . Dad? Daddy? Oh my God, has he— Then a sudden throaty gasp and the rhythm of life returns. His eyes focus on mine for a moment – recognition? – before drifting away once more. It's as if he's in a glider, high up there, silently, elegantly, effortlessly circling, peeking out of cottonwool clouds for a moment before disappearing out of view. Calm, content, I like to think. But always at the back of my mind is the inevitability of descent.

Moments of lucidity follow. Lulu and Felix arrive, possibly to say their last goodbyes, but who knows? I watch my son closely in case he falters on seeing his grandfather so diminished, now in Shakespeare's seventh age of man. But Felix seems more curious than upset, at least at this moment anyway. Grandpa recognises him and smiles, and as they leave Dad kisses my wife's hand, ever the gentleman, although the words he tries to form are lost as the muscles needed to express them are weakening by the moment.

It's not going to be long now.

Circling, high up there, taking in the view of patchwork green fields.

Shallow breaths.

On Valentine's Day he turns ninety-four. I have to leave the room when the carers bring him the cake because I know this is the last time that "Happy Birthday" will be sung in his honour.

Two short afternoons later we are alone again, and for the fourteenth or maybe fifteenth time I recite the poem for which he had given me £10 on the day, aged eleven, when I was able to repeat it aloud without stumbling . . .

If you can keep your head when all about you

Thank you for the incredible opportunities you gave me, Dad.

Are losing theirs and blaming it on you.

For your calmness, your modesty, your courtesy and your patience.

If you can trust yourself when all men doubt you
But make allowance for their doubting, too . . .

The standards you set, which I could never match.

If you can wait—

The soft, liturgical mood is interrupted by the door opening. In scurries Johanna, the sweet Polish nurse with the jet-black bob of hair who has doted on Dad for months. Her voice is incredibly high-pitched, like Minnie Mouse.

"Your daddi is like my daddi to me," she says gently. She tells me again that she lost her own father at fifteen. "I luff your daddi veri much."

I know she means it. I nod in sympathy and gratitude, my bottom lip trembling now. She looks at Dad and sighs. Then she looks at me, nervously.

"Misty Hugh, Misty Hugh!" she says suddenly. "You maybe not come here no more soon, and I maybe no see you no more. So, please . . . would it possible you to make autograph?"

I am teetering on the edge of a pool of tears yet I can't help but smile. I am immediately Roald Dahl in the hospital corridor when the junior doctor asks Patricia Neal for her signature.

Johanna looks puzzled. "Why you smilin'?"

I sign the bit of paper she hands me and then, quietly, she leaves. I send a text to the director of *To Olivia*.

"Life imitating art imitating life," I write.

Barely a minute later the glider gently comes in to land.

Acknowledgements

This is the first time I've written a book and I've found the process scary and cathartic in equal measure. Many people have helped me along the way, especially Rory Scarfe of The Blair Partnership, who cajoled me into doing it in the first place. He would ring me every few months and ask how it was going. For a long time it wasn't, at all. His patience and perseverance deserve a standing ovation.

Everyone at Little, Brown for guiding me through this strange process, especially Richard Beswick, for telling me he didn't favour a fuck in the first chapter and for chiselling my lumpy material with wisdom and good humour.

My day-job agent, Donna French, who has allowed me to tease her a bit despite having had to tolerate my rants for some three decades. Una Maguire, my publicist, for being the best wing woman in the world. Two brilliant people I am honoured to call friends.

Flora Ogilvy has been a superb researcher and dispassionate scrutineer, while Catriona Whitefield, who runs my online archive and social media, has been equally helpful, reminding me of projects and timelines I had long forgotten.

As for the friends and colleagues who have either granted permission to publish their copyright material, confirmed the veracity of particular passages, or simply told me to bloody well get on with it, I think alphabetical order is safest, since it will avoid tears over billing – their input and support have been invaluable: Sir Kenneth Branagh, Patrick Brennan, Laura Carmichael, Shane Collins, Richard Curtis, Simon Curtis, Nigel Daly, Richard Dillane, Michelle Dockery, Frank Doelger, Greg Doran, Dominic Dromgoole, Sir Richard Eyre, James Faulkner, Izzy Fraser, Donna French, Andrea Galer, Iain Glen, Sally Hawkins, John Haynes, Guy Henry, Karl James, Allen Leech, Richard Lintern, Tim McInnerny, Sir Ian McKellen, Michael Maloney, John Morton, David Nicholls, Richard Olivier, Pooky Quesnel, Paul Schlesinger, Michael Simkins, Tamar Thomas, Liz Trubridge, Anthony Ward, Clare Williams and Donal Woods. And above all, first in line with advice and encouragement as well as a lifetime of patience, my darling wife and son, Lulu and Felix Williams.

Index